# TOWARD
# A NEW
# POLITICS

Edited by
## William A. Harper
Gordon College

Assisted by
Theodore R. Malloch

---

**MSS Information Corporation**
655 Madison Avenue, New York, N.Y. 10021

This is a custom-made book of readings prepared for the courses taught by the editor, as well as for related courses and for college and university libraries.  For information about our program, please write to:

MSS INFORMATION CORPORATION
655 Madison Avenue
New York, New York  10021

MSS wishes to express its appreciation to the authors of the articles in this collection for their cooperation in making their work available in this format.

**Library of Congress Cataloging in Publication Data**

Harper, William A.          comp.
    Toward a new politics.

    CONTENTS:  Zylstra, B.  The individual Gospel. — Zylstra, B.  On Christian social action in a pluralist society. — Pierad, R. V.  The golden image of Nebuchad-nezzar.  [etc.]
    1.  Christianity and politics — Addresses, essays, lectures.  2.  United States — Politics and government — Addresses, essays, lectures.  I.  Title.
BR115.P7H354          261.7'0973          73.12924
ISBN 0-8422-5122-7
ISBN 0-8422-0345-1 (pbk.)

# CONTENTS

31115

## SECTION IV

SECTION I

# THE INDIVIDUAL GOSPEL

## Sources
## and Shortcomings
*by Bernard Zylstra*

The Christian Labour Association of Canada is now entering its third decade of witness to the healing Lordship of Jesus Christ in labour relations. At this moment we are intensely grateful to our heavenly Father Who has opened a highway for a small band of Christ's disciples to follow the Master in one of the most difficult and complex areas of life: the world of production, money, machines, technology, assembly-lines, strikes, bargaining, unemployment, poverty, alienation, salesmanship, advertising, excessive consumption of material goods. In that world the Spirit of Christ is largely absent. In that world the spirit of antichrist is hard at work. This is the Spirit that denies that Jesus is of God, and that this Jesus, crucified at Calvary but risen from the grave, is the Lord of lords and King of kings to Whom all power and authority belongs, also in matters of money, wages, labour, production, the market, and consumption. (cf. 1 John 4; Matt. 28: 18)

## Part One.
## DEFINING THE DIFFICULTY

The Christian Labour Association of Canada has encountered many obstacles during its first twenty years of life. In this article I want to focus on one set of problems that the CLAC shares with other movements that attempt to carry Christian witness into the social and cultural arena.

### 1. A complexity of obstacles

The obstacles I have in mind are these: (a) the problem of political and legal recognition and equality of Christian social organizations, specifically the issue of the recognition of the CLAC as a bona fide trade union; (b) the general absence of support for a program of Christian social and cultural action in the Canadian and American Christian community; and (c) the criticism that Christians, if they are at all interested in social, political, and educational matters, should not pursue their aims in organized unity but in the avenue of individual witness and action. The entire history of the CLAC has been a constant struggle against these obstacles. But one encounters them just as vehemently in the area of education where Christian schools are generally subject to intense political and hence financial discrimination. Further, the presence of these obstacles makes the birth and growth of a Christian political movement in Canada and the USA extremely difficult. Finally, the force of these obstacles explains, to a great extent, the monopoly of secular principles in the area of medical care, family counseling, social health, and the professional organizations (law, medicine, etc.).

### 2. A common root

One can approach these obstacles from various vantage points. But I believe that one can better understand them in the light of a common root, a common source that explains their power in today's society. The source or root I have in mind is *the individual gospel* which exists in polar tension with *the social gospel* in many seg-

THE GUIDE, April/May, 1972, vol. 20, no. 4/5, 21-25.

ments of Christendom. For the purpose of this article, "the individual gospel" is sufficiently described as the view (a) which holds that man is first and foremost an individual being whose humanity lies in an identity separate from other men; and (b) which looks upon the Gospel of Christ mainly as a power for the salvation of the souls of individuals.

## 3. Will the social gospel do?

In subjecting the individual gospel to a critique it must be clear at the outset that my alternative does not lie in the social gospel, which (a) holds that man is first of all a social being whose humanity lies in his relations to his fellow-men; and (b) which looks upon the Gospel as the source of inspiration for improving and restructuring these relations. The error of the social gospel is not that it sees man constantly interacting with his fellow-men in the execution of his tasks in culture and society. We also acknowledge that. For the very notion of mankind as a community brings us to that conclusion. However, the uniqueness of Biblical revelation on this score lies herein, that this community is founded on mankind's covenantal bond with the Creator. For this reason the *first* and *great* commandment of the Christian religion is: "You shall love the Lord your God with all your heart." The implication of this is that man is not first of all a social being; he is a religious being whose life is service of God. This service includes obedience to the *second* commandment: "You shall love your neighbour as yourself." Love to God demands love to neighour. But the motivation for love to neighbour does not lie in the first place in our neighbour himself but in God Who reveals that our neighbour is a fellow-creature whom we must respect and honour in his creatureliness. The interpersonal love requires a supra-personal reference-point and norm. That, I take it, is what we must learn from the first letter of the apostle John, summed up in these words: "If God so loved us, we also ought to love one another." (4:11) For this reason humanitarian concern for our neighbour is not to be equated with love to God. That is the error of

the social gospel. Biblically based social action is not identical with social philanthropy. The lasting impact of any Christian social endeavour lies in the implementation of the Biblical conception of a genuinely *open society* whose members are imagers of God and whose final point of reference lies beyond the social-horizontal relationships in Christ Jesus, to Whom all power belongs. A conception of society whose final point of reference is either autonomous individual man or autonomous humanity cannot provide a lasting foundation for an open society: its horizon is too limited. And the absolutization of limited horizons is idolatry: service of the creature rather than the Creator. (Rom. 1:23-25).

## 4. Is conversion necessary?

Yes, conversion is necessary. The difficulty with the individual gospel does not lie in its emphasis on personal repentance from sin, conversion and regeneration and commitment to the Lord in the joy of faith. The scriptures make it quite clear how men, brokenhearted because of sin and idolatry, can again become members of the spiritual community which is the Body of Christ. They must surrenderingly pray with David: "Create in me a clean heart, O God. . . . Take not thy Holy Spirit from me." (Ps. 51) The individual person will get lost in society unless the Lord teaches him His way so that he can walk in the Truth, unless his heart is again *united* to fear—not creatures—but the Name of Jahweh. (Ps. 86:11f)

But why is personal conversion so important? Because the Kingdom of Christ can only enter human life and society via the avenue of radically changed heart commitments. The heart is the motor from which are the issues of life. It must be regenerated, filled with the new life of the Holy Spirit, before a person can acknowledge Christ as Saviour and Lord. Nicodemus, a fine representative of doctrinal purity and moral uprightness in the church, had to be told by Christ: unless one is born anew he cannot see the Kingdom of God. (John 3:3) Paul makes it very explicit: "No one can say 'Jesus is Lord' except by the Holy Spirit." (1 Cor. 12:3)

6

This brings into clearer focus the real problem of the individual gospel and the aims and strategies of its adherents. For the latter have not sufficiently understood that conversion from a life of sin must lead to a new life of Kingdom service. They have not fully seen *the context of repentance* since they tend to sever the link between individual rebirth and the totality of God's Kingdom plan for the entirety of creation, culture and society, where the Father wants to establish His gracious, sovereign, and loving rule. They neglect to notice, at least in part, that *the motive for rebirth* is the coming of the Kingdom, as Christ so clearly stated throughout His entire ministry: "Repent, for the Kingdom of heaven is at hand." (Matt. 4:17; cf Mark 1:14)

# Part Two.
## CAUSES and CONSEQUENCES

Over against the Biblical motive of regeneration and conversion as a first step in a life of sanctification, that is, a life of integral discipleship and service to the glory of God, the individual gospel posits *the motive of the salvation of individual souls*. In the Scriptures, the soul is the life of the body in all of its earthly activities. How are we to understand the loss of the vision of the Kingdom of God and the reformation theme of *soli deo gloria* — to God alone be the glory? When did this vision and this Scriptural theme become narrowed down to the salvation of man's soul?

### 1. John Locke and individualism

In order to answer this question we will have to look at some of the conceptions of a great British philosopher, John Locke (1632-1704). We can only highlight a few basic points.

Locke developed a conception of society which supplied both elements of the individual gospel as described above. To begin with, he maintained that society is a collection of individual beings whose humanity lies in an identity separate from other men. In defending this position, Locke in effect opposed the Scriptural revelation that God created mankind as a spiritual community which is restored through the reconciling work of Christ, the Head of the Body of believers. The foundation of society in Locke is no longer Jesus Christ but the will of the individual.

The will of individual man is the key to Locke's conception of society since only through its expression can human *needs* and *interests* be met. There are all kinds of human interests and needs, but they fall into two basic categories. Man has *earthy* needs, since man has a body. He has *heavenly* needs, since he also has a soul.

### 2. The acquisition of soul salvation

Man's heavenly needs concern the salvation of the individual soul. Souls must get to heaven. Religion and the church must meet this human interest in salvation. A man's soul can be saved only by the proper expression of a man's individual will. In Locke's famous *Letter concerning Toleration* (1689) he writes: "The care . . . of every man's soul belongs unto himself, and is to be left unto himself. . . . Nay, God Himself will not save men against their wills." A person does not become a member of the Church of Jesus Christ by the operation of the Holy Spirit but by the voluntary expression of his human will. He should be able to choose any sect that suits him best since there are "several paths that are in the same road" to heaven. Religion in Locke has been largely reduced to 'the man-centered search for salvation. Very little is left of the Scriptural view that religion is man's loving service of Christ, Saviour and Lord.

### 3. The acquisition of private property

Man does not only have a soul. He also has a body. That body, too, must be taken care of. How can one best meet the needs and interests of the body? It is highly significant to note that the answer Locke gives to this question runs parallel to the answer concerning soul salvation. In both cases the answer lies in an expression of the individual will. The individual person, in trying to meet the needs of the body, must learn to shift for himself by *acquiring private property*. If you've got something you can call *your own* you can begin to take care of your earthly needs.

The Bible teaches certain basic principles about "property". Some of these are: (1) man belongs to the Lord Who created him; (2) the earth belongs to the Lord; and (3) man's use of the earth is a matter of stewardship over a possession inherited from the gracious heavenly Father. Man's use of the earth, in agriculture, industry, and trade, is placed in the context of the covenant between God and man which provides the conditions of responsibility within which man may utilize the resources of creation for the welfare of family and for the welfare of those who are in need: the orphan, the widow, the alien, and the poor. In this covenantal setting the notion of absolute private property is absent.

Locke rejects this Biblical normative setting. In the chapter on property in the *Second Treatise on Government* he teaches (1) that man has a property in his own person; (2) that he has a property in the labour of his hands; and (3) that the fruit of the earth can only fulfill a person's needs if it belongs to him, that is, it must be "a part of him, that another can no longer have any right to it."

On reading these passages it is not surprising that several modern scholars have called attention to the relation between religion and the rise of capitalism. As a matter of fact, for many the founders of Protestantism — Luther and especially Calvin — are supposedly the real originators of today's acquisitive society. I believe that this is a gross error. The roots of modern society cannot, I think, be properly understood unless one makes a clear distinction between the early reformers of the sixteenth century and the later seventeenth-century developments in which the spirit of an un-Biblical individualism twisted Christian thought and action into a direction foreign to the Gospel itself. The Gospel does not know an unfettered individual who can rely on individual will and reason to shift for himself in the acquisition of soul salvation — neo-

Pelagianism and traditional Arminianism — and the acquisition of absolute private property — capitalistic liberalism. John Locke was not a Calvinist. His friends in England and in Holland were not the divines of the Presbyterian and Reformed Churches. His friends were the rationalists among the Arminians, the forerunners of the later enlightened deists and the modern liberals — in theology and politics!

## 4. Separation of religion and politics

There is another matter on which Locke exercised an immense influence. It is the relation between religion and politics. Having neatly divided human interests between heavenly and earthly because of the "separation" between soul and body, Locke found a way of keeping religion out of politics. "The church itself is a thing absolutely separate and distinct from the commonwealth. The boundaries on both sides are fixed and immovable." In this way Locke could find a foundation for the secular state of classic liberalism which exists to preserve private property. Locke is the founder of the religion of absolute private property. He is the father of *laissez-faire* doctrines not so much in the sense of keeping politics out of property questions (the state exists to protect property relations) but in the sense of keeping God and the Bible out of property relations.

## 5. Intolerant toleration

Having thus limited religion to matters of soul salvation, having cut the body out of Biblical religion, Locke can readily propose toleration between the various sects of Christendom: private religious opinions should not in any way affect the affairs of society. Society could be established on the basis of rational agreement between individuals pursuing the same end: property. Since most men are endowed with a spark of reason, toleration and consensus can readily be achieved. Persons not so rationally enlightened are permitted to find a basis for social morality in private religion. That kind of a basis is better than no basis at all. In other words, besides serving as the avenue of soul salvation, Christianity could also function as a *civil religion,* as the *support of a particular political order after that order had been secularized,* severed from the fountain of life in Christ Jesus.

However, Locke made it very clear that the political order had to determine the range of influence of the Christian religion; for only in that way could toleration be maintained. Here toleration becomes intolerant: if the Christian religion would come into conflict with the political system, the Christian religion had to surrender. In this way Locke formulated the essential ingredients of the relation between the social-political order and the Christian faith that we find today in Canada and the United States: "no opinions contrary to human society, or to those moral rules which are necessary to the preservation of civil society, are to be tolerated by the magistrate."

## 6. The individual gospel as civil religion

The results of the conception hastily sketched here are these:

a. The polite totalitarianism of liberal rationalism reduced the catholic claims of the Gospel of Christ to matters literally out-of-this-world. The sweet reasonableness of this totalitarianism determines the decision-making process in education, the trade unions, the political parties, and most professional organizations. Witness the legal battles of the CLAC! And the struggle for educational justice!

b. American and Canadian Christians, also those in the orthodox churches, have grown more and more accustomed to this reduction of Christ's Lordship over life. The wall of partition between religion and the state, established by the enlightened deists of the eighteenth century (Voltaire, G e o r g e Washington, Thomas Jefferson, etc.),

has now become a bulwark of mainline orthodoxy itself. Behind that bulwark the churches and "sects" were allowed to pursue their programs. What was accomplished must not be despised. But the thrust of these accomplishments, in revivals, in missions, in evangelism, in Sunday Schools, was largely limited to the salvation of individual souls and the well-being of the isolated and fragmented denominations.

c. The individual gospel, implicitly or explicitly, proceeds from the assumption that the individual person or at least the individual soul can somehow be lifted out of the context of God's creation. That context is then left to itself, neutralized, or avoided as the devil's domain. But what do we see in recent decades? The proponents of the individual gospel become proponents of an individualistic social order as well. And their methodology of "social action" is a methodology of "individual witness and action". This is not surprising since human life is indeed *of one piece.* A basic conception defended in one area of life will soon influence one's thinking in remaining areas. Careful commentators have indeed correctly concluded that it is precisely the religion of individual soul salvation that is now becoming the civil religion of the United States. Billy Graham and Richard Nixon are fast friends.

The Christian religion, without the wide horizons of Christ's redeeming Kingship over men and nations, narrowed down to man-centered soul-salvation, has become for many the moral justification for nationalism, the "American way of life," and all that it stands for in the world today.

Precisely *here* we must listen to Christ Himself: "My Kingdom is not of this world." (John 18: 36) Or to the Apostle John: "Little children, keep yourselves from idols." (1 John 5: 21)

ON CHRISTIAN SOCIAL ACTION IN A PLURALIST SOCIETY

Foundations and Directions

Bernard Zylstra

## Introduction

In 1972 citizens in Canada and the United States will
witness intense political campaigns in which both Prime
Minister Pierre Elliott Trudeau and President Richard Nixon
stand for re-election.  In these campaigns, the citizenry,
constitutionally co-responsible for the affairs of state,
does not have a Christian political option.  Hence, the
Gospel's vision of justice is not structurally and lasting-
ly related to the process of political decision-making.  It
also means that Christian citizens are in a political limbo.
They have, as it were, returned to the land of Egypt, enslaved by the pharaohs whose revelation comes from the
highpriests and whose power lies in chariots.  Christians
today, to employ another Biblical image, are captives of
the mighty in a secular Babylonian exile; their voice is
not heard loud and clear in the places where our lands are
given direction.  Do we now hear the expected song of la-
ment from God's People:  "How shall we sing the Lord's
song in a foreign land?"  (Ps. 137)  Hardly.  Instead, we
find God's People limping with two opinions, confusedly
listening to their leaders who seek to worship Jehovah
while adjusting to the demands of Baal.  (cf. I Kings 18:21)
     When it comes to the area of the relation between the
Christian faith and politics, most Christians, including
orthodox evangelicals, fall into three groups.  (1)  Some
assert that the world of politics is largely neutral with
respect to the claims of Jesus Christ; that it can well
run its own affairs without specific Christian involvement.
(2)  Others claim that politics belongs to the world of the
devil, and that Christians should stay away from it as far
as possible.  (3)  Then there is the third group, increasing
rapidly today in both Protestant and Roman Catholic circles,
which argues that Christians should not avoid the social
and political arena but that they should join forces with
the best elements of humanism, either in its capitalistic
or socialistic form (or some half-way house in-between), in
order to see if together we can't make this world a bit of
a better place to live in.
     These answers, I think, are not worthy of the Gospel
of Christ, and for this reason I would explore an alternative with you.  My alternative is this:  the organization
of a Christian political movement in both the United States

ORIGINAL MANUSCRIPT, 1973.

and in Canada. In each country the purpose of the movement would be twofold: (1) the establishment of a center for Christian social and political reflection where the building blocks for a practical political option would be developed; and (2) the establishment of an action division responsible for the implementation of a political program first in those states and provinces where sufficient support can be found among Christian citizens, and subsequently at the national levels in Washington and Ottawa.

The realization of this alternative is an immense undertaking because of the immensity of political concerns. The vast scope of politics in 1972 would distinguish Christian action there from action on other fronts. That vast scope also makes the birth of a new political movement so frightfully difficult. Christians, with sincere commitment, ingenuity, financial backing, and persistance, can set up a local church, an evangelism campaign, a foreign mission, a Christian school, or a Salvation Army project, without altogether too much ado. This is possible because the thrust of such actions is usually local. But that simply isn't the case with politics, even if politics also does have local dimensions.

Whenever we properly use the word "politics" we refer to the action of states, of entities like the US, India, China, Canada, or their parts. A state is the community of citizens responsible for the administration of justice within the state's territory in cooperation with other states for the administration of justice in international relations.

It is my conviction that the Gospel of Christ has very much to do with politics, with the action of states. Since it is impossible to give a full account of that conviction in a single speech, I will limit myself to two points: (1) the Biblical foundation for Christian social and political action; and (2) direction for the future.

Part I.   BIBLICAL FOUNDATIONS

A. The Government:   the Lord's Servant

One of the most famous and debated passages in the Scriptures deals with government. It is found in Paul's letter to Christians in Rome, the center of world politics two thousand years ago. This very passage already indicates that the Bible itself certainly does not exclude the life of states from its concerns. What do we read?

"Let every person be subject to the governing authorities. For there is no authority except from God, and

11

those that exist have been instituted by God. Therefore he who resists the authorities resists what God
has appointed, and those who resist will incur judgment. For rulers are not a terror to good conduct,
but to bad. Would you have no fear of him who is in
authority? Then do what is good, and you will receive
his approval, for he is God's servant for your good.
But if you do wrong, be afraid, for he does not bear
the sword in vain; he is the servant of God to execute
his wrath on the wrongdoer." (Rom. 13:1-4)

This passage has often been interpreted to mean Paul's
passive acquiescence to the power of the Roman empire. It
means no such thing. Instead, this passage - along with
the entire letter to the Roman Christians - in effect de-
stroyed the spiritual foundations of the Roman empire. For
the essence of that empire was this: the citizen exists
for the good of the state. Paul turns this around, and
does so totally: the state and its authorities exist for
the good of the citizen. This, in a nutshell, is the evangelical, the Gospel's message for politics: all political
authority exists for the benefit, the good, the welfare,
of the citizen.

Further, Paul does not arrive at this conclusion on
the basis of conceptions which have been so universally
accepted especially in the Anglo-Saxon world: the conceptions of popular sovereignty, government by consent of the
governed, government of and by and for the people. For
these conceptions make the government the servant of the
people. Here again, Paul's argument is exactly the opposite:
the government is here for your good because it is God's
servant.

So in one brief passage Paul rejects the two most influential theories of the state that have plagued Western
civilization from the time of Plato to the period of Hitler,
Stalin, de Gaulle, Mao Tse-tung, Nixon and Trudeau: (1) the
authoritarian conception of authority, viz. that might is
right; and (2) the democratic conception of authority, viz.
that government is of the people (in principle the rule by
majority vote). Paul's alternative to these basic conceptions is clear: all those in authority over us can use
their power for the good of men in the final analysis only
when they are servants of the Lord. What does this mean?
This question confronts us with the entire Biblical understanding of the Kingdom of God, His Word, and the Church.

B. The Kingdom of God

If Christendom is to become again a vital force in modern life it will have to listen anew to the Scriptural teachings concerning the Kingdom of God. Yes, listen anew, since

12

our acceptance of the individualistic conception of the Gospel during the last two hundred years has made us strangers to this central theme of the Kingdom in the Bible. It was central in the Old Testament. It was central also in Christ's ministry as we learn from Mark's description of it: "Jesus came into Galilee, preaching the Gospel of God, and saying, The time is fulfilled, and the Kingdom of God is at hand; repent, and believe in the Gospel." (1:14f) It must similarly be central in our life. In our prayers: "Thy kingdom come, Thy will be done, on earth as it is in heaven." And in our deeds: "Seek first His kingdom and His righteousness." (Matt. 6:10, 32) Only if we seek first the Kingdom can we hope to receive the rest, can we hope to be socially and politically relevant. What is meant by the Kingdom?

## 1. The Word of God

The Bible speaks of the Kingdom in two basic ways. First, it is the Reign or Rule of God over the entire creation by His Word; second, it is the Realm where this Word is heard, obeyed, and done. An understanding of the Kingdom of God implies an understanding of the Word of God. The first chapter of the Gospel of John reveals that the Word of God was in the beginning and that all things were created by that Word. What is that Word? The Word, the voice of the Lord is power(ful). (Ps. 29:4) God's Word is His power creating all things. (cf. Ps. 33:6f;II Pet. 3:5f) It is also His power upholding all things, once created. (Hebr. 1:3; cf. Col. 1:16f) Further, it is His power directing all things, once created, to their final end, which is God's own glory. God's Word is thus the very life of all things. "In Him was life." (John 1:4) In a humanly halting way one might describe the Word as God's calling creation into being-for-service. God's Word is thus God's Kingdom as His Rule over creation.

## 2. The covenant

Because of the very nature of the Word of God we should understand that the Scriptures present a certain frame of reference within which we can know something of the relation between God, man, and the world. That is the frame of the covenant. In this covenant, this 'contract,' there are basically two parts: the Creator and the creation. The Word of God is the link between these two part(ner)s. On the one hand there is God Who speaks the Word: He makes, molds, patterns, structures and destines the creation. He has the 'say' over all things. What does He say? One can put it somewhat as follows: "I, the Lord, have made you, my creation, so that you may serve Me. If you obey Me, if you listen to My Word, then you will have life and joy. Then I will bless you." On the other hand there is the required response from the creation to the Word. The Word requires an answer. an _Antwort_. The covenant is the comprehensive arrangement between God and His creation with the Word as the communicating link.

## 3. Creatures are servants

Since the Word of God patterns the very nature of all reality, the meaning of reality is service of God. This is the Psalmist's song: "Forever, O Lord, thy Word is firmly fixed in the heavens. . . . For all things are thy servants." (119:89f) Creatures simply are servants. This is true not only of man, whose very freedom lies in being a slave of the Lord. (cf. Rom. 6:18) It is also true of what we call 'nature,' which in its diverse ways fulfills the Word of the Lord. (Ps. 148:8) Finally, it is true of social institutions, like the government, which are specifically called ministers of the Lord, as we saw in the passage from Romans 13.

To be a creature, therefore, is to be wholly dependent upon the Lord. Nature, man, and human institutions have no life apart from the Word of the Lord. His Word is their very life. (cf. Deut. 32:46f; Lev. 18:3f) Obedience to the Word gives joy and peace. Disobedience leads to disintegration, frustration, curse and final death. (cf. Deut. 11:26f; chs. 27 and 28)

In this light we can already begin to understand Paul's statement about government; it too, in its own way, is a servant of the Lord for our good. Paul is saying that the very life of governmental authority lies in listening to the Word of the Lord. If it does not listen, it is a curse, to itself, and to the citizenry.

## 4. Man in the symphony of God's creation

God has formed the earth to make man's unique service possible. The Lord did not create the world a chaos; He formed it to be inhabited, to be a home for man (cf. Isa. 44:18), the climax of God's creative activity. (cf. Ps.8) Within the all-embracing inescapablle covenant-Kingdom bond between God and creation, the Lord assigns a place to man where four fundamental and inseparable relations obtain:

a. God and man. Here we find man in his relation of utter dependence upon and service to God. Summed up simply: man is God's man. (cf. II Tim. 3:16; I John 4:6)

b. <u>Heart and functions</u>. Here we find the relation between the central religious unity of man's person and the diverse aspects of his life on earth. The central religious direction of man's manifold functions is found in the heart of man. After sin, man's spiritual rebirth is a matter of the heart, which is the motor directing his life's actions. "Unless one is born anew, he cannot see the Kingdom of God." (John 3:16)

c. <u>Man and fellow-man</u>. Here we find man in his relation to his fellows, to the whole of mankind, which - before sin - is the People of God.

d. <u>Man and the earth</u>. Here we find man in his relation to the rest of creation, to its many creatures which serve man and over which he is to have dominion. Under God, man is king of the earth. That is his mission, his mandate.

The uniqueness of the Christian religion lies in the Biblical revelation that the harmony among these four dimensions is <u>life</u> for man. This harmony in effect is the positive relation between God's Word and man's response in the covenantal bond. It indicates the presence of the Kingdom both as Reign (Word) and Realm (obedience, service). Here one finds the coherence, wholeness, joy, and peace of paradise, God's home for man.

5. <u>God's Word for Man: Love!</u>

The specific service which man is asked to render his Creator is found in the Word addressed to man: "Love the Lord your God with all your heart, and with all your soul, and with all your mind. This is the first and great commandment. And a second like unto it, You shall love your neighbor as yourself. On these two commandments depend all the law and the prophets." (Matt. 22:37f) Together these two commandments constitute the Word, the creation-ordinance for man, made in the likeness of God, Who is love. (I John 4:8) These two commandments make mankind a community, a fellowship of love, God's People, His Body.

In order to understand properly the Biblical foundation of social and political activity, two points must be stressed here. (1) These two commands, distinguished by Christ but inseparable, sum up all that is required of man. The many statutes and ordinances that one finds in Holy Writ are not additions to but explications of what love means in the actual life of men. For this reason we should not assume that <u>besides</u> love we also owe justice to our

neighbor. For justice is a specific way of loving our
neighbor. (2) In the second place, love is to be expressed
in many ways. The Bible speaks of the one Word but also of
the ten words, the ten commandments. The central and _pri-
mary_ creation-order of love embraces and gives meaning to
all of the _secondary_ orders directed to mankind in its task
of unfolding creation in history. Some of these secondary
and derivative Words or orders are: justice, morality,
economy, stewardship, language, science, culture technique,
nurture, schooling, etc. The relation between primary unity
and secondary multiplicity in the Words which God gives to
man is parallel to the unity (heart) and multiplicity (functions) of man's person.

For our problem it is crucial to understand that human
institutions - like the state, the family, industry, the
school - are avenues in which man serves the Lord, in which
he expresses love to God above all and to his neighbor, a
fellow-creature. If these institutions are not channels of
this kind, they are not servants of the Lord but a curse.
For they, one and all, are founded on God's creation-order
for mankind, to be realized in history, man's path through
time.

## 6. The total character of sin

Sin is man's declaration of independence from God.
It is radical. It affects the root of human existence and
thus the direction of the entire creation in history. Sin
is total. For it does not merely break man's link with God.
Since that link is all-embracing, the disrupting effect of
sin shatters the shalom-harmony in the entire covenantal
setting of creation. (1) It breaks asunder the integrality
of man's person, leaving him broken-hearted. (2) It dis-
rupts the love-relation towards fellow-man, destroying the
community of mankind as God's People, God's Body. (3) It
introduces a tension between man and the earth, which now
produces thorns and thistles. (Gen.3) Sin spreads alienation all around. It makes man a stranger to the covenant,
having no hope and without God in the world. (Eph.2:12)
The sin of Adam, mankind's father, means that the Garden
of Paradise will not be the start for building of the City
of God, the Kingdom of service and praise.

## C. Jesus Christ: Saviour and Lord

Sin is not the last 'word' in history. For the Word
of the Lord - and it only - stands forever. (cf. Isa. 40:8;
I Pet. 1:23f) The light continues to shine in the darkness.
(John 1:5) For the Word of the Lord is never spoken in vain.
(Isa. 55:10f) The darkness of sin has not overcome the

Light, the Word. Rather, the Word became flesh in Jesus
Christ, fit for hanging on Calvary's tree.

## 1.  No dualism between creation and redemption

At this point in our deliberations everything comes
to a head. For the crucial question is:  What think ye of
the Christ?  Conflicting answers to that question have divided Christendom since its birth, and today an improper
understanding of Christ's place in history has eroded the
strength of His followers.  Only a few things can be said
here.  But the following must be said:  in Christ God the
Creator is bringing His plans with the entire creation to
fruition.  "The will of the Lord shall prosper in His hand."
(Isa. 53:10)  This means that whatever we have said about
the Word of God for creation, about the covenant, and about
the Kingdom, must now be said again in connection with Jesus
Christ.  There is no conflict in the Scriptures between
God's order of creation and His order of redemption.  There
is no dualism between a Kingdom of power and a Kingdom of
grace.  There are not two realms in God's plan, one for
mankind in general and one for the church in particular.
There is not a realm of common grace for society and a realm
of special grace for the church.  There is not a will of
the Lord for society in distinction from His will for the
individual.  There is no special mission mandate for the
salvation of souls in distinction from a general cultural
mandate for the operation of society.  There is not a sacred
realm where the Scriptures supposedly are supreme next to
a secular realm where we can rely on general reason or natural law or common sense.

## 2.  Christ is Creator and Redeemer:  Alpha-Omega

In short, the Word of God for creation is total; sin
affects the totality of creation; and Christ's atonement at
the cross is total.  "For God so loved the world that He
gave His only begotten Son, that whoever believes in Him
should not perish but have eternal life.  For God sent the
Son into the world, not to condemn the world, but that the
world might be saved through Him."  (John 3:16; cf. 1:29;
1 John 2:2)  That world is not just the collection of saved
individuals.  It is the cosmos, which was made through
Christ the Word made flesh.
For Christ, like the Father, is "the Alpha and the
Omega, the first and the last, the beginning and the end."
(Rev. 22:12; cf. Isa. 44:6)  The cosmic signifigance of
Christ's role in creation and re-creation is revealed in
Paul's incisive letters to the Ephesians and the Colossians.
(1) Christ is the first-born of all creation; all things

17

were created through Him and for Him, and in Him all things
hold together. He is the cohesive link in the chain of the
entire symphony of creation. He is the Alpha. (2) But
Christ is also the head of the Body, the church, the New
Mankind. He is also the beginning in the economy of redemption, the last Adam, the firstborn from the dead, so that
He might be pre-eminent in all things. He is the Omega.
In Christ all the fullness of God was pleased to dwell -
in creation. Then, after sin disrupted the peace of creation, God in Christ is reconciling all things, restoring
peace. In the fullness of time God is again uniting all
things, in Christ. Thus He is our peace. How? Christ
made peace by the blood of the cross. (see Col. 1:15f; Eph.
1:9f; 2:14f)

## 3. The Lamb of God is King of Kings

So the key event in history is Golgotha; for there the
Prince of Darkness was dethroned. Hence Christ could say:
It is finished. (cf. Luke 10:17; John 12:31; 16:11; Rev.
12:7-11) The crucifixion means that the creation in principle is restored to its original intent, to sing the
praises of God and the Lamb: "Then I heard every created
thing in heaven and on earth and under the earth and in the
sea, all that is in them, crying: 'Praise and honour, glory
and might, to him who sits on the throne and to the Lamb
forever and ever.'" (Rev. 5:11f) The Lamb Who was slain
is Lord of Lords and King of Kings. (Rev. 17:14) Because
of this Christ's last words to His disciples bring together
the 'cultural mandate' of Genesis I and the 'mission' mandate of the pentecostal era. Since all authority has been
given to Christ, the church must go and make disciples of
all nations, teaching them to observe all that Christ has
commanded. (Matt. 28:18f) That means: the Word in its
entirety. That brings us to the task of Christ's disciples
today.

## Part II. DIRECTIONS FOR THE FUTURE

Turning now to the second part of my theme - directions
for Christian social action - I really want to focus mainly
on the question: What does it mean to be members of the
Body of Christ? What is it to be People of God, to be
Church, in these last days? Paul describes the task of
God's People in 2 Cor. 5:16-21. God, he writes, was in
Christ reconciling the world to himself. We, who have heard
the Word of the Gospel and accepted it, have been reconciled.
Therefore we, who are in Christ, are already a new creation;
the old has passed away, behold the new has come. But then
there are still so many who have not heard of the Lamb Who

18

is King of Kings.  There lies the task of Christ's disciples:  to them has been given the ministry of reconciliation. "So we are ambassadors for Christ, God making His appeal through us."

Now there are certain norms for God's people which they must meet if they are to be a proper vessel of the Word.  These norms are the marks of the Church, confessed in the Apostles' Creed and in the Nicene Creed:  "I believe one holy catholic and apostolic Church, the communion of saints."  If the Church attempts to meet these marks it will understand its responsibilities in the entire area of social and political action.  In other words, all that we have to be today is:  Body of Christ, Church.  In the measure that we are not that, we are in need of a reformation.

A.  The Church is a Communion of Saints

1.  Christ is our Life

If the Church is to be an agent of reconciliation - peace-making - in the world, it must be a communion of saints.  Now at the very outset it must be clearly understood that when the Bible speaks of the People of God or the Body of Christ or the Church (ecclesia), it does not refer to what today we call the institutional church.  Precisely because we have narrowed down the meaning of 'church' to institutions now called denominations we no longer know how to relate the Word of God to the entirety of our earthly life.  The Church is the body of those men and women who have in faith accepted the call of the Lord to serve him anew.

Though the Gospels do not refer much to the 'church,' Christ described it profoundly:  "Abide in me, and I in you. As the branch cannot bear fruit by itself, unless it abides in the vine, neither can you, unless you abide in me.  I am the vine, you are the branches.  He who abides in me, and I in him, he it is that bears much fruit, for apart from me you can do nothing." (John 15:4f)  The body of people that wants to do nothing apart from Christ - in their personal life, their schooling, their politics, their economics, etc. - is the Church.  Paul puts it succinctly:  our bodies, that is, our entire earthly existence, must become members of Christ. (I Cor. 6:15)  It is dangerous to say that we are members of the church, that we share in the communion of the saints.  For as soon as we say that we must be willing to confess with Paul:  "I have been crucified with Christ: it is no longer I who live, but Christ who lives in me; and the life I now live in the flesh I live by faith in the Son of God, who loved me and gave himself for me." (Gal. 2:20) I take that phrase - the life I now live in the flesh - to

19

refer to all of our actions and decisions and plans here on earth. Our life in Christ is not the life of the 'soul,' but the life of the body: our work, our homes, our loves, our voting, our playing. That is the radical and total meaning of redemption.

## 2. The Church is a community of love

If that is clear, then we can also turn to the other side of the church: it is a communion of saints, that is, it is a community where we are members one of another. (Eph. 4:25) It is a community of love. That means: it is the New Mankind, the New Humanity (Eph. 2:15), where the creation ordinance of Love to God above all and Love to Neighbor as ourselves is heard, and done. This may sound drastic, but nothing more than the radical character of Peter's statement: "Once you were no people but now you are God's people." (I Pet. 2:9f) The church is that spiritual community where we can be genuinely human again, where men and women can be doers of the Word. The Church is the citizenry of the Kingdom. After all, God the Father "has delivered us from the dominion of darkness and transferred us to the kingdom of his beloved Son, in whom we have redemption, the forgiveness of sins." (Col. 1:13)

## 3. The Church has many members

The church is God's agent of reconciliation. The intent of that reconciliation is to bring mankind back to the all-embracing Word of the Lord. That Word has many dimensions. That means that the church has many tasks: as many as there are walks of life. For this reason the church has many members, each with different gifts and talents, so that the total program of the Kingdom can be witnessed to, so that the Word of the Lord may speed on and triumph. (2 Thess. 3:1) Some members preach on pulpits, some teach in the schools, some are home-makers, some are politicians; others work in industry, in art, in journalism. Whatever their individual task is, together they must form a body fitly framed together, experiencing the communion of the saints on the job, strengthening one another in the faith, "sharing with one another in Jesus the tribulation and the Kingdom and the patient endurance," (Rev. 1:9) knowing that "all who desire to live a godly life in Christ Jesus will be persecuted." (2 Tim. 3:12) The persecution doesn't matter; the witness, the mission matters. That brings us to the next mark of the church.

## B. The Church is an Apostolic Movement

## 1. Mission and Missions

at the cross.  Without that, society disintegrates.
Concretely, without a foundation in Christ's atoning
work, states, industries, families, universities, will
indeed disintegrate until finally the 'man of lawless-
ness,' the Anti-Christ, who takes his seat in the temple of God, proclaiming himself to be God, is revealed.
(2 Thess. 2:3f)

b.  And what is the institutional church?  It is part
of society.  It is human.  It is an institution.  It
is founded, with all other institutions, on God's order
for creation.  Its specific mission is the ministry of
the Word in proclamation and sacrament.  It proclaims
the Word so that men and nations can serve the Lord.
It is not an end in itself.  It simply proclaims the
Good News, so that the life of people in the state, in
the economic sector, in the labour unions, in the
schools, may be the life of Christ.  The institutional
church is the vanguard of the apostolic Body of Christ.
It should always be in the forefront of history, har-
nessed with the Word of Truth.
    The institutional church must carefully limit it-
self to its specific mission.  In pulpit and pastoral
care it has but one aim:  to bring men to repentence
and service.  But it will avoid taking over that service itself.  It will not want to engage directly in
political and educational and cultural matters.  Instead, it will challenge its members to assume service
in these areas as part of a life of sanctification.
The church preaches so that its members will assume
responsibility in the area of social action.

C.  The Church is Catholic

1.  Individual gospel vs. social gospel

    The word 'catholic' originally meant:  according to
the whole.  That is the meaning it ought to have when we
talk about the mission of the Body of Christ.  The 'whole'
that is of importance here is the entire setting of man in
God's creation, where the four basic relations obtain that
we spoke of earlier:  (1) God-man, (2) heart-functions, (3)
man-fellows, (4) man-earth.  In view of what has already
been said above I do not have to repeat here the impossibility of lifting the individual man with an individual 'soul'
out of the concrete earthly setting in which God has placed
him.  That impossibility is the mistake of individualism.
The Gospel is covenantal.  And the dilemma of an individual
gospel of a social gospel represents a fundamental distortion of the Biblical message.

21

God is one.  His Word is one.  Christ's Body is one.
The mission of that body is also one.  Its mission is to
bring the Gospel - by word and deed - to all men in their
live's totality.  But that all-encompassing mission has
many dimensions; it is concretely expressed in many diverse
and distinct missions.  These missions in principle are as
many as there are distinct areas in human life and culture.
Bringing the Gospel with its healing effect to any area of
human endeavor is possible and meaningful because God is
reconciling the entire world in Christ.  The exclusion of
any area of life from the Gospel implies unfaithfulness to
the Lamb, Who is Lord of Lords, Who seeks pre-eminence in
everything.

## 2.    The Institutional Church and Society

For this reason, I think, the prevalent separation of
the task of Christians in the institutional church from
their tasks in society is un-Biblical.

> a.  For what is society?  Society is the complex of
> the totality of human relations intertwining with
> each other in a hundred ways.  Society is human.
> Society is a complexity of institutions and associa-
> tions in a particular culture.  Institutions and asso-
> ciations, in turn, are avenues in which men realize
> specific Words (norms) of the Lord.  For example, in
> industry men are called to respond to the divine norm
> of stewardship.  In the state, the divine norm of jus-
> tice.  In the home, the divine norm of nurture.  In the
> school, the divine norm of education in truth.  In the
> university, the divine norm of scientific analysis.
> But we have seen how these norms are but partial expli-
> cations of the over-arching Norm of love to God and
> neighbor.
>      Society therefore, in the light of a radical accep-
> tance of the meaning of creation and redemption, may
> only be the historical realization of the Kingship of
> Christ, to Whom all power and authority in these social
> relationships belongs.  Outside of that redemptive
> Kingship, society has no lasting meaning.  It is not
> a law unto itself; its law is the Word of the Gospel.
>      With reference then to its concrete historical
> reality, human society must simply be the Body of
> Christ, differentiated in many ways.  The foundation
> of that Body is the Word of the Lord now made known in
> Christ, whose Name is the only name by which men can
> be saved, by which they can be wholly human.  The foun-
> dation of society is that same Word.  What other foun-
> dation could there possibly be?  The very possibility
> for human society - for the state, for industry, for
> the family - is Christ's redemptive reconciliation at

## 2. The Gospel of the Kingdom for the Whole Man

This rejection of an erroneous dilemma, which really stems from the polar tensions within humanism (individualism and socialism), also implies a re-setting of mission priorities and strategies. The latter must be determined by the Gospel of the Kingdom for the whole man, for the 'catholic' man. A mission program that is concerned with decisions for Christ without proclaiming and giving evidence of Christ's saving Lordship for man's concrete creaturely and earthly existence does injustice to God's human personality. Such a program may well in the long run increase the frustration that individual persons experience in a technological society instead of alleviating such frustration. Here we have to learn from Moses and the prophets and the apostles who preached the renewal of life in Christ in whatever setting the converts were found. Moses stipulated carefully what the new rule of love meant in matters of trade, law, agriculture, hygiene, temple worship, etc. The prophets hurled the Word of the Lord to an apostate Israel that confined religion to Sunday services without seeking justice and correcting oppression. (cf. Isa. 1:13-17) Paul concluded practically every one of his epistles with practical guidelines for masters and slaves, parents and children, governors and subjects. When the Lamb of God will judge the nations, He will give the kingdom to those who fed the hungry, clothed the naked, and visited the prisoners. (cf. Matt. 25:31f) The Gospel is good for mankind. It picks men up right where they are to restore them to true creatureliness.

## D. The Church is One

### 1. The Many Denominational Fragments

The marks of the Church - unity, catholicity, apostolicity and holiness - pertain in the first place to the Body of Christ as the New Mankind, the spiritual community of those whom the Lord calls His own. But these marks are the central religious norms for every undertaking of that body in society. This implies, to begin with, that the institutional church must be one. That is God's norm. We do not meet that norm today since the institutional church is fragmented into hundreds of pieces. How can the one Lord, Who has one Gospel, Who requires one faith, use us as His reconciling agent if we are divided, schismatic, sectarian?

### 2. Unity in Christian social action

The unity that must characterize the Body of Christ

should be evident also in its non-ecclesiastical endeavors. The communion of saints must be present in whatever God's people undertake in social action. The traditional stance especially of evangelicals has been that involvement in social and political and educational tasks should follow the avenue of individual witness and action. This is, I think, contrary to the NT teachings about the corporate bond that ties Christ's disciples together. In the midst of all the tensions in Corinth, Paul exclaims: "Now you are the body of Christ and individually members of it." (I Cor. 12)

Moreover, the notion that Christians should shift for themselves in society is a grave strategic error. For in doing the work of the Lord we are to be members one of another, we are to be a hand and a foot to each other. We need each other. Let's make this specific. In concrete social and cultural tasks the measure of cooperative unity among Christ's followers depends upon the job at hand. If it is a small task, a small team will do. If it is a large job, a large team is required.

There are a host of tasks in Canada and America that cannot meaningfully be tackled via the avenue of individual witness and action. These tasks are in the area of politics, primary and secondary education, university, the economic sector (both on management and trade union sides), journalism, the media. These tasks should not be given to the institutional churches since they lack competence and authority there. Instead, Christ's people in America and Canada should begin to form organized reflection and action fronts in these sectors of modern culture in order to more effectively channel the healing power of the Gospel to the centers of decision-making. Since limited insight and limited resources require a system of priorities, I would suggest that the first tasks to be tackled by evangelicals in North America in the seventies should be: (1) a Christian educational movement; (2) a Christian political movement; and (3) a Christian daily.

E.  The Body of Christ is Holy

1.  The Spiritual Antithesis

The final mark of Christ's Church is this: it must be a holiness movement. Perhaps everything that I have tried to convey can be summed up in that one characteristic. Holiness does not entail that God's People step out of this world, that they must leave it to the devil's devices. This is our Father's world. Holiness means that the Father asks for total dedication of that world to Him. So that brings us back to our starting-point: For from Him and through Him and unto Him are all things. (Rom. 11:36) The world is holy when it serves the Maker. We are to be holy not in ascetic isolation (as if sin has its source outside of men's hearts!) but right in the simple and concrete earthly setting of our daily life. The motor of your car and the toaster in your kitchen must be holy, says the Lord. (cf. Zech. 14:20) The Bible doesn't know our separation between a sacred and secular part of life.

But the Bible does know of a very profound antithesis between the dominion of darkness and the Kingdom of Jesus Christ. (cf. Col. 1:13) That antithesis is total with reference to the spiritual-religious direction of men's hearts and lives. That is the antithesis between the gods of this world and Jahweh, the one Lord, Whom we are asked to serve with single devotion. Holiness entails a negative aspect: " Do not be conformed to this world." Holiness also entails a positive aspect: "But be transformed by the renewal of your mind, that you may prove what is the will of God, what is good and acceptable and perfect." (Rom. 12:2)

Christ's little ones must not be conformed to this world. They must not listen to the words - lies - of the gods of this age. These are the gods who speak their words in the papers we read, on the TV screens that are in all of our homes, in the classrooms of our educational system, in the programs of our political parties, in the goals of the economic sector, in the promises of the trade unions. They are the gods of reason, toleration, science, technology, industry, material welfare, success. They are the gods of what this world calls progress. We listen to the words of these gods because we do not want to be holy. European man, American man, Canadian man wants the welfare and comfort and ease which these gods afford. No matter how much the worship of these gods destroys in human lives, in warfare, in the ecological balance, in the lives of the poor, the Third World, in the metropolitan centers.

## 2. Revolution, conversion, reformation

Some acknowledge the destruction that capitalism has brought upon our lands, and seek an alternative in a social revolution of the economic and political systems. The real problem, of course, does not lie in the first place in the social systems but in man who built these systems.

You have asked me to speak on Christian social action in a pluralist society. Have I done that? Yes and no. I am deeply concerned about a drastic re-direction of the social system in Canada and in America. Our economic and and political structures become less human, and thus less godly, as this century rushes to its end. In Toronto we are now working on a Christian political movement. But I know that no lasting and fundamental change in the social system will occur unless western man returns to the Lord, unless those who are still members of Christian churches experience a reformation. Our life in this world, our life in society, our 'social action' must be holy, dedicated to the Lord. It must be part of a life of sanctification, of conversion to the Lord. For millions in our lands it may be the first conversion. For all of us it is a daily necessity.

O land, land, land/America, America/O Canada, O Canada Hear the Word of the Lord! That He may have dominion from sea to sea! (Jer. 22:29; Ps. 72:8)

# THE RADICAL RIGHT & THE RISE OF THE

# FUNDAMENTALIST MINORITY

## DAVID DANZIG

EARLY IN FEBRUARY of this year a group of leading Protestant ministers and laymen in Dallas, Texas, were invited to form the core of a local chapter of "Christian Citizen," a new national organization whose announced aim is to train Christians in the techniques of practical politics. The founder of Christian Citizen, Mr. Gerri von Frellick (a Denver real estate developer and a Southern Baptist lay leader), spelled out the program of his movement as primarily an educational one whose purpose is to foster Christian principles in the nation's government and to combat "an increasing sense of futility and apathy in America." Qualifications for membership require only that the recruits must "give testimony of their personal experience with Christ" and must "accept the Bible as the infallible word of God." Once having joined, the "Christian Citizen" will be given an extensive training period at the precinct level and then go to work in the political party of his choice. The organization itself, according to von Frellick, will not endorse any candidate or take partisan stands on controversial issues. Appropriate action will be left to the "graduates" who will organize Christians to vote as a bloc and thus "participate effectively in the nation's political life." It is von Frellick's expectation that the movement will eventually become influential enough to "take over a majority of the precincts in this country."

As to actual political objectives, von Frellick has insisted that these are open and unspecified, the ideology of Christian Citizen being that "the democratic process has room for all viewpoints." When questioned about his position on certain key leaders and groups of the much publicized "radical right," von Frellick said that Dr. Fred C. Schwarz's Christian Anti-Communist Crusade was a "terrific" organization and "doing a fabulous job." He also said that the John Birch Society has "made a tremendous contribution to alerting the American people to the problem of Communism." The main difference which the Denver realtor finds between his organization and these others is that they lack "a positive approach"—whereas Christian Citizen can be "a means of launching an offensive in the ideological struggle with Communism."

Behind the vague and pious slogans, then, what we have here is the most recent formation of a cell nucleus in the growing organism of the extreme right. Christian Citizen also offers a particularly clear example of the relation of the more extreme wing of Protestant fundamentalism to the new ultra-conservative movement—a relationship that has frequently been overlooked or scanted by writers in their haste

COMMENTARY, April, 1972, 170-181.

to explain the movement in purely political terms and to find its roots in the same general rightist tendencies that produced the politics of Father Coughlin or of Senator McCarthy or Senator Goldwater, as the case may be. While it is true, of course, that Senator McCarthy is taken by the John Birch Society as its second great martyr, there are some significant differences between McCarthyism and the new radical right—one of the most decisive of which has precisely to do with the connection between this radical right and extreme Protestant fundamentalism.

Fundamentalism, when noticed at all by our popular journals, is usually patronized as a colorful fragment of an older, vanishing way of life. But the truth is that fundamentalism is a growing socio-religious force in America. While its more moderate wing has been attempting to work out a position of "classic orthodoxy" in theology and an over-all *modus vivendi* with liberal Protestantism (particularly of the National Council of Churches variety), its more extreme wing, defined in good part by a belligerent opposition to liberal Protestantism and deep hostility to the NCC, has by no means lost ground. It is only of this latter group that we shall be speaking in the following pages.

Fundamentalism is not a sect or a denomination or a specific church; it is a rigorously orthodox point of view which completely dominates some Protestant denominations and has adherents in many others, including even the Episcopal church. Among its basic doctrines are the inerrancy of the Bible, salvation by faith alone, and the pre-millennial return of Christ. On religious questions, it takes a stand against any attempts at revisionism and modernism. This emphasis upon literalness and purity of doctrine makes the fundamentalist look upon pragmatism in the social world with the same suspiciousness and distaste with which he views revisionism in religious doctrine. His commitment to Biblical prophecy, moreover, results in an anti-historicist perspective

which readily supports the conspiracy theory of social change. Given all this, and given the association that came to be developed between the "Protestant ethic" and the ideology of 19th-century capitalism, it is not surprising that fundamentalism should always have had a strong disposition to regard the revisions of this ideology (which were partly inspired by Protestant liberals) as the work of heretics and atheistic radicals, infected with and spreading false doctrines in a conspiratorial manner.*

In fundamentalist eyes, departures from 19th-century capitalism have carried with them the corruption of virtually sanctified socio-economic doctrines and have consequently helped to undermine the Christian society. Thus, the fundamentalist's apocalyptic conception of the world as strictly divided into the saved and the damned, the forces of good and the forces of evil, has readily lent itself to reactionary political uses. Fundamentalism today supports a super-patriotic Americanism; the conflict with Communism is not one of power blocs but of faiths, part of the unending struggle between God and the devil. The danger of Communism, therefore, is from within—from the corrosion of faith by insidious doctrines. That is to say, by "collectivism"—the modern fundamentalist's secular counterpart of atheism.

THE INHERENTLY CONSERVATIVE bent of fundamentalism has been further reinforced in America by regional factors. The fundamentalist population has always been located predominantly in the South, the border states, the Middle West, and in several Western states. It was partly as a spokesman for this population that William Jennings Bryan could talk of the East as "enemy territory," and express

* In his *History of Fundamentalism*, Stewart Cole speaks of fundamentalism as "the organized determination of conservative churchmen to continue the imperialistic culture of historic Protestantism, within an inhospitable civilization dominated by secular interests and a progressive Christian idealism."

their economic plight in the fundamentalist imagery of the "cross of gold" speech. In Bryan, as later in Huey Long, the hatred of finance capitalism, or "Wall Street," by a rural population could produce the reforming spirit of Populism without appreciably liberalizing the impacted prejudices of fundamentalist social attitudes. As H. Richard Niebuhr has said:

The fundamentalist movement was related in some localities to . . . intense racialism or sectionalism. With them it shared antagonism to changes in the mores which the war [World War I] and its consequences, the rise to power of previously submerged immigrant or racial groups and other social processes, brought forth. The political effectiveness of fundamentalism was due in part to this association and *to the support which it gave to political leaders,* who found in it a powerful symbolism representative of the antagonism of political and economic minorities against the eastern or northern urban industrial majority.

The influence of fundamentalist ideas on the political and social life of these regions is seen in the fact that the states in which the movement predominated were the ones that passed—or nearly passed—statutes forbidding the teaching of evolution in the schools and that first enacted prohibition laws. Similarly, fundamentalism's ancient and unregenerate hostility to Catholicism was in good part responsible for the heavy losses which the Democrat Al Smith suffered in 1928 in these regions.

THE STATES that repudiated Darwinism and Al Smith are today prominent among those nineteen that have passed "Right to Work" laws. Since World War I the social base of fundamentalism has shifted markedly, though few political writers have apparently noticed the shift. Its constituency is no longer mainly made up of sharecroppers and poorly educated villagers. Many fundamentalist churches are modern and imposing, financed by wealthy oilmen from Texas and Oklahoma and prosperous farmers in the wheat and corn belts. Rich and influential lay leaders such as J. Howard Pew and von Frellick now make their influence felt in the power structure of the community and state. The fundamentalists also operate a vast network of colleges, training schools, Bible institutions, Bible prophecy conferences, prayer meetings, and study groups. They have many large publishing houses which blanket small towns with conservative tracts and pamphlets. An increase in Protestant orthodoxy has added members to their churches at a more rapid rate than the liberal churches have been able to show. Though still more numerous in the small sects and local churches such as the Pentecostal and Seventh Day Adventists* and among the Southern Baptists, the fundamentalists, in some areas, are also found in the Presbyterian and Methodist churches, and to a lesser degree, in the Episcopal and Congregationalist ones. For example, the members of a Congregationalist church in Los Angeles and an Episcopal church in Fort Worth, both cities with powerful fundamentalist traditions, are likely to have a stronger affinity with these traditions than with those practiced by their sister church memberships in the large New England cities.

Population movements, affluence, and mass culture have all, of course, obscured some of the distinct regional features of fundamentalism. But it would be a mistake to view the more prosperous and integrated surfaces of contemporary fundamentalism as indicating any real loss or modification of its identity. Though it has become increasingly middle class, this has not changed its profoundly conservative character, and its vast wealth and growing respectability have mainly served to broaden the base of its traditional antagonism to modern reform capitalism. Its

---

* Many of these small sects are affiliated with the National Association of Evangelicals which claims a total membership of about ten million.

29

local and regional character has insulated it from the influence of religious pluralism; still mainly Anglo-Saxon, it has preserved—unlike Catholicism and liberal Protestantism—an ethnic homogeneity that shields it from the liberalizing social adjustments invariably created by contending ethnic interests.

WITH THE CONTINUING world crisis, fundamentalism is finding a new political relevance for its doctrines and an arena in which it can exert its growing influence. As *Christian Century*, the leading organ of liberal Protestantism, observed recently: "Now the fundamentalists have apparently decided that the time has come to break out of their isolation and to contend for the soul of American Protestantism." A special target of theirs has been the National Council of Churches—the citadel of modern Protestantism. On the whole the attacks have come in the rural areas rather than the large cities, by means of local media rather than national. (One exception was an Air Force manual charging that the National Council of Churches was infiltrated by Communism, which had the effect of driving the Fourth Baptist Church of Wichita, Kansas—the largest local church in the Baptist convention—to withdraw from the convention in protest of its affiliation with the Council.) In those regions populated with churches, schools, publishing houses, and study groups that are dominated by fundamentalists, liberal Protestantism has been subjected to an avalanche of bigotry and calumny exceeded in intensity only by the worst period of anti-Catholic propaganda.

In analyzing the motives behind these attacks, Dr. Truman B. Douglas, formerly vice president of the Board of Home Missions of the Congregational Churches, has explained that "what they really want is to silence the witness of the Church *on all social problems and issues. . . .*" That is to say, on all social issues and problems other than Communism. However, as we began by indicating, the fundamentalist mentality and temperament—in the extreme, unregenerate forms that we are discussing in this article—is unable to view the threat of Russian or Chinese Communism in pragmatic and realistic ways. For the fundamentalist mind the great menace of Communism is less in its military power than in its *doctrines,* and the main threat of these doctrines is not that they operate abroad but at home. Like the "papists" of America who, the fundamentalist continues to believe, have never ceased in their insidious and cunningly concealed attempts to undermine the faith and institutions of Protestant America and to deliver the nation up to Rome, the Communists today are everywhere at work disseminating under such subterfuges as "liberalism" and "middle-of-the-road progressivism" the heretical doctrines of collectivism that are poisoning American faith and subverting its social order. Instead of a puissant and pure Christian America marching resolutely toward its apocalyptic encounter with the Soviet anti-Christ, the nation, drugged with false doctrines and blinded by traitorous leaders, is being carried down the road to appeasement and, eventually, capitulation.

It is not surprising to discover, then, that Robert Welch, who has built his organization to fight a conspiracy which numbers President Eisenhower among its members, should have come from a strong fundamentalist background, or that John Birch himself first prepared for his martyrdom in China by being suspended from college because of the extremist zeal of his fundamentalist activities. Much of the affinity of fundamentalism for what is today called the radical right derives from the attempt to wed Protestant zeal and reactionary animus which developed and took shape during the New Deal years. The leader of one such group, the Christian Freedom Foundation, wrote a diatribe which was titled *The Menace of Roosevelt.* During the same period of the middle

1930's, an organization called Spiritual Mobilization was established "to check the trend toward pagan statism." In coming out of their "isolation," as the *Christain Century* puts it, the fundamentalists are not only "competing for the soul of Protestantism" but are also trying to reassert the traditional cultural and political supremacy of conservative Protestantism. Its leaders—men like the Reverend Billy Joe Hargis, the Reverend Fred C. Schwarz, the Reverend James Fifield—are no less aware than the late Senator McCarthy was of the demagogic possibilities inherent in an anti-Communist crusade. But they enjoy an advantage that McCarthy did not have: a massive potential following which is prepared to accept the belief that a restoration of the influence of the old-time religion must be accompanied by a return to the pre-New Deal era of free enterprise and isolationism if the country is to be purged of its disabling doses of collectivism and internationalism. Thus the fundamentalist movement provides both potent political images and popular support to rally other disaffected Americans of different backgrounds who nonetheless feel that they, as well as the nation as a whole, have been losing power, and who are united not only in their hostility to Communism but in their anti-minority, anti-city, anti-labor, and anti-international attitudes.

THE ELECTION OF A Catholic to the Presidency has signalled the change in America from a Protestant nation with a prevailing Anglo-Saxon tradition to a pluralistic nation with a Protestant tradition. The defeats that the South has been suffering in civil rights mark the demise of white supremacy in its own sectional stronghold. Given current population trends, increasing urbanization, the organizational growth of minority groups, these changes are not likely to be reversed. Not long ago a leading figure in Spiritual Mobilizers, who also heads a large and wealthy Los Angeles church, articulated part of what the fundamentalist position amounts to in socio-ethnic terms when he reportedly said, "We are not going to give the city away to the Jews, Negroes, and Mexicans." Such cities as Houston, Miami, and Los Angeles were always fundamentalist strongholds, but the fact that they are now also centers of rightist politics is at least partly to be explained in terms of local responses to a growing Catholic minority, a growing Jewish community, and rapidly increasing Negro or Spanish-speaking minorities.

While the election of Kennedy reflected a decline in bigotry in some quarters, his campaign stimulated a recrudescence of it in others; and his career as President is likely to provoke an increase in self-consciousness among our religious communities and a heightened awareness of their sources of contention—in other words, it is likely to deepen the pattern of religious pluralism in America even further. The fundamentalists' reaction to the ascendancy of pluralism is double-sided. As Anglo-Saxon Protestants, in the main, they are reacting to the loss of the political dominance that came from their majority position. As *fundamentalist* Protestants, however, they are a particularly fervent and committed religious *minority* and one growing in wealth and numbers and ambition. As such, they are behaving more and more like other important minorities in America—demanding more time and space in the media, and devoting more energy to organizing their constituencies for social and political action. Whatever else may develop, it is abundantly clear that the Protestant fundamentalists have now taken their place among the other distinct groups—the Catholics, liberal Protestants, Jews, Negroes, and secular humanists—that make up the pluralistic socio-religious pattern of America.

In trying to convince the community that America's interest will best be served through their leadership, many fundamentalist religious and lay leaders have been moving into the seats of power which have opened on the radical right. Insofar as militant anti-Communism today has a socio-religious cast, fundamentalism has replaced Catholicism as the spearhead of the movement.* None of this is to say, of course, that the radical right has become identified with the aspirations of a single group—it would hardly have got off the ground if it had. The radical right cuts across all groups in varying degrees, and no doubt there is still a hard core of Catholic McCarthyites who have followed his sanctified image into the radical right movement. Father John F. Cronin, the author of the pamphlet issued last month by the NCWC attacking the new "extremists of the right," was indeed quoted by the New York *Times* as saying that "quite a few Catholics" belong to the John Birch Society.

B UT SUPPORTERS of Senator McCarthy were, on the whole, a much more variegated and dispersed group than the constituency of the radical right today seems to be. Though many Catholics found in the Senator an expression of their militant anti-Communism, McCarthyism never became a "Catholic movement." It drew the bulk of its support from the traditional "isolationist bloc"—pro-German and anti-British—who had opposed an alliance with Communist Russia against Nazi Germany. McCarthy also had a sizeable following in the large cities, in the national veterans' organizations, and in working-class groups—particularly those with roots in countries now behind the Iron Curtain.

From his famous first speech in Wheeling, West Virginia, McCarthy clearly played up to the minority groups, who were attracted by his hard anti-Communism, which they saw as posing no threat to the economic gains they had made during the New Deal. For the most part, McCarthy managed to attack New Deal liberalism for allowing itself to be infiltrated by Communists, without directly challenging the policies and practices of

reformed capitalism that had been achieved by the Democratic coalition and had come to be supported by the middle-of-the-road consensus in America. Seen in historical perspective, McCarthyism was the final phase in the repudiation of our wartime alliance with Russia; the charges of treason and disloyalty were aimed vengefully by those who had always considered Stalin a greater menace than Hitler against those who had taken the opposite position and engineered the alliance with Russia, and who might therefore be held responsible for the postwar predicaments which had flowed from that alliance. However, McCarthyism was virtually devoid of social and economic content as well as religious inspiration, and so lacked stable bases of local, popular support. With an all but inevitable logic, McCarthy was forced to play out his role in the national arena where his main concerns lay. Once his performance there had been discredited by the changes in international policy that were already in progress when his star appeared on the horizon, and by his unchecked hostility to the Executive branch that was now in the hands of his own party, McCarthy collapsed. And with no further issues and grass-roots support which his followers could exploit, McCarthyism, in effect, collapsed with him.

The radical right, as we have been seeing, is a very different affair, one

* Father Robert A. Graham, among others, has called attention to this change in a recent issue of *America:* "It was not so long ago that Catholics were regarded as the most active foes of Communism. This can no longer be said today. Dr. Fred C. Schwarz's anti-Communist Christian Crusade is of predominantly Baptist inspiration. The National Education Program of Dr. George S. Benson [of the Church of Christ], is another fundamentalist operation. It is no accident that the key centers of the John Birch Society are in the fundamentalist South and Southwest." An even more authoritative indication of the fact that the new radical right does not lean on a predominantly Catholic base is the campaign begun last month by the National Catholic Welfare Conference—the central administrative body of the American Bishops—to discourage participation by Catholics in extreme anti-Communist movements.

with a definite political, economic, and social purpose, and able to capitalize on the growing power of an important religious group which has long felt the denial of its rightful share in shaping the policies of the nation. To be sure, fundamentalist conservatism is today by no means a monolithic ideology. Even as von Frellick was attempting to recruit prominent ministers and lay leaders in Dallas for Christian Citizen, a leader of the Baptist General Convention of Texas was publicly reminding them of the recent recommendation of the Convention that "Baptists . . . exercise caution when asked to support efforts to mobilize Christians into a political power." But despite this recommendation, and despite warnings by other Baptists and moderate fundamentalists, it remains clear that large numbers of fundamentalists *are* being "mobilized" and that their religious and regional conservatism is converting readily into the ideology of the radical right and swelling the chorus of reactionary and apocalyptic voices in the land.

THE MAIN STRENGTH and appeal of fundamentalist conservatism lies in its nativist nationalism. In the "gray atmosphere" of America's tense, cautious international power struggle with the Soviet Union in a nuclear age—an atmosphere made even more troubled by the rise of the minorities within the society—its program of "Americanism" becomes a way of explaining the nation's loss of supremacy and autonomy; it also provides a set of crusading directives for the road to Armageddon that dispels uncertainty and discharges both national tensions and local frustrations. On the international scene, it identifies America's "decline" and the Communist ascendancy with the loss of the West's four-hundred-year monopoly of power and with the passing of Anglo-Saxon dominance. The immense strengthening of America's world position since the war counts for nothing in the light of our failure to assume the world dominance

which Great Britain has relinquished. The shock which followed Sputnik has doubtless helped to bring on the somewhat delayed discovery by certain people in the hinterlands that the American century had been lost, just as the Supreme Court decision on desegregation and the election of Kennedy woke many of the same people to the fact that political power in America was also passing out of their hands.

The appeal of the new nativist nationalism, however, need not remain confined to the rabid—as McCarthyism, being a form of revenge politics, necessarily was. The redistribution of power both abroad and at home has disheartened many moderate people—those who gladly might have settled for less than a monopoly if they could be sure that the Russians (and the Chinese) would do likewise, and who might have accepted the claims of the racial, religious, and ethnic minorities (and of labor), so long as these did not encroach upon their own lives, and so long as their own interests continued to be dominantly represented. Feeling that all of this is no longer the case, the nativist segment of the Protestant population becomes a prey of those who would like to replace the pluralistic orientation which has led America to a precarious co-existence by a doctrinaire, chauvinistic Americanism seeking to achieve a *"Pax Americana."* In Protestant fundamentalism, imbued with nationalism—not unlike the case of pre-World War II German Lutheranism—many formerly moderate people find a powerful rationale and symbolism for this complex of attitudes. The practical program to support the "Americanist" effort in foreign affairs has the further attraction of asking for the abolition of the welfare state, which the Protestants in question see as benefiting mainly the minorities whose rise to prominence has begun to threaten their control within the society and reshape their America in a different image. Thus they are susceptible to a program which by calling for a return to a 19th-century type of capi-

33

talism and an end to collaboration with our allies on an equal basis, will bring into power those native groups who can restore their traditional position in the scheme of things. It is on such anxieties and impulses that the radical right has battened.

Whoever has taken the radical right as amounting to nothing more than the fulminations of a few crackpots, or the temporary prominence of the lunatic fringe achieved mainly by publicity, would do well to ponder the matter further. More thought had better be taken, also, by those who have concluded that since the radical right is unlikely to take over America, it can be disregarded as a growing power bloc and a potential influence for harm.

WHILE IT IS PROBABLY true that the new-found strength of reactionary ideas cannot be said to indicate a turn toward conservatism in the population at large, it does seem to indicate that American conservatism is being pulled to the right. This in itself represents a gain for the ultras. But what gives them an even greater potentiality for influence is the fact that they operate at the local and state levels, where a minimum of pressure can exert a maximum of effect, and where there is no necessity for taking the risk of an all-or-nothing gamble—as McCarthy, working at the national level only, was forced to do. This does not mean that the new ultras are interested only in local affairs. On the contrary, as a distinct and now politically self-conscious minority within the pluralistic pattern, they are de-manding a greater voice in the shaping of national policy, which they hope to achieve through a strategy of interlocking local pressures. (The effectiveness of such a strategy can be seen from the enormous amount of attention Manager Mitchell attracted through his attack on public welfare programs in the city of Newburgh; a similar attack in Congress would probably have fallen flat.)

So far as foreign policy is concerned, there is even an advantage to the ultras in being an out-of-power faction: they can conduct their programs with wild irresponsibility, blanketing the country with small undercover cells, repressing free discussion, and imposing a doctrinaire conformity. The effect of all this is to reduce the government's opportunities for a flexible handling of delicate problems such as we now face in Germany, in the UN, in Africa. Perhaps most important of all, the ultras make it very difficult for the country to dissociate itself from the imperialism and white supremacy in which the Anglo-Saxon world has figured so prominently in the past. It is ironic, if not yet tragic, that having more or less united the Western world around the belief that the best way to oppose Communism is through the promotion of social reform and the development of international pluralism, America should now be the scene of a nativist movement which would substitute for this idea a belligerent nationalism, one whose socio-religious mystique is not very different from that with which certain European nations recently experimented and in so disastrous a fashion.

# The Golden Image of NEBUCHADNEZZAR

RICHARD V. PIERARD

Portrayed in Daniel 3 is the action of King Nebuchadnezzar of Babylon in erecting a huge golden idol. He ordered that when an assembled orchestra of musical instruments sounded, all inhabitants of the kingdom were to bow down and worship. Those who neglected to do so were to be thrown alive into a burning fiery furnace.

Three Hebrew young men, Shadrach, Meshach, and Abednego, who had been inducted into the king's civil service but nevertheless had remained true to their faith, were accused by their enemies of disobeying Nebuchadnezzar's command. When the king confronted them with the charge, the courageous youths, taking no thought for their own safety, replied forthrightly: "O Nebuchadnezzar, we have no need to answer you in this matter. If it be so, our God whom we serve is able to deliver us from the burning fiery furnace; and he will deliver us out of your hand, O king. But if not, be it known to you, O king, that we will not serve your gods or worship the golden image which you have set up."

In Revelation 13 we read about another object of adulation, a beast that rises out of the sea. Men worship him, saying, "Who is like the beast, and who can fight against it?" This beast makes war against the saints, and it exercises authority over the peoples of the earth. Those who refuse to worship the beast and to receive its mark are slain.

Both passages speak of an idol—an image, a beast that God's people are commanded not to serve, which oppresses all those who refuse to worship and serve it.

What is an idol? Perhaps the best definition is that

THE REFORMED JOURNAL, December, 1972, 9-13.

it is anything that occupies the first place in one's life—the object of highest loyalty. Of course, nobody in the Western world bows down to an idol of gold, stone, or wood anymore. We are too enlightened and sophisticated to do anything so barbarous and demeaning as that. Nevertheless, we have our idols today.

One of the most insidious but yet pervasive forms of idolatry to be found in the present-day United States is the worship of America itself. By this I do not mean something quite so tangible as the state or the president but rather the *nation itself*. This is the golden image, the beast that rises out of the sea. Unfortunately, most American evangelicals are unaware of the pernicious nature of this civil religion—the religion of Americanism.

Let me first cite three examples of manifestations of this religion that evangelicals will readily recognize. Then I shall attempt to define more closely what is meant by civil religion—and suggest what we should do about it.

•       •       •

One of the most dramatic religious events of 1972 was EXPLO '72, staged in Dallas during June by Campus Crusade for Christ. An event of particular significance to our discussion was the patriotic ceremony sponsored on June 14th. A reporter for *Worldwide Impact*, the official organ of Campus Crusade, described the service held on that evening in the following terms:

> Wednesday, June 14, was Flag Day in the United States, and it didn't go unnoticed at EXPLO '72.
>
> High ranking officers of the United States military commemorated the occasion ceremoniously at the evening Cotton Bowl session while military chaplains, former astronaut James Irwin and families of prisoners of war and those missing in action looked on.
>
> Gen. Ralph Haines, commander of the U.S. Continental Army Command, gave a brief history of Flag Day and the foundation of the U.S. Army and drew cheers when he told the crowd, "I have dedicated my life to Christ. . . ."

A color guard representing each military service carried flags into the arena, and delegates participated in a salute to the Stars and Stripes and the customary pledge of allegiance.

After giving his testimony about asking Christ into his life, Rear Adm. Francis L. Garrett, chief of Navy chaplains, gave the opening prayer.

The event was interrupted briefly by a small group of anti-war protestors whose chants were promptly quieted by other delegates.

Said one youth, "This isn't the right place for that. EXPLO doesn't have anything to do with politics."

*EXPLO did not have anything to do with politics.* What follows is that this session, with its display of militarism and the ritual of the flag salute, was a *religious act.*

In the same vein Evangelist Billy Graham was asked at a press conference at EXPLO whether he considered a pro-Vietnam War stand compatible with Christian tenets. What was his response? "Explo is a *religious* gathering, not a political forum." Concerning that comment, Roger L. Dewey, of the Evangelical Committee for Urban Ministries in Boston, wrote in the Christian civil rights magazine *Inside* (July 1972 issue):

> The trouble is that Explo *was* a political forum, both (as they say) by commission and by omission. Shut out of the mammoth display area was the American Friends Service Committee—called a "lunatic fringe group." Included, however, were the Chaplain Corps of all branches of the armed services. A lengthy telegram from President Nixon was read publicly, assuring those present of his "prayers." Later Graham introduced a "spokesman" from South Vietnam—to a standing ovation—who described the situation, at length, as a holy war against the Viet Cong. And what was the effect of having everyone recite the pledge of allegiance?

Here, then, is one illustration of a *religious* action that glorified America—not political, but according to its authors, religious.

A second example is the Honor America Day *religious service* (precisely the expression used by *Christianity Today,* July 31, 1970, p. 988) that took place in Washington, D.C. on July 4, 1970. This was a huge demonstration organized by comedian Bob Hope and *Reader's Digest* president Hobart Lewis, which many commentators interpreted as a show of support for the Nixon administration and conservatism in general.

Featured speaker at the nationally televised gathering was Billy Graham. To the thousands assembled before the Lincoln Memorial he declared: "We honor America because there is woven into the warp and woof of our nation faith in God." He urged his listeners "to raise your voices in prayer and dedication to God and to recommit yourselves to the ideals and dreams upon which our country was founded." The goal and vision of our forefathers must be ours as well, namely, "one nation under God, where men can live together as brothers." After urging the assembled patriots to honor the nation, respect our institutions, and shun extremism, he concluded, stabbing his finger in the air: "I say to you today, 'Pursue the vision, reach the goal, fulfil the American dream—and as you move to do it, never give in! Never give in! Never! Never! Never!' "

The *Newsweek* magazine reporter who viewed the spectacle accused Graham of fashioning a "common-denominator faith" and "lending his own powerful voice to the civil religion in America" (July 20, 1970, p. 55). This was clearly an expression of the religion of Americanism, but the evangelist in his zeal to show his patriotism and sincere love for his native country failed to recognize the trap into which he had unwittingly stumbled.

A third instance of the religion of America is the decision of President Richard M. Nixon to hold religious services in the White House. Why did he do this? In the introduction to *White House Sermons* (Harper & Row, 1972) the president stated: "I feel that it is entirely in order to convert the great East Room—which has seen the making of so much American history—into a 'church' on Sunday mornings. It serves as an appropriate reminder that we feel God's presence here, and that we seek His guidance here—and that ours is, in the words of the Pledge of Allegiance, 'one nation, under God, indivisible. . . .' "

President Nixon went on to say: "I wanted to do something to encourage attendance at services and to emphasize this country's basic faith in a Supreme Being. It seemed to me that one way of achieving this was to set a good example. What better example could there be than to bring the worship service, with all its solemn meaning, right into the White House?" (p. vi).

Interestingly enough, the sermons preached here are almost completely devoid of prophetic content. Instead of an Amos or Isaiah, we hear Norman Vincent Peale affirm on Father's Day that it is "a privilege to preach in the presence of the first father of the nation" (p. 56) and Rabbi Louis Finklestein pray that "the future historian looking back on our generation may say. . .that in a period of great tribulations, the finger of God pointed to Richard Milhous Nixon, giving him the vision and the wisdom to save the world and civilization" (p. 68). The Cincinnati Fundamentalist Baptist preacher Harold Rawlings declared, in all sincerity, that the Constitution of the United States came out of a "prayer meeting" and its "laws and policies are based largely upon the Word of God" (p. 104). Billy Graham talked about America's "soul," which he defined as "patriotism, morality, respect for law, faith, social justice, brotherhood among people of diverse backgrounds." He implied that "our soul" must be "renewed and restored" and asserted that Jesus asked the question, "What shall it profit a man or a nation if they gain the whole world and lose the soul?" (p. 136).

With regard to the president's frequent practice of publicly expressing his religious views— of which the White House services are an egregious example— Charles P. Henderson writes in his new book *The Nixon Theology* (Harper & Row, 1972, p. 193) that the chief executive "systematically appropriates the vocabulary of the church—faith, trust, hope, belief, spirit—and applies these words not to a transcendent God but to his own nation, and worse, to his personal vision of what that nation should be. . . . lacking a transcendent God, he seems to make patriotism his religion, the American dream his deity."

These are rather strong words, words that many admirers of the president would categorically reject as a gross distortion of his actual stance on religion. But, the very fact that such a statement would be made at all is symptomatic of the deep spiritual crisis affecting our body politic and American evangelical Christianity in particular. EXPLO '72, Honor America Day, and President Nixon's public religious expressions are recent cases in point that strike especially close to home for those who profess evangelical Christianity. Certainly many others could have been singled out as well.

●     ●     ●

What is this "civil religion"? How does it relate to Christian Americanism? Why should it be a matter of concern? The eighteenth-century political thinker Jean-Jacques Rousseau introduced the concept in *The Social Contract,* defining it as

> a purely civil profession of faith, the articles of which it is the business of the Sovereign to arrange, not precisely as dogmas of religion, but as sentiments of sociability without which it is impossible to be either a good citizen or a faithful subject. . . . [Its dogmas are] the existence of a powerful, wise, and benevolent Divinity, who foresees and provides the life to come, the happiness of the just, the punishment of the wicked, the sanctity of the social contract and the laws.

Sociologist Robert N. Bellah brings out that the specifically American civil religion is not worship of the nation-state *per se,* but an understanding of the American experience in the light of ultimate and universal reality. It is not anti-clerical or militantly secular, and it has borrowed so selectively from the Christian religious tradition that few people notice any conflict between the two. America has been chosen to carry out the divine mission in the world and thus is worthy of God's benevolence. He is a God of law, order, and justice and he has a special concern for America, which is Israel, his covenant people. The God of the founding fathers was

40

actively involved in history and America was the special object of his concern.

The American revolution was the final event of the exodus from the Egypt across the Atlantic, the Declaration of Independence and the Constitution were the sacred scriptures, and George Washington the Moses who led his people from tyranny to freedom. The Civil War added the themes of death, sacrifice, and rebirth to the civil religion, and a "new testament" was introduced into the national consciousness by Abraham Lincoln (Donald R. Cutler, *The Religious Situation 1968,* Beacon Press, 1968, pp. 331-93).

As Lowell Streiker and Gerald Strober emphasize, the American civil religion is highly pietistic in nature—"zealous, enthusiastic, individualistic, and messianic." Americans see themselves as the "New Order of the Ages," a unique and superior society which is ordained and protected by God. The American creed stresses both the exemplary character of the nation—the Puritan city on a hill or the revolutionary affirmation that all men everywhere have certain inalienable rights—as well as its sense of mission—manifest destiny, make the world safe for democracy, or protect defenseless peoples from the tyranny of Communism. The churches are vitally involved in sanctifying the aims, ideals, and standards of the implicit common faith and condemning those who deviate from them (*Religion and the New Majority,* Association, 1972, pp. 172, 175).

It should be obvious that the popular image of Christian America has little to do with genuine faith in Jesus Christ, but instead is simply a manifestation of civil religion. After all, Jesus gave his life primarily so that human beings might be reconciled to God; and conversion is an individual matter, not a national one. The dream of "national repentance" so often expressed by pastors and evangelists across the land is only that—a dream. The application of II Chronicles 7:14 ("If my people who are called by my name humble themselves, and pray and seek my face, and turn from their wicked ways, then I will hear from heaven, and will forgive their sin and heal their land") to America is a profoundly arrogant act. What right do we as Americans with our corrupt and sin-ridden society have to claim that we are the people of God? The realization of a truly Christian nation lies yet in the future, after the coming of Christ and the establishment of his perfect rule on earth.

Thus, the concerned follower of Christ should have nothing to do with the false doctrine of Christian Americanism. It has been cultivated and exploited by rightists of every stripe, and as a result genuine patriotism has been weakened and American democracy distorted. Take, for example, the virtual deification of the American flag. Arthur Stivaletta, an organizer of the "Wake Up America" rally in Boston in April 1970, declared, according to *Time* magazine: "I see the flag as I see God: a supreme being." The same article quoted Billy Graham: "The American flag is what the black man means when he says Soul. It's like the Queen of England—the flag is our Queen" (July 6, 1970, p. 15).

Christian Americanism is also dangerous because it blurs the delicate line of separation between church and state. The involvement of churches in the promotion of the civil religion sidetracks them from performing their primary tasks of preaching the gospel and meeting human needs. The continuing struggle over religion in the public schools and the quest for a "prayer amendment" to the United States Constitution are manifestations of this distraction. Of course, the possibility that the churches could be taken over by the state and transformed into mouthpieces for official policy always lurks in the background. As the history of Nazi Germany so clearly reveals, a church whose primary allegiance is to the civil religion cannot be expected to resist pressures to knuckle under to the dictates of the state.

•　　•　　•

Every dedicated follower of Jesus Christ should recognize that the doctrine of Christian Americanism is a form of idolatry, and he should expose it for what it is. It equates the American system with God's will and in effect demands a final allegiance and prior loyalty which belongs to God. The deity and religion are used to serve national interests and purposes. By linking Christianity to American nationalism, the role of the faith in society is vitiated. The truly national sins—race prejudice, poverty, social injustice, immoral business practices, environmental pollution, warmongering—go uncriticized and unjudged. The Christian who dares to speak out against these is labeled as subversive and un-American. He is told to "love America or leave it." Nevertheless, we cannot avoid the reality of the biblical teaching that one is first a Christian and then an American or member of some other nationality (Matt. 6:33).

Writing in the fall 1972 issue of the provocative evangelical publication, the *Post-American,* Robert Sabath stresses that "when political powers demand the worship of unconditional obedience that assumes men should assign them ultimate value, then the worship of God and the assigning of ultimate value to his kingdom becomes a radical act, a political threat" (p. 8). This statement has profound implications for every sensitive believer.

Although Romans 13 intimates that the governing authorities are ordained of God, Christians are never instructed to continue rendering allegiance to them when the state transgresses on the territory that is God's. That is what the deification of America does—our nation is enthroned alongside God.

That we must resist—even if it requires facing a modern-day equivalent of the fiery furnace. Desperately needed are more courageous evangelicals like the young folks from the People's Christian Coalition who took their stand for the faith at the "colosseum" of EXPLO '72. At the Flag Day service we mentioned above, as the U.S. Navy chief of chaplains rose to pray, they unfurled two banners—one reading "Cross or Flag?" and the other "Christ or Country?"—and began chanting "Stop the War!" (*Reformed Journal,* July-Aug. 1972, p. 16). They were only a tiny minority, but the suspicion lurks that these youths were more in the line of the Old Testament prophetic tradition than the promoters of this spiritual extravaganza in Dallas.

Or, more churches should follow the lead of the Redeemer Lutheran Church of Seattle, Washington, which recently voted to discontinue the practice of displaying the American flag in its sanctuary. The church's council affirmed that this change was not an act of national disrespect but a declaration "that our love and loyalty to God must be the greatest," and that in the church "people are 'neither Jew nor Greek.' " This was indeed a commendable action, because the presence of the flag in the chancel of a house of worship does much to foster the notion that Christianity is the religion of Americanism (*The Banner*, Oct. 6, 1972, p. 15).

If we as evangelicals do not stand up for righteousness, if we fail to separate piety from patriotism, if we persist in using the symbols of our religion to sanctify the status quo, then we ought not be surprised when our traditions of personal freedom and social justice are extinguished by a beast, a monster state, that professes to be acting on behalf of the American nationality.

That was the experience of German Christians during the holocaust of the Third Reich. Of course, it is common knowledge that few Lutherans offered any meaningful resistance to Nazism, but a recent study has revealed that one of the most orthodox of all the German Christian groups, the Baptists, also loyally supported the regime and even welcomed Hitler's accession to power (David Priestley, in R. D. Linder, ed., *God and Caesar*, Conference on Faith and History, 1971, pp. 101-23).

It is not hard to understand the passiveness of the German Christians once the Third Reich's totalitarian control apparatus had been imposed upon the land, but what had they done before 1933? German historian Hannah Vogt criticized her countrymen, and rightly so, for trying to excuse themselves by saying they did not know about the Nazi crimes nor did they want them to happen. To her fellow Germans she put the penetrating question: "Where were we when we should have opposed the beginnings?"

44

Her response to her own rhetorical statement should be taken seriously by every thoughtful American Christian:

> We let the flame of hatred rise and did not extinguish it while there was still time. We allowed posters and songs to spread hatred and abuse while we were still at liberty to fight against them. This first sin of omission gave rise to all the later crimes (*The Burden of Guilt,* Oxford U.P., 1964, p. 234).

Furthermore, speaking of the experience of believers in Nazi Germany David O. Moberg warns that "people within a nation may be honest, loyal, Christian citizens and yet support national evils which are a disgrace to mankind and a violation of the ethical teachings of the Christian Scriptures" (*The Great Reversal,* Lippincott, 1972, p. 125).

The conclusion is inescapable that although we will want to love our country and appreciate its contributions, we as Christians must never become so tied to the nation that we are no longer able to exercise a prophetic ministry. We must ever be ready to speak out against the evils perpetrated by our country and its leaders—including the atrocity of Vietnam and social injustice at home—and to demand repentance.

We still have opportunity to offer resistance to those who wrap themselves in the flag and slogans like "national honor." Shall we languish in conformity and accommodation or shall we bring the power and presence of Christ to bear on our national crises?

This, then, is our hour of decision. What shall it be—God and country, or God over country?

# CHRISTIAN ECONOMICS?

## by Bob Goudzwaard

Recently VANGUARD co-editor Robert Carvill sent me a copy of *Christian Economics*, a magazine which was unknown to me until I received this issue. Its subtitle reads: "A better America through Christian principles in Action". Eagerly I began to read, very anxious to discover its contents. It isn't every day that you come across a magazine whose title immediately associates economics and the Christian religion. You don't often find a publication that refuses to reserve the Christian religion for Sunday worship and ecclesiastical activities; even rarer is the periodical which understands that the Good News of Christ is of universal importance, penetrating to the very core of all aspects of contemporary life.

But what a disappointment when I began to read! Perhaps I can best illustrate my disappointment by quoting and then discussing the magazine's basic foundation — its underlying confession printed every month in the editorial section: "We uphold the Constitution of the United States and the limited government which it inaugurated; we believe in the free market economy and the faithful application of Christian principles to all economic activities."

You might ask yourself, "What's so disappointing about that?" Why am I concerned? Isn't it a very good thing to confess that people should execute "a faithful application of Christian principles to all economic activities"? And why would anyone be against "upholding the Constitution of the United States"? And isn't the free market economy clearly preferable to totalitarian economic systems?

The reasons for my disappointment can only be understood if we look at this confession (that which we believe!) more carefully. Doesn't something strike you as odd in the order of arrangement of these *confessional* tenets? That's right ——the *application* of Christian principles is mentioned, not as an all-determining point of departure, not as the dominating norm, but as that which is in third place, of only tertiary importance. What *does* have priority? First, the *limited* competence of government, according to—not the Bible—but the Constitution of the United States; and secondly, *belief* in the free market economy. Only in this arrangement of priorities and in line with these suppositions is the *application* of Christian principles mentioned. In other words, it's implicitly presupposed that these Christian principles are in full harmony with the limited task of government, and with an unhindered free market economy. Limited govern-

VANGUARD, October/November, 1971, 17-18.

ment and an unrestricted free market remain beyond discussion. Why? Because these two items are of a religious nature. They're part of what these men *believe*. Only after you've already accepted these beliefs in the free market and limited government in the socio-economic realm, can you then consider (other!) *applications* of Christian principles. Note the term *application* — a technical term which reminds us of attempts to *instrumentalize* the Good News in the same way as you *adapt* technical directions in your daily work.

What's my confession? My confession is of a quite different nature from that given by *Christian Economics*. I believe that the Good News of Christ is of universal significance for the whole of life, and that it impells us—indeed, relentlessly drives us, to continually lay our whole lives at the feet of our Saviour, without holding anything back. Therefore, *neither* the Constitution of the United States, *nor* our ideals of a free market economy (with a limited task for government) can avoid being subjected to the critical power of the Word of God. When, for example, the Christian Freedom Foundation declares at its Convention that "we believe in: the Bible— U.S. Constitution—private property system—economic freedom — church and private welfare" then that declaration is (perhaps unintentionally) already in its formulation a violation of God's second commandment, which directs us to serve God, and Him alone, and not to serve other gods we have alongside Him. Furthermore: even in the Apostle's Creed the words *believe in* are reserved for our confession of faith in the Trinitarian God Himself; we *believe* the Christian Church and eternal life, but we believe *in* God. And yet the CCF declaration tells us to believe *in* the Bible *and* the private property system. In a word—horrible!

If we take the second commandment seriously, we'll see that it mandates us to take an approach to Christian economics that is diametrically opposed to that taken by the Christian Freedom Foundation and *Christian Economics* magazine. Our approach, if it is to be at all Christian, has to begin its development in the light of God's Word *alone*. From the very beginning we have to thoroughly examine *if* and how *far* a strongly limited governmental task in socio-economic affairs and the maintenance of a free market system in all its aspects, is really in accord with God's Word—a Word which is able to renew not only our own lives, but also the systems of human society.

To answer these penetrating questions there's an urgent need for real Christian reflection. However, I can't avoid the strong and growing impression that the main cause of the many troubles in present western societies is exactly this: the search for an increasing individual saturation with market goods under a vigorous free market system has become *far more* than only *one* aspect of human development—this search has grown into the dominating *religion* of man and society. Racial problems, environmental pollution, patent deficiencies in essential public expenditures in the social sector —they all point to an incongruous *over*-development in the sector which produces the market goods and an *under*-development in nearly all other sectors of human life. These results are the consequences not of the *system*, but of the *idolatry* of the free market—the worship of the free market as an end in itself.

Please read over the confession of *Christian Economics* again. I hope that you'll agree with me that it's nothing but the sublimation of an attempt to create an impossible synthesis: linking the *service* of Christ and the *service* of Mammon.

# SECTION II

# Conservatism

By Jasper B. Shannon

ABSTRACT: Conservatism has played a significant role in the development of American politics notwithstanding the revolutionary tradition in the United States. In the absence of a crown and a nobility, conservatism has centered around the Constitution and the institution of private property. Deeply perturbed by the appearance of New Deal and Fair Deal welfarism, many conservatives hoped the security state was a passing phenomenon. The persistence of the Cold War and the acceptance by the moderate Eisenhower regime of the New Deal reforms have left many conservatives profoundly disturbed. Anticommunism developed around the investigative function of Congress as the chief device used to combat liberalism. Since 1960 a secret organization, the John Birch Society, has been created which advocates radical action, such as the impeachment of the Chief Justice. The Supreme Court is the current focus of criticism. The strategy of the extreme right appears to be the splintering of the Republican party. Amply financed by the *nouveaux riches,* especially the oil beneficiaries of special tax privileges, widespread propaganda is being spread to inflame the unthinking masses. The radical right has some resemblance to fascism but should not be so regarded unless stronger leadership and more violence develop.

---

THE ANNALS, November, 1962, 13-24.

CONSERVATISM as a distinct political term is 130 years of age, coming into general usage after the Great Reform Act of 1832 in Great Britain. The word meant opposition to reform. In general, conservatives wish to preserve present or past values rather than to create or adopt new ones. Oddly enough, etymology gives little help in defining the term. For example, conservatism and conservation go to the same basic Latin roots but, in American political history, they have opposite connotations. Conservationists in both the Theodore Roosevelt and the Franklin D. Roosevelt eras were regarded as radical, or at least liberals or progressives. In Europe, conservative parties generally have stood for loyalty to the monarchy, for King and Country, and the traditional national way of doing things. In America, the colonial conservatives were likely to be loyalists, followers of the Crown, Tories, in the language of their day. Members of the governor's council were generally large landowners, frequently seeking larger grants. They were likely to be officials in the accepted clerical hierarchy in the established church of the dominant denomination, and, not infrequently, they were officers in the colonial militia.

The anomalous position of the Daughters of the American Revolution as modern conservatives is frequently dwelt upon. Descendants of revolutionists, they are embarrassed ideologically in opposing the application of the sweeping doctrines of the Declaration of Independence, the essence of the contemporary propaganda of liberals, especially of minorities seeking civil rights and admission to full citizenship upon a basis of equality.

## THE CONSTITUTION AND PROPERTY

The Constitution, since American conservatives have no crown as a rallying point, stands in its place. Inasmuch as there is no native American nobility or monarchy and both are prohibited by the American Constitution, American advocates of inequality have usually fallen back upon the institution of private property as a bulwark against egalitarianism. The American conservative has found in the doctrine of liberty a defense against equality. Property is necessary to undergird liberty of conscience. Free enterprise is essential to the freedom of the soul or the mind. As a wall of separation was erected by the Bill of Rights against the interference of the state in the realm of religion, so the followers of Adam Smith found in the natural law of society and a free market a bulwark against interference in the economy by the state. However, the sweep of nationalism, especially economic nationalism, in the form of tariffs gave an ambivalence to this argument. To Hamilton and Clay, the contention was that a balanced society required industry and commerce to offset the uniformity imposed by Jeffersonian agrarianism. Against the centralizing force of technology, the South fell back upon states' rights as a bastion of support against industry, equality, and technology. It was upon the Constitution with its safeguards against interference with private property, even in human beings, that John C. Calhoun, Stephen A. Douglas, and Roger B. Taney relied when assailed by the glittering generalities of the Declaration of Independence. Conservative Republicans were recruited primarily from the old Whigs who were later pitted against radical Republicans who wished to abolish slavery immediately. Lincoln placed his policy upon nationalism and order as established in the Constitution, and Charles Sumner and Thaddeus Stevens pushed the Declaration of Independence to the point of revolutionizing southern society by incorporating former slaves into the electorate with full rights of franchise.

## ROOTS OF CONSERVATIVE DOCTRINES

Historically, the Constitution was established out of a reaction to the radicalism of the Declaration. Early American conservatives and liberals both owed a great deal to John Locke whose treatises on government were written to expound views congenial to the great Whig landowners and merchants of the seventeenth century. Locke was an advocate of both liberty and property. The Declaration of Independence leaned toward liberty, but the framers of the Constitution were motivated by a desire to create stability and security, especially the security of property. In fact, Locke lay down as the fundamental purpose of the state the protection of property. This appears to be the foundation stone of capitalism, but it is not clear that he meant individual property. He probably intended to defend collective property whose title was in all mankind as children and grantees of God.[1]

The matter becomes complex, however, when Locke decrees that the value of property depends upon the amount of labor incorporated in it. This view was later apparently accepted by Abraham Lincoln, one of the founders of the Republican party, when he declared in a message to Congress: "Labor is prior to and independent of capital. Capital is only the fruit of labor; and could not have existed if labor had not first existed. Labor is the superior of capital and deserves much the higher consideration." [2] Moreover, it is not clear whether primitive communism was a part of the golden age, the Garden of Eden, or whether it was an evidence of original sin. Within the American tradition, it seems to have been all three, whether simultaneously or seriatim is not always clarified.

## HUMAN NATURE

Conservatives are likely to be skeptical of the rationality of men, especially when they act in groups. From Edmund Burke and Alexander Hamilton to Herbert Hoover, they have distrusted the capacity of any generation to reconstruct society by logic or reason. Convention and experience are safer guides than experiment, statistics, and inference for the foundation of human institutions. Human nature is a frail reed upon which to depend for judgment upon values. Power corrupts human nature. Lord Acton's famous aphorism concerning the absolute corruption of power is cited by a prominent spokesman for contemporary conservatism, who emphasizes the danger of the concentration of political power and defends the original doctrine of limited power as established by the Constitution.[3]

If an institution exists, that existence is prima facie evidence of its validity. The burden of proof is always upon the advocates of change. Yet there are the stubborn facts of social change. One of these is the increase in the number of human beings upon the planet. Population of the world doubles within the life time of its current inhabitants, largely as an outgrowth of science and technology. Material change is the perpetual solvent which alters human environment. The person of threescore years has seen most of the changes wrought by mass production of motor cars and the introduction of airplanes. Obsolescence, even planned obsolescence,

[1] Peter Laslett, *John Locke: Two Treatises of Government* (Cambridge: Cambridge University Press, 1960), pp. 102–103.

[2] Archer H. Shaw (Ed.), *The Lincoln Encyclopedia* (New York: The Macmillan Company, 1950), p. 181.

[3] Barry Goldwater, *The Conscience of a Conservative* (Shepherdsville, Ky.: Victor Publishing Co., 1960), pp. 22–23.

is a part of our economy. Adjustment and readjustment is a certainty in an increasingly uncertain world. There is a steady erosion on the human nervous system which increases the nostalgia for simpler ways of life. A half century ago, Graham Wallas raised the question of man's adaptability to his environment. Environment changes rapidly, human nature very slowly, if at all. The resulting stress and strains upon human nerves and psyche are enormous. We are daily reminded of the growing incidence of mental disease, juvenile delinquency, divorce, and crimes of violence. A few anthropologists intimate that the simple human mechanism cannot survive the complex technological environment of atomic fission. Like other animals, man may be doomed to extinction, especially since his scientific knowledge is so superior to his ethical achievements. The pressure of all these facts may give pause to the most optimistic liberal. What it does to the pessimistic or emotional temperament may be well-nigh catastrophic. Escapism and scapegoatism appear to be well-established human behavior patterns. The incurable romantic escapes into a utopian future, the creation of his perfervid imagination. The incurable pessimist escapes into a nostalgic utopian past. Both are equally unrealistic. The liberal blames the *status quo* for his failures; the conservative ascribes his lack of success to social change.

Even if they agreed on ends and purposes, conservatives and liberals may disagree on means. Conservatives as well as liberals may disagree among themselves on means. Theodore Roosevelt characterized visionaries and dreamers as the lunatic fringe. Today, the phenomenon of the radical right has emerged—those who would alter existing institutions because they have gone too far to recognize strange minorities or have yielded too much to mass majori-

ties. Aristotle ascribed all change or revolution to too little or too much equality.[4]

## THE AMERICAN TRADITION

It may be worth while to examine a few of the fundamental premises in the American tradition. First, these emerged from the American Revolution and its antecedents in Great Britain. In fact, although advanced by the liberals in the seventeenth and eighteenth centuries, the doctrines were children of both theology and practical experience. Governments were regarded as inherently evil. Were it not for the evil nature of man, government would not exist at all. The fact that the governments complained of were monarchical or autocratic was glossed over, and all government was categorized as bad. The notion of government as a referee, primarily a restraint upon violence, is deeply embedded in the American tradition. The fact that this ideology was a by-product of an agrarian, self-sufficient society is ignored.

## CORPORATE GROWTH AND PARTISAN POLITICS

In the impasse which resulted from Reconstruction, a new group of men obtained strategic control of the economy. The power of the rulers of the economy was rapidly concentrated into the hands of great masters of technology and credit who utilized the corporate structure to the fullest. The new economic rulers created devices for controlling credit through centralized banks and transportation by means of banker dominance of railroads. Subsequently, by the consolidation of the process of refining oil so necessary to a motorized

[4] "Thus inferiors become revolutionaries in order to be equals, and equals in order to be superiors." Ernest Barker, *The Politics of Aristotle* (London: Oxford University Press, 1946), p. 207.

51

economy and by the invention of holding company ownership of the natural monopoly of electricity, the masters of the economy became vastly more powerful than the politicians who operated the *laissez-faire* state. Through financing the propaganda to gain consent of the electorate, as well as by controlling the procedure of selection of candidates, who in turn appointed office holders subservient to the masters of economic organization, the political state was reduced to a subordinate position among the agencies of social control. In the meantime, the development of the Darwinian hypothesis with its conception of continual struggle and conflict offered the new elite a ready justification of their power in the economic hierarchy. Natural law was a convenient rationalization whenever religious conscience became troublesome. An ethic was founded upon the medieval Christian doctrine of trusteeship. Men of great wealth were guardians of earthly goods for the benefit of others. They could do for people what they would or could not do for themselves in the areas of culture, art, music, libraries, and education.

## THE DEMOCRATIC PARTY

Between 1866 and 1896, there was little to choose between the major political parties. The Democrats were largely dominated by a mystical attachment to the feudal doctrine of locality. Samuel J. Tilden and Grover Cleveland were *laissez-faire* advocates even more than the Republicans who were ideologically embarrassed by their economic nationalism, namely, the tariff. Tilden planned to make the leading exponent of social Darwinism, William Graham Sumner, his Secretary of the Treasury. Cleveland could and did use national power to crush a railway strike, relying upon the equitable dogma of government property in railroads and the mails. He abjectly surrendered credit control to the sovereignty of the House of Morgan. He was a devout worshiper at the throne of the gold standard.

Meanwhile, farmers found their property expropriated by the economic sovereigns who controlled credit, price, and transportation. They never fully understood what was happening to them, but they struck out blindly against their exploiters and sought in a very un-Jeffersonian manner to use national or federal power to regulate railroads (Interstate Commerce Commission) and trusts (the Sherman Act). When William J. Bryan merged Populists and Democrats in 1896, the Hills, Clevelands, Carlisles, and Whitneys, as well as Breckenridges and Buckners and Wattersons, deserted the Democratic party. Failure in attempts to assume the old Democratic conservative roles in 1904 and 1924 pointed the road for party disaster to Franklin D. Roosevelt in 1933.

## THE IMPACT OF TECHNOLOGY

Farms and rural culture, the original basis of American political institutions, are disappearing. The voter who is sixty has seen the agrarian and self-sufficient way of life largely disappear. From 1910, when the United States was almost equally rural and urban, to 1960, with only one person in twenty actually farming and then by high-powered motor driven tractors instead of with human and horse power, is an astonishing period of transformation. A technological revolution has transpired in three decades. It is not unlikely that the consequences of this agarian revolution will be greater than those of the enclosure system on medieval England. The shift from an America of isolated self-sufficient farmers to one of megalopolis has already had dramatic political results. The presidency goes to the party which can carry the great industrial states. This was demonstrated in 1944, 1948, and 1960. Congress is governed under seniority by one-party regions dominantly rural. Seniority and gerrymander are parts of our over-all constitution, by prescription if not by solemn compact. When the Supreme Court struck a blow at racial segregation in 1954, it was altering the prescriptive constitution more sharply than the written document, hence the violent resistance of so many conservatives. A further blow was struck in 1962 when the Supreme Court laid the foundation for federal judicial control of reapportionment. Since World War II, strenuous efforts have been carried on in the heartland of Republicanism, the center of economic nationalism—the Midwest—to establish a two-party system.

## The Midwest

Michigan has a Democratic party, largely labor union, created as a by-product of the motor technology of Detroit. The last bastion of conservative opposition was the gerrymandered and unrepresentative state senate. Determined to hold power against the political doctrine of one man, one vote, the Republican party succeeded in getting the state voters to adopt area as well as population as a basis of representation. The Senate blocked the passage of a state income tax and forced an increase in the sales tax by endangering the existence of all public services. Wisconsin voters approved a similar amendment, but the Wisconsin Supreme Court ruled the amendment unconstitutional.[5] However, a selective sales tax was forced upon the Democratic governor as a compromise to keep public services operating. Thus, the historic

[5] The amendment was first voted down in the regular election of 1952, but, when resubmitted at a spring primary in which there were few urban contests, a majority of a very small turnout approved. The Farm Bureau was one of the chief groups pushing the area proposal.

position of Progressive Wisconsin was changed from progressive to regressive in taxation. Similar efforts at area representation were proposed in Minnesota, Iowa, and Nebraska. Liberal Democrats have two senators and a governor in Michigan and two senators in Minnesota and a governor and a senator in Wisconsin. They had governors in Iowa (four years) and Minnesota (six years) and in Nebraska two Democratic governors in succession in spite of Republican ascendancy in the delegations to the federal House and Senate. The growth of industry followed by unionization spells the ultimate triumph of liberalism, unless some constitutional bulwark is established like the House of Lords to block the growth of union welfarism. No conservative, however, has undertaken to defend government aid to agriculture as a means of preserving the economic base for rugged individualism Conservatives rather support the technological revolution, which is destroying the very people and institutions they profess to admire.

## Political Institutions

The doctrine of separation of powers is founded upon the belief that all government is dangerous. The Constitution grants only limited powers, and these powers are channeled into three separate compartments. Only in wartime can all these be directed into the same channel. Energy can be supplied chiefly by the executive, hence the presidency becomes the agency through which direction can be given to the state. Jackson, Lincoln, Wilson, the two Roosevelts, and, somewhat belatedly, Truman pressed for social change. Lincoln paid with his life, because he symbolized, in the paranoid mind of John Wilkes Booth, the exercise of tyrannical power. Theodore Roosevelt split his own party; Wilson wrecked his health; Franklin D. Roosevelt broke the

third-term tradition and probably has-
tened his own death by becoming indispensable to the liberal movement. The
political strategy of conservatism is to
equate governmental power exercised by
the executive with the old tyrannical
power of a monarch. The fact that
these newer exercises of power have
popular consent only makes the power
the more arbitrary to conservatives.
Conservatives do not approve of concentrated power in public governments.
In the name of liberty of free enterprise,
they may approve of concentrated power
in the economy in the exercise of economic sovereignty over the lives and
work of millions of people. When the
President of the United States intervenes
in behalf of his conceptions of the
general interest, his actions are described
as dictatorial. The debate is shifted
from economic terms, the competition
for wealth and prestige, to political
terms, the right of the citizen against
a tyrannical political leader. Rarely is
the discussion based on the nature of
monopoly or economic private governments.

## Taxation and Conservatism

Aside from any ideological base is
the fact of wealth against poverty. Unable to destroy monopoly and imperfect
competition, liberals employed progressive taxation as a weapon against concentrated wealth. Progressive taxation
has existed for almost a half-century,
but the burden of taxation was so light
before World War II that the economics
of taxation was less important than the
pattern of taxation imposed by the
Second World War and its aftermath,
the prolonged Cold War. Not only is
the burden heavy, starting with a one-
fifth bite in the lower brackets, but taxes
are withheld from payrolls. A glance
at one's nominal income compared with
his income after taxes is a traumatic

exercise in any income bracket, but, in
the highest echelons, it is an almost
lethal shock. Keeping in perspective the
fact that parliamentary government
came into existence because of differences about taxation and that "taxation
without representation" was an important factor in the American Revolution, it is little wonder that high income-
tax rates become personally poignant
to people in all brackets. The fact that
a large number of state legislatures have
approved a proposal to repeal the in-
come-tax amendment is evidence of the
visceral resentment to high taxes. The
consequences of a repeal may be catastrophic, but, to emotional conservatives,
the appeal is very attractive. Economic
conservatives have fought a long battle
of strategic retreats since the economy
became centralized in the years following the Civil War. For thirty years,
conservatism in the new industrial
society dominated both political parties.
The advocates of social change had to
undertake to form new parties, a well-
nigh impossible task under the American
constitutional system. The Greenbackers
and the Populists, not to mention the
Socialists, Prohibitionists, and Single
Taxers, might control a balance of power
but never majority power itself. When
William Jennings Bryan merged the dis-
satisfied Populist farmers with the
Democratic party in 1896, with credit
the central issue, he changed not only
the character of his own party but that
of the Republican party itself.

## The Republican Party

When accident made Theodore Roosevelt president, he found himself the
nominal leader of a party which did not
accept his Lincolnian liberalism. The
Supreme Court, the senatorial group led
by Nelson P. Aldrich, combined with
the centralized political power in the
hands of Speaker Cannon, prevented

drastic change. When George W. Norris successfully led the movement to curb Cannon and the Constitution was amended to elect United States Senators directly and the costs of war were shifted from sales taxes (tariffs) to income taxes, formidable breastworks of conservatism were penetrated. However, the Republican party organization renominated Taft. With the control of the organization remaining in the hands of Penrose, the economic conservatives were able to nominate and elect Harding, Coolidge, and Hoover in the 1920's as the cynicism of reconstruction followed World War I. The Progressive revolt of 1912 among Republicans opened the way for many liberals to join the Democrats as Woodrow Wilson pushed the union of farmers and workers even further into a national effort to produce a "new freedom" from centralized economic government.

## THE ATTEMPTED WELFARE STATE

When the depression of 1929-1933 shook confidence in existing institutions, Franklin Roosevelt undertook to establish a welfare state to replace land as the basis of individual security in the United States. Conservatives established the Liberty League as a weapon of defense as former conservative Democratic leaders John W. Davis and Alfred E. Smith deserted the party. Following the landslide of 1936, Roosevelt carried his fight to the Supreme Court, one of the principal defenses of the opponents of change. The conservatives won a pyrrhic victory, partly through the accident of the death of majority leader Joseph Robinson. The Democratic party was rent in two by the fight. Roosevelt then sought unsuccessfully in the 1938 Democratic primaries to purge the Democratic party of its conservative wing, which was deeply intrenched in southern constituencies. A conserva-

tive Republican-Democratic coalition emerged which has held power in Congress for nearly a quarter-century. Southern sectional conservatives, the residual legatees of the old southern Bourbons, have embedded themselves in Congress behind committee seniority, local gerrymandering, failure to reapportion, and the one-party system to furnish an effective political bastion against any form of creeping or galloping welfarism. The entente between Big Business and racial white ascendancy has brought the wave of reform to a standstill.

## COURT DESERTS CONSERVATISM

In the meantime, the time bombs Roosevelt left on the Supreme Court, Hugo Black and William O. Douglas, have exploded again and again. Under their leadership, and prodded by world events, they have joined with Eisenhower's appointees, Republican liberals generally, to reconstruct the role of the Court, once a sheet anchor of conservatism, into a phalanx of liberalism. By shifting its concern from the shibboleths of property to the symbols of liberty, the Court has wrought a constitutional revolution. Not since the days of John Marshall has the Court been the instrument of political centralization and broadening of national power. The Court has made the national government into the haven of civil liberty, in contradistinction to Jefferson's belief that local governments and the states were the effective protectors of individual rights and freedom of the mind. This reversal of roles by the highest Court has resulted in much-changed views from both conservatives and liberals. Liberals, who once denounced the "nine old men" as defenders of property, now approve of the new frontiers of civil liberty carved out by the nine younger but now aging members. Frightened by the encroach-

55

ments upon property and status made by the new Court, the believers in racial separation and the defenders of prescriptive property rights have joined in denouncing the Supreme Court as soft on communism. Even the American Bar Association, which once worshiped at the Court's shrine, has restrained its enthusiasm for the Court, once the embodiment of security, stability, and respectability.

## ANTICOMMUNISM

The frenzied frustration of the Cold War made Marxian communism the symbol of every kind of wickedness. Unable to destroy the enemy abroad, many conservatives turned to a real or fancied enemy within. Not content with warning against the diminishing number of official members of the American Communist party, baffled conservatives broadened the definition of communism to include anyone whose views they regarded as dangerous. Liberals and even moderate conservatives fell under the sweeping charges of what one may call the emotional conservatives. Some of these radical-right persons clung to General Douglas MacArthur as a forlorn hope for the presidency in 1952. Embittered by MacArthur's failure to win a considerable following, they supported Robert A. Taft. When Taft was defeated by Eisenhower, the wrath of these inflamed rightists turned against Taft for not throwing his delegates to MacArthur. No language was too strong to be applied to either Taft or Eisenhower in this moment of agonized disappointment.[6]

The failure of Eisenhower to destroy communism abroad or to dismantle the New Deal and the welfare state at home

[6] The writer personally observed this behavior in a Chicago hotel close to the MacArthur for President headquarters at the time of Eisenhower's nomination.

further disappointed the voters of the far right. Finally, the censure of Senator McCarthy, the hero of visceral conservatism, combined with the Supreme Court decisions extending to defendants charged with subversion the cloak of due process, threw fuel upon the flames burning in the breasts of the passionate patriots. The deaths of Taft and McCarthy and the nomination of Nixon, by his iron control of the party organization as he adopted parts of the Rockefeller program, enraged some voters who belonged to the Republican right. Mr. Nixon became alarmed by the fact that money from the right wing was being diverted into splinter right organizations instead of the party coffers. Nixon's narrow defeat by a youthful Boston Irish Catholic further enraged the sensitive right-wingers. They displaced their frustrations upon Mr. Nixon, advancing the myth that Nixon's betrayal of conservatism led to his defeat. The vocal popularity of Senator Goldwater at the 1960 Republican convention continued after Nixon's defeat.

## CONSERVATISM IN BOTH PARTIES

The general conclusion that Eisenhower had won for the Republican party in 1952 and 1956, Nixon's loss in 1960, and the fact that congressional leaders Dirksen and Halleck presented something less than a glamorous facade for the Republicans led moderate Republicans to seek to improve their national image in 1962, as the Democrats had in 1953–1954. The establishment of a Republican Citizens Organization in the summer of 1962 aroused bitter comment within the party, especially from Senator Goldwater, head of the Congressional Republican Campaign Organization.

These developments brought into sharp focus the fact of presidential party and congressional party divisions in both major parties. The left wings of both parties win the executive and the right wings of both parties control Congress. A combination of the right wings in the legislature succeeds in frustrating presidents of both parties. Both Eisenhower and F. D. Roosevelt toyed with the idea of forming liberal or moderate parties to overcome the deadlock against change in the pyramids of power created by the seniority system in Congress. Influenced by one of his political-science advisers, retiring President Eisenhower issued a solemn warning against the entente of the military and businessmen.

In some respects, President Eisenhower, in his farewell address, appeared to be sustaining the thesis of C. Wright Mills in his somewhat sensational book, *The Power Elite*.[7] In fact, readers might recall the contentions of Franz Neumann in his analysis of *Behemoth*[8] of the coalition of large merchants, manufacturers, great landowners, and the Prussian Junkers to the ultimate support of German Nazism. Though there may be a similarity of facade, the more precise facts do not sustain the charge, at least not at this time. The character of military men varies. The vivid contrast between the consciously charismatic MacArthur and the self-evidently more modest Eisenhower illustrates the point. The difference between an unsophisticated General Walker and the overly sophisticated Admiral Hyman Rickover is another case in point.

The forces which bind together the military, big business, and big bureaucracy are evident and powerful. In the Cold War, the conquest of space, and the competition for mastery of technology, the federal government is forced to spend a major portion of its income,

[7] C. Wright Mills, *The Power Elite* (New York: Oxford University Press, 1956), chaps. 7 and 9.
[8] Franz Neumann, *Behemoth: The Structure and Practice of National Socialism* (London: Oxford University Press, 1942), pp. 13–14.

roughly three-fourths, on war and national defense, past, present, and prospective. As the chief consumer of products, the federal government plays a significant role. President Kennedy demonstrated this economic power in his quick victory over Big Steel.

However, top bureaucrats in business, government, and the military come to have a managerial outlook upon society. All resent interference with action by workers who quit work to increase their economic advantage. The soldier is taught and disciplined in duty. Civic bureaucrats may not strike, and, of course, the elite of corporate managers is indoctrinated in the values and purposes of the particular organization. The corporate manager is the organizational man par excellence.

The interchange among the three is of considerable interest. Top business executives come in at the top of the government bureaucracy. Top bureaucrats leave government to take top positions. Under the practice of early retirement for the military, particularly in the Air Force, relatively young men have much active life after their retirement. As procurement officers, military men may not be unwilling to "see" the point of view of corporate management and thereby earn a good will which will pay personal dividends later. The former military officer may, as corporate manager, have peculiar insights into the military mind and many contacts with the strategically "right" people in the military bureaucracy. The power of these interlocking groups is sometimes shown by the insistence upon using outmoded equipment. Powerful congressional friends and manufacturers may be as potent as the Commander-in-Chief and the Secretary of Defense. Likewise, intrenched adherents of the National Guard may, through state governors, overpower the Secretary of Defense. Though efficiency is a frequently declared value of conservatism, it may lose its value in the conflict of special interests posing as the general good.

## INTOLERANCE

Intolerance is no stranger to American experience. Witchcraft trials, the Alien and Sedition Acts, suppression of liberty of expression in the pre-Civil War South, the rise of Know-Nothingism, the prevalence of Klu Kluxism after the Civil War and following World War I when the politics of many southern and a few middle western states was dominated by the secret order are reminders of the influence of hatred in the midst of professed tolerance and devotion to liberty. Since the 1930's, congressional investigations of so-called un-American activities have proved an important tool in counteracting liberal propaganda. Mr. Nixon's work in uncovering Alger Hiss's peculiar actions and the ensuing trial and conviction of the former State Department adviser did much to excite suspicion of all liberal activities.

The well-known "investigations" carried on by Senator Joseph McCarthy followed by his encounter with the Eisenhower Administration and the Army demonstrate the power of congressional bodies. The relationship of Texas oil producers to the junior Senator from Wisconsin has frequently been discussed.

## CONSERVATIVE PROPAGANDA

The fast growth of the vast state of Texas as the industrial revolution took over the commonwealth from agriculture exposed a seething cauldron of contradictory forces. An industrial society based upon machinery depends upon oil, as does mechanized warfare. The necessity for oil offers the justification for the famous 27 per cent depletion allowance set up in federal tax laws to furnish incentive to the oil producers. The successful ones are the new crop of oil millionaires and even billionaires who finance the radical right. They have been able to find a plentiful supply of talent for sale. For several years, the listening public was regaled with a *Facts Forum* which pretended to give a balanced view of burning political issues. The astute moderator could effectively marshal his arguments in such fashion as always to produce a conservative victory. A former professor of English at Harvard, he was very skillful in his presentations, but radio audiences either did not listen or became bored, for the project died rather abruptly.

The sponsor was not disheartened, for he has kept up, under various guises, the barrage of propaganda against welfarism. He himself wrote a utopia of his own in which he proposed to revise the American Constitution and make men of wealth the political guardians of the country. He reportedly spends about a million dollars a year in his rightist propaganda, but he is not quite certain of the amount.[9] Part of his publicity is put on in the nature of religious activity. One widely broadcast program begins and ends with the old crusader hymn, "Onward, Christian Soldiers." One spokesman, obviously aware of the dangers of libel laws, condemns the "mistaken" rather than communism.

## THE JOHN BIRCH SOCIETY

In 1961 something of a sensation was created by the announcement of the existence of an organization called the John Birch Society. Its founder was a Boston manufacturer who set up his group upon the same principle as the Communist party, namely, hierarchy and democratic centralism. This means that the leader can purge the membership when any of them deviate from the views of the leader.

[9] Fred J. Cook, "The Ultras," *The Nation,* June 30, 1962, p. 581. This is an excellent study of the radical right.

58

The Birchites have created what might be considered a tempest in the Republican teapot. In California, they have embarrassed Richard Nixon in his effort to come back as a presidential possibility. The Birchites had infiltrated the Young Republicans sufficiently to prevent a complete denunciation of the Birch Society—a more lukewarm declaration against its leadership was accepted.

In New York State, the extreme right threatens to nominate a candidate of its own in order to reduce Governor Rockefeller's expected majority in November. With one third of the electors necessary to a majority in the electoral college coming from California and New York, the importance of any minority, however small, may be greater than would be the case in the national electorate. The prospect of the nomination of Rockefeller in 1964 is very distasteful to the right-wing Republicans.

APPRAISAL OF THE EXTREME RIGHT

The extreme conservatives are not conservatives at all. Edmund Burke, usually regarded as the conservatives' wisest and most eloquent spokesman, makes continuity a leading principle of conservatism. Certainly, the exponents who would destroy free speech and the Supreme Court and who would establish a government of, by, and for the recently rich are acting upon an idea incompatible with the essence of the American tradition. Only once has the United States surrendered to the extremists, and that resulted in the Civil War, a precedent unlikely to excite repetition. A group so anti-Communist that it disallows any intermediate course and which sees no choice except atomic war and atomic aggression is nihilistic, not conservative. There is not much evidence that this type of superpatriotism has become widespread.

There is no charismatic leadership in prospect. Retail merchants, however handsome, and political-science professors, however vocal, scarcely fit the role. The effort to make a martyr out of General Walker was a miserable failure. His lack of political sophistication when he was presented before a national audience was too much. Even in Texas, General Walker ran sixth in a race of six candidates. The failure of any candidate of popularity to present himself against Senator Fulbright of Arkansas, who had questioned the activities of rightist-minded generals who indulged in political propaganda, further reduced the practical political potency of the far right. It would be easy to discover the tenets of fascism in the combination of right-minded generals, frustrated intelligentsia, and men of great wealth, but, at present, the potential is not very great. Liberals do well not to exaggerate the fear of fascism in the same way their opponents make domestic communism into a monster of overpowering strength. The Cold War requires a mastery of the mind over the viscera. The yen for attention for publicity seems to be the common denominator which links extremists of right and left. They long to lose the anonymity of "the lonely crowd."

# Abraham Kuyper's Answer to "Liberalism"

### DIRK W. JELLEMA

## I

AT A TIME WHEN ORTHODOX CHRISTIANS ARE FOUND who support the far right for what they sincerely believe to be good reasons, we might note an orthodox Protestant leader who developed a political philosophy on a Christian foundation. We refer to the great Dutch Calvinist Abraham Kuyper (1837-1920). Kuyper, known as well for his leadership in the establishment of a free Reformed Church in the Netherlands, was one of Holland's greatest statesmen. He organized a Calvinistic political party, went on to become prime minister, and put his own stamp indelibly on Dutch politics of the twentieth century.

Along with building a political party and developing a political philosophy on Christian principles, Kuyper launched a basic Christian critique of the right-wing political grouping that dominated Dutch politics prior to Kuyper. Kuyper was opposed to "rightism," either of the Conservative or Liberal type. In Europe in the nineteenth century, "liberalism" had a definite meaning, different from its general usage today. In somewhat over-simplified terms, a "liberal" was one who supported "rugged individualism," who favored unrestricted free enterprise, carried on by unrestricted free individuals. The government, a "liberal" would say, should "keep hands off" economic affairs, which should be left to individuals ("laissez-faire"). Thus the nineteenth-century "liberal" whose ideas Kuyper attacked would be found today supporting what most Americans would call the political "right," or even "far right." Kuyper, in brief, is attacking what many

THE REFORMED JOURNAL, May/June, 1965, 10-14.

Americans would call "Goldwaterite" ideas. (For the same reason, some "Goldwaterites" claim to be "true liberals" — meaning the nineteenth-century definition of "liberal").[1]

We go on, then, to note three things about Kuyper's answer to the "right" of his day. First, the "liberalism" which Kuyper opposed was, he said, the evil fruit of the French Revolution; and it turns out to be strikingly similar to the views held by the "right" in America. Second, Kuyper's own view on society implies social and economic programs that the "right" of today would vehemently oppose. Third, acceptance of the social and economic views of "liberalism" did *not* automatically mean that a man was an atheist. A pious and devoted Christian could still be a "liberal" — but, if so, because he had not thought the matter through. "Liberalism" does not refuse the right to have Jesus as personal Savior; but it does fall far short, in Kuyper's view, of the full-fledged Christian vision of society. And, further, if a pious and evangelical Christian accepts the social and economic views of "liberalism," he is accepting views that do not really stem from Christianity. Thus, an evangelical Christian whose social and economic views are "liberal" is inconsistent.

## II

WHAT WAS THE "LIBERALISM" WHICH KUYPER FOUGHT so bitterly? It was, in his mind, basically anti-Christian.

[1] In the March issue of *The Guide*, the organ of the Canadian Christian Labor Association, Bernard Zylstra makes somewhat the same point. He speaks of the "laissez-faire individualistic liberalism of the last century" with its "non-Scriptural view of the social order." Unfortunately, he says, "this view is still often found in evangelical circles, as the Goldwater candidacy revealed." Such a view implies that "the state cannot alleviate the people's socio-economic wants, for that is a matter of benevolence to be exercised by individuals and voluntary agencies such as the church." But, says Zylstra, this "negative" view of the state, upheld by "liberalism and neo-liberalism, defended today by political conservatives . . . does not sufficiently do justice to the full implications of the demands of the Gospel for the political order." And acceptance of this "liberal" view of the state has hindered Christianity's witness against Communism. Zylstra concludes with an appeal for Christian social action, and a giving up of "liberalism" in favor of a view that would recognize the state's responsibility to intervene wherever socio-economic injustice exists.

It came, he said, from the French Revolution and the Enlightenment. It was based on Reason rather than on Revelation. In religion, it tended to be "modernist" rather than evangelical. And yet, its political and socio-economic views had seduced many pious Christians.

These views, he said, were seductive; and yet, false. Indeed, the "liberal" and the Marxist ideas of society are basically alike. Furthermore, as between the two, the Marxist is the more consistent and thorough-going. The "liberal" does not follow through: "he makes a wholly arbitrary stop on a road which in accordance with his own system must be followed further. . . . as over against the Socialist, he is in the wrong."

What both the "liberal" and the Marxist do, essentially, is to attempt to dethrone God. The Marxist does it more openly. Yet the socio-economic views of the "liberal," likewise, really imply the idea that God is not sovereign. "The sovereign God is dethroned, and man with his free will is placed on the vacant seat of authority. All power, all authority, proceeds from man." Marxism says this openly. Yet "liberalism" also refuses to accept the sovereignty of God. And despite this fact, many pious and evangelical believers accept many of the political and social views of the "liberals."

How does "liberalism" deny the sovereignty of God, even though many misled evangelicals accept its socio-economic views? Basically, the "liberal" — just as the Marxist — does this by trying to build a social system, a political system, and an economic system, in which God is left out. The "liberal" may leave room for piety and prayer on Sunday, but God is left out of the affairs of society.

Kuyper is attacking, of course, the "liberalism" of the nineteenth century. Before his death, Kuyper saw this nineteenth-century "liberalism" modifying some of its social and economic views: but, as he saw it, not basically. And, because of that, it still cannot get at the root of modern problems. It has no answer, really, for dictatorship and Caesarism and Marxism. It shares too many of their presuppositions and approaches. Though it may leave room for *personal* piety, *personal* witnessing, *personal* charity, and *personal* worship, it banishes Christianity from the affairs of *society*. And thus it has no real answer against Marxism. And thus it has no answer to the deep-seated crisis of the modern world. Indeed, it must bear a large share of responsibility for the crisis.

The crisis is deep. Listen to Kuyper in 1891: "There are thousands upon ten thousands who would rather demolish and annihilate everything rather than continue to bear the burden of existing conditions. . . . we have arrived at a radical breach with the Christian tradition of the past. . . . [we have] a political and social life characterized by the decay of parliamentarianism, by an ever stronger desire for a dictator, by a sharp conflict between pauperism and capitalism — while heavy armaments on land and sea become, even at the price of financial ruin, the ideal. . . ." Kuyper feared the rapid decay of Western civilization unless the "poison" of Marxism and "liberalism" was countered: "Rome collapsed . . . and so, too, our Western civilization will succumb, unless" — unless what? "Unless Christianity intervenes to redeem it."

How did "liberalism" help bring about this crisis? Basically, because it denied the sovereignty of God over all spheres of life. It tried to banish God from the life of society. It tried to confine God to, at most, the revival meeting and the prayer closet. It dreamed of making God little. It dreamed of building its own society without considering God — except perhaps as a personal Savior. It dreamed of a politics without God, a social life without God, and an economic system without God — and thus, says Kuyper, it stands with the Marxists.

What sort of economic and political system did "liberalism" try to build? Briefly, as follows. Though the "liberal" would allow revival meetings, politics and economics would be built by man, without concern for God's Holy Word. The economic system would be unrestricted capitalism. The political system would be one in which the capitalist could dominate. Not Christ, but the "natural laws of economics" and "freedom of contract" would determine economic policy and the form of economic institutions. Not the Christian idea of the state as the vicar of God, but rather the "liberal" idea of the state as the protector of property rights and freedom of contract, would determine political measures

63

and the forms of government. The rich would treat the poor not as fellow men created in the image of God and still bearing some of its glory, but rather as "machines of flesh" (in Kuyper's graphic phrase), whose role is to make profits for the bourgeoisie.

How, then, can the "liberal" answer the Marxist? He cannot. For the Marxist and he agree in too many things. The Marxist merely goes further. Once agreed that God shall not be considered, and agreed that the strongest shall determine how things are run — the Marxist says merely that the proletariat, the masses of producers, shall control. Agreed that "freedom" rather than "responsibility to God" shall be the watchword — the Marxist demands freedom for the masses to rule the capitalist. Agreed that the use of violence is justified to gain power for one's economic class (as, says Kuyper, the bourgeoisie did in the French Revolution) — the Marxist promises a violent revolution that will make the slaughter of the nobility seem mild in comparison. Agreed that material values are all-important in practice and that riches are what men need — the Marxist says the masses of producers rather than the small group of capitalists shall have riches. Agreed that (as Kuyper put it) "money was the standard of value . . . and the law of the animal world, dog-eat-dog, became the basic law for every social relationship" — the Marxist merely claims that the capitalist, finally, is the weaker dog.

As Kuyper's mentor, Groen Van Prinster, had said in 1848, "it will do no good to give power to the bourgeoisie. They are a new aristocracy and a new privileged class, and it will only be a change."

In summary, then, the "liberalism" that Kuyper attacked as the evil fruit of the French Revolution was a view of society which, as he saw it, did not really base itself on Christian principles. And thus the practical political, social and economic program that it favored does not give a real answer to Marxism. But this practical program demands the same things that the far right today demands: a capitalism unrestricted by the state, and a "rugged individualism" unrestricted by society. It is difficult to avoid the conclusion that the "liberalism" Kuyper attacks survives today on the "far right" of American politics.

64

# III

IF "LIBERALISM" CONFINES CHRIST TO A CORNER, AND builds society on the basis of the "free individual" unrestricted by the state, what is the alternative that Kuyper suggests? What social views reflect the teachings of God's revelation?

To begin with — and Kuyper emphasizes this point over and over — we must see society in a far different light than the "liberal" does. Society is *not* made up of isolated individuals, acting in "freedom," and making social arrangements merely through "contracts freely arrived at." The individual is *not* "free" in that sense. Rather, society — as well as the individual — is bound by the law of the Holy Triune God. Not only the individual must obey this law, but also society. And not only society, but also the state. The state's function is *not,* therefore, merely to preserve the "freedom" of individuals who act in isolation from each other, bound together only by contract arrangements. The state's function is to carry out the Will of God. And this is a far different task, in Kuyper's view, from that which the "liberal" would give it.

Society, cries Kuyper, is not made up of isolated individuals acting in "freedom." It is an organism. It is a body. It is made up of intimately associated social groups. Each man is closely related to each other man. No man can exist in isolated "freedom." Society is an organism, like the body; and no part of that organism can "freely" ignore the welfare of the other parts.

If the capitalist insists on "freedom of contract" alone, without taking measures for the welfare of the worker, then the body social will decay. If the capitalist insists that society is merely made up of individuals associated by contract, then the body social will decay. For society is organic, related, and each group is bound to each other group, and no man may insist on his "rights as a free individual" if this hurts the welfare of another.

Listen, says Kuyper: "The social question [the gulf between rich and poor] has become the burning issue. . . . it is the assertion of the organic nature of human society. . . . the social problem will permit nations no rest until a solution is found. . . . socialism is in the air. . . . if you do not apply *your* [Christian] principle to the problem, it will nevertheless be brought to a con-

65

clusion, but in a spirit hostile to you. . . . every true Christian aspiration must condemn the actual condition of society. . . . [no relief will come] from the palliatives of 'liberalism,' which would offer the people a lecture in political theory, offer the worker a smoking room and a reading chamber, which has no other cure-all than the savings-bank and the public school. . . . the social question [rich and poor] arises from a fault in the very foundation of our society. . . . it cannot be exorcised through the cultivation of more piety, or greater friendliness, or more charities. . . . I see improvement, only in — and I do not hesitate to use the word — a socialist direction, provided that by socialism is understood [not Marxism but] the idea that society is an organism, a God-willed community. . . . rejuvenation can come only through the old and yet ever-new Gospel. . . . once before [in the Roman era] it was by His gospel alone that the society of that day was saved from certain destruction. . . . there is this which partly bridges the gap between us and the Socialists: both we and they have pity for the suffering of the oppressed, and both we and they try and improve this state of affairs. What inexorably divides us is this, that they lift not their hand to the salvation of the eternally lost, while we, as confessors of the Christ, always look at the strife against social injustice in conjunction with [the even greater need for] the Kingdom of heaven."

To escape the rapidly deepening crisis of Western society, says Kuyper, we must return to God. And God must not be restricted to occasional appearances at revival meetings, nor be thought of only at prayer breakfasts. Our political ideas and our economic ideas and our social ideas must be based on the Revelation of God. For He rules the cosmos, and any society that does not reckon with Him must perish. He rules not only in the hearts of individuals; He rules society.

Society, then, is not a hit-and-miss collection of isolated individuals acting in "freedom," unrestricted by the state. Society is an organism, a body. The basic building-block of society is not really the isolated individual, as the "liberal" (and the Marxist) claims. It is rather the individual-in-relation, the individual-as-part-of-society. Man was not created to be an individual-in isolation-and-"freedom." He was created to be an individual-in-community, related to his neighbor. Society is made up of communities, or "social spheres."

Each of these "spheres" has its own laws of being, its own code of regulations; and these are not given to it by agreements between isolated "free" individuals; nor are these laws given to it by the state. The laws governing the "spheres" of society are given by God, at creation. They rest, ultimately, on the nature of man, on the nature of man as image-bearer.

As society develops, more and more of the rich potential which is implicit in the "spheres" unfolds. The basic "sphere" (community) is the family. There are also others, which appear as society becomes more complex. Labor, business, education, the arts, science — all these, and many more, are separate "spheres" whose laws of being are given by God. The state interferes with these laws at the peril of harming the welfare of society; and an over-emphasis on the "rights of the free individual" will also harm the spheres, and thus hurt society. It is a law given by God that the father may chasten the child; and it is, in another sphere, a law of God that the laborer is worthy of his hire. In neither sphere is there "unrestricted freedom."

What is the role of the state? To administer justice. What does justice mean? It does *not,* for Kuyper, mean the protection of "unrestricted freedom." For this would merely mean that the strong would exploit the weak. It means, rather, that the state's duty is to see to it that the social spheres (communities) grow strong. And this may imply far-reaching state intervention, to protect a sphere (community) against exploitation at the hands of the over-strong "free individual."

Thus, over a hundred years ago, Kuyper demanded that the sphere of labor be given the right to organize, and the right to manage its own affairs. Despite "liberal" denunciations of Kuyper as a man who was moving towards "socialism," he continually insisted on the rights of labor-as-community. He saw the duty of the state as implying, among other things, the active encouragement of the growth of this sphere. This led him to support the growth of labor movements, and labor unions — despite "liberal" opposition to them as interfering with the "freedom of the individual." He supported a far-reaching plan of state-sponsored health and old-age insurance — despite "liberal" outcries that he was opposed to the "freedom" of the individual to buy or not buy insurance. He supported state legislation setting down maximum hours of work — despite the impassioned speeches of "liberals" insisting that this violated the "freedom" of the employer to work his men as long as he wanted.

Despite anguished outcries from "liberals" who said that business should be "free" to make whatever arrangements it wanted in Dutch colonies, Kuyper pushed through state measures that began to protect the East Indies from exploitation. Despite emotional appeals from outraged "liberals" that religious schools should be supported "freely" on a voluntary basis, Kuyper pushed through legislation giving tax money to religious schools. Despite angered "liberal" appeals to the glories of "free" and unrestricted individualism, Kuyper's party began to push the concept of "co-determination" (*medezeggenschap*), which would give labor the rights of a partner with management in the running of a business. Despite a constant drumfire of "liberal" denunciation of him as an opponent of "freedom," as a "radical," a "left-winger," a "socialist," and worse, Kuyper stuck to his guns and continued to push for what he viewed as a social program that would recognize the Kingship of Christ.

The result was a program of far-reaching social and economic reform. Michael Fogarty, in a recent book, hailed Kuyper's Antirevolutionary or "Christian Democratic" movement as "one of the most successful, and in many ways the most instructive political, economic and social movements to be found anywhere in the Christian world." It surely bears closer study by evangelical Christians today.

## IV

IN SUMMARY, THEN, IT SEEMS DIFFICULT TO AVOID THE following conclusions. First: the "liberalism" that Kuyper denounced implied a social and economic program very similar to that which the far right proposes today. Second: the social and economic program that Kuyper favored as a program that would recognize the demands of Christianity would be denounced as "socialist" by the far right today.

This should not, in our opinion, deter us from or make us fearful about examining Kuyper's approach (or Calvin's). And, at very least, it surely bears careful consideration as an important attempt at working out an orthodox Christian theory of society, and a practical program based on it.[2]

[2] For more extensive accounts, see *Review of Politics,* 1957; *Church History,* 1948; and Michael Fogarty, *Christian Democracy in Western Europe* (Notre Dame, 1957). A good popular biography is that of Frank Vandenberg, *Abraham Kuyper* (Eerdmans, 1960). For his political and social thought, see further Kuyper's translated works *Calvinism* (Eerdmans, 1943) and *Christianity and the Class Struggle* (Grand Rapids, 1950; available from the Calvin College Bookstore).

# Contemporary American Liberalism

By Alan P. Grimes

ABSTRACT: Liberalism in America has been at a low ebb ever since the Second World War. This is evident in the decline in circulation of liberal periodicals as well as in the decline in influence of politics of the left. The decline of politics of the left is attributed to postwar reaction, the Cold War, the rhythm of politics, excessive loyalty enthusiasm, and defense prosperity The extent of this prosperity, however, is questioned. The absence of an effective and aggressive left has modified the force of moderate liberalism in both ideology and politics. A survey of college students at Michigan State University reveals that, while liberalism is still the accepted ideology of a majority of students, it is probably neutralized by an acceptance of the political role of conservative reference groups.

---

THE ANNALS, November, 1962, 25–34.

IT was of scant comfort to contemporary liberals to learn in 1960, in the closing months of the Eisenhower Administration, that Senator Goldwater felt that liberals still ruled in Washington and had been there ever since the New Deal.[1] Barry Goldwater saw liberals the way Joe McCarthy saw Reds, yet the fact of the matter was that liberals were having difficulty in recognizing each other. Nor was it much comfort to learn from the liberal historian, Eric Goldman, that "If the intellectuals were discussing a 'new conservatism,' " during the 1950's, "the new conservatism was heavily streaked with the old liberalism."[2] This seemed only to confirm the caustic judgment that yesteryears' liberalism had become, like many of its once youthful disciples, middle-aged, middle class, and muddled. In ideas, as in politics, the age of the Cold War and defense prosperity, of McCarthyism and conformity, of bumbling platitudes, of Madison Avenue, of the flip-top box and the flipped lid had played havoc with American idealism and, with it, its natural vanguard, liberalism.

The decline—or perhaps dormancy would be a better expression—of liberalism since the Second World War has been evident not only in politics but in the circulation figures of the little liberal magazines. In 1945 *The Nation* listed a circulation of 37,425, which rose to 39,439 in 1950; in 1960 its circulation had dropped to 23,148. In 1945 *The New Republic's* figures were 37,253; in 1950, 52,022; in 1960, 23,663.* *Commonweal* rose from a circulation of 14,000 in 1945 to 20,563 in 1960, but *The New Leader* dropped from a high of 43,000 in 1945 to 15,900 * in 1960. *The Progressive*, with a circulation of

30,000 in 1945, ceased being a weekly in 1948 and had a circulation of only 26,000 in 1960. *Commentary* was established in the optimistic climate of 1945, yet in 1960 it had a circulation of only 22,923. The significant exception, other than the slight gain made by *Commonweal*, to the general decline in circulation of the liberal magazines has been *The Reporter*. This slick-covered magazine with its *New Yorker*-style format was established in 1949 and soon rose to fame in liberal circles with its exposé of the "China lobby." In 1950 its circulation was 25,000, certainly on a par with its liberal competitors; however, over the decade its circulation skyrocketed so that in 1960 it stood at 122,942.[3]

Something of the changing character and constituency of modern liberalism may be seen in the above circulation figures. Twenty years ago, a liberal could know what his liberal friends were thinking by looking at the table of contents of the current issues of *The Nation* or *The New Republic;* today, most liberals are more likely to find that their friends have read *The Reporter.* *The Reporter* now has a circulation approximately equal to, if not above, that of *The Nation, The New Republic, The New Leader, Commentary, Commonweal*, and *The Progressive* combined. Liberals, particularly academic liberals, seem less impressed today with the snappy, strident prose of what they often term "visceral liberalism" than they were two decades ago; they prefer instead the sober and sedate prose, the less ideologically oriented style of the sustained article which deals with the

[1] Barry Goldwater. *The Conscience of a Conservative* (New York: Hillman Books, 1960), pp. 3–4.

[2] Eric Goldman, *The Crucial Decade—And After: America, 1945–1960* (New York: Vintage Books, 1961), p. 290.

[3] With the exception of the two asterisked figures, the circulation figures are taken from the *Directory of Newspapers and Periodicals* (Philadelphia: N. W. Ayer & Sons) published in the years indicated above in the text. The two asterisked figures were found in *The Progressive*, January 1960, p. 2, as they were not given in the *Directory*.

complexity of political life. This may well mean that traditional fire-eating liberalism finds little favor today among the intellectuals of the middle class. Most of these liberals would no doubt insist, however, that their views are no less liberal than they once were but only that they have become more thoughtful and less ideologically oriented.

Twenty years ago, there was a multi-colored political spectrum for those of the leftist persuasion, with numerous parties offering rival candidates for public offices and a veritable snowfall of handbills from feverishly active mimeographing machines. True, few people voted for these minor parties, but the parties helped through their campaign to keep ideas in circulation and to make men think. At that time, the Communists had not been read out of the American left, except in a few sophisticated Socialist circles; at that time, the genial and seemingly inexhaustible Norman Thomas still gave leadership to the Socialist party as its quadrennial presidential candidate. After the war, however, the situation changed markedly. In 1948 the Communists threw their support to Henry Wallace in the abortive Progressive movement. Following this political fiasco, their exposure by the Americans for Democratic Action (ADA), and their prosecution under the Smith Act and similar legislation, the Communists ceased to be a significant force on the American left. Ironically, the Socialists, their bitter opponents, all but collapsed along with them. In 1948 Norman Thomas, in his last presidential campaign, polled nearly 100,000 votes; in 1952 the Socialist candidate for president polled less than 5,000 votes; in 1956 the Socialist vote dropped to slightly over the incredibly small total of 2,000. The Socialist Labor party somehow hangs on, continuously offering a presidential candidate every four years since 1896, but the 45,000 votes

their candidate received in 1956 was unlikely to disturb the slumber of even a General Walker, for they seemed permanently dedicated to a "no-win" program. In short, the voting habits, like the reading habits, of American liberals have changed since the Second World War. What was once an active aspect of the left is now left out of the liberal political spectrum. For all practical purposes, the active "left" of American liberalism is occupied by the Americans for Democratic Action.

## POSTWAR DECLINE OF THE LEFT

In order further to assess the character, strength, and appeal of contemporary liberalism, it is necessary also to see it in the setting of recent history. The brief and energetic era of domestic reform under the New Deal had actually ended by 1938. Since then, Americans have lived under the imminent awareness of global war and the threat of war. War, whether of the hot or cold variety, has never provided a congenial climate for the growth of liberalism; yet, for the last twenty-four years, such has been the climate in which liberalism has struggled to survive. Invariably, the appeal to patriotism and national security produces a closing of the ranks behind the more conservative forces in society and, thus, a subtly insistent demand for a departure from such liberalism as might disturb the *status quo*.

It was hoped by many liberals, as the Second World War drew to a close, that a rebirth of the New Deal might follow along global lines. Yet, for all of Truman's valiant, if many times awkward and uncertain, efforts to keep the nation's focus on a Fair Deal, he was, as James Wechsler has observed, "incapable of giving continuity or new direction to the movement of liberalism." [4]

[4] James Wechsler, *Reflections of an Angry Middle-Aged Editor* (New York: Random House, 1960), p. 49.

72

It was asking too much of both history and Mr. Truman. "Every war brings after it a period of materialism and conservatism," Franklin D. Roosevelt wrote shortly after the First World War; "people tire quickly of ideals and we are now repeating history." [5] The Civil War produced the administration of Ulysses S. Grant; the First World War gave us Harding, Coolidge, and Hoover; the Second World War led to the Eisenhower era. And, as though the aftermath of the unsettling upheavals of the war were not enough to explain the return to conservatism, there was the theory of the cyclical course of history. In the December 1939 issue of the *Yale Review*, historian Arthur M. Schlesinger, Sr., pointed out the cycle of liberalism and conservatism in America in an article entitled "Tides of National Politics." These periods of change averaged out at about fifteen or sixteen year intervals. Arthur M. Schlesinger, Jr., calling attention to this pattern of politics, saw liberalism in the saddle from 1900 to 1920, conservatism from 1920 to 1930, liberalism from 1930 to 1950, and conservatism from 1950 to 1960. Our recent history, he observed,

would suggest that there is an *inherent cyclical rhythm* in our national affairs—a predictable (and understandable) · swing from positive government to negative government; from periods of intense activity which accomplish a lot of things but finally wear the people out to periods of apathy and passivity which go on until the national energy is replenished and forward motion can again be resumed.[6]

## Cold War and Communist threat

Whatever may be the merit of a cyclical theory of politics with predict-

[5] Quoted in Arthur M. Schlesinger, Jr., *The Crisis of the Old Order* (Boston: Houghton Mifflin Company, 1957), p. 366.
[6] Arthur M. Schlesinger, Jr., "The Coming Shape of American Politics," *The Progressive*, September 1959, p. 23.

able periodic sequences of liberal and conservative triumphs or of the inexorability of reaction as the predictable offspring of war, there can be no doubt that the conscious overriding consideration which bolstered post-World War Two conservatism was the Cold War and the challenge of Soviet communism. The consequences of the Cold War and the Soviet threat were threefold.

In the first place, there was the call to patriotism and preparedness and, with it, the concomitant appeal to conservatism and conformity, such as would have occurred no matter who the enemy might have been. Reform, both global and domestic, the hallmark of liberalism, became of secondary consideration to national security and defense.

Secondly, the American Communist party became recognized as an instrument of Soviet power and, therefore, in the global struggle, an instrument of American subversion and was accordingly declared out of bounds by both law and consensus. There is no need to dwell here on the nature of the Communist conspiracy on the one hand or the methods of its exposure and control on the other. The fundamental point here is that the deletion of the Communist alternative from the political spectrum automatically narrowed the scope of the spectrum by removing what had traditionally been seen as the far left. This affected liberalism in the same manner that conservatism would be affected today if its radical right were declared out of bounds. The presence of the extremes of both right and left has always provided the horrible examples for those who delight in reasoning by *reductio ad absurdum*. Liberalism has always steered its course somewhere in that vast uncharted area between the radical left on the one hand and conservatism on the other, just as conservatism has been defined by the boundaries of liberalism and the radical right. To navigate safely in the 1950's, liberalism had to keep in view the shoreline of conservatism.

Finally, the challenge of Soviet communism produced a period of considerable confusion in the ranks of liberalism itself, which made it exceptionally vulnerable to attacks by unfriendly critics. This was most clearly seen in the inability of many liberals shortly after the Second World War to recognize the enormity of the Soviet threat to liberal principles in the world and the unsavory aspects of the Communist party in the United States. The Wallace movement of 1948 remains the best evidence of this confusion. Non-Communist leftists were caught in a cross fire from both left and right.

In 1947 the Americans for Democratic Action—then sometimes facetiously called "the New Deal government in exile"—was founded to give leadership to a non-Communist liberal movement. However, even ADA liberals with long records of anticommunism were to be smeared as fellow-travelers for advocating liberal programs which might also be supported by known Communists. Consistently since its founding, the ADA has articulated a liberalism that has at once eschewed communism and advocated reform.

Yet the belief has persisted that, generally, liberals have been inadequate on the issue of communism. For example, in April 1962, *The New York Times Magazine* carried an article entitled "The Liberals Have Helped the Radical Right." The article declared: [7]

The real tragedy of the American anti-Communist movement, lies in the fact that American liberals, who know the Communists best because they fought so many successful battles against them in the union movement, veteran's organizations and the

[7] Harvey B. Schecter, "The Liberals Have Helped the Radical Right," *The New York Times Magazine*, April 29, 1962, p. 13.

political arena, for more than a decade have been silent on the question of communism.

## Decline of socialism

A further aspect in the changing character of liberalism following the war was the decline of socialism as a persuasive ideology. This, too, may have been at least in part a consequence of the Cold War and a prosperity built in large measure on defense spending. The billions the government pumped into the economy in the name of defense, which probably would not have been put into the economy in the name of social welfare, promoted a sense of prosperity which seemed to forestall the ability of socialism to creep, let alone stand up and walk. J. K. Galbraith aptly labeled the new era "the affluent society," and thousands of Americans proved some measure of their affluence by purchasing Galbraith's book. There was, however, some serious question as to the general distribution of this postwar prosperity and its concomitant assumption of a broad equalization of wealth. Early in 1962, Robert S. Lampman published a report entitled *The Share of Top-Wealth Holders in National Wealth, 1922–56* [8] which might prove as disturbing in its findings as the Berle and Means analysis of *The Modern Corporation and Private Property* had been to an earlier generation. In spite of the wide sale of common stocks during the 1950's, Lampman found a greater concentration of ownership of common stock among the very rich in 1953 than had existed in 1929. In 1953 some 1.7 million Americans held estates valued at $60,000 or more, and the richest one per cent of American adults held nearly 28 per cent of the nation's entire personal wealth. Although all evidence indicated a swelling in the ranks of the very rich, it was usually

[8] Princeton University Press.

also argued that the poor had also risen in wealth and had now passed into the middle class. Michael Harrington, however, surveyed this other extreme in *The Other America*[9] and found that forty to fifty million Americans were poor by whatever standard was used. And, generally, Gabriel Kolko independently corroborated both of these findings. Kolko wrote, before the appearance of the works of Lampman and Harrington: [10]

Most recent studies of American society assume that since the end of the Great Depression, in 1939, the nation's wealth has been redistributed and prosperity has been extended to the vast majority of the population. . . . But this assumption is nonetheless fallacious, for despite the obvious increase in prosperity since the abysmal years of the Great Depression, the basic distribution of income and wealth in the United States is essentially the same now as it was in 1939, or even 1910. Most low-income groups live substantially better today, but even though their real wages have mounted, their percentage of the national income has not changed.

As a result of his findings, Kolko declared that "well over one-third of the nation's households subsist on incomes too meager to provide minimum standards of health and decency."[11] Furthermore, he found that, "Throughout the 1950's, the income of the top tenth was larger than the total for the bottom five income-tenths—about the same relationship as existed in 1910 and 1918."[12] The concept of affluence in the society of the fifties was thus seriously questioned by the statistical analyses of the early sixties, and, accordingly, the explanation of widespread affluence for the collapse of socialism is also open to question.

In retrospect, it would appear that much of the meager following of socialism prior to 1950 was a personal following of Norman Thomas and, when he ceased to serve as "Mr. Socialism," the movement all but expired. It is doubtful, however, that even with a younger Norman Thomas the climate of opinion in the fifties would have been favorable to the growth of socialism. Increasingly, in the conservative press, "socialism" proved to be a successful derogatory epithet rather than a descriptive label for a meaningful political alternative, and, increasingly, Socialists were less certain themselves of the panacea quality of their solutions. Over the years, American socialists had departed from the doctrinaire ideological line of socialists of the past. As early as 1931, Norman Thomas had declared that socialism "must not degenerate into dogmatic creedalism."[13] Early in the fifties, Thomas re-emphasized this point, declaring that socialism "must unite the social actions of men of varying beliefs on the common denominator of a conviction that through cooperation men may win plenty, peace, and freedom. Inspired by this faith, socialism must be experimental rather than rigidly doctrinaire."[14] If this made good sense, as it did to many, it also indicated the decline of socialism as an ideology. No longer was there some mysterious magic in industrial nationalization as the pathway to an economy of abundance nor was unilateral disarmament the certain pathway to peace. And many former

[9] New York: The Macmillan Company, 1962.
[10] Gabriel Kolko, *Wealth and Power in America: An Analysis of Social Class and Income Distribution* (New York: Frederick A. Praeger, 1962), p. 3.
[11] *Ibid.*, p. 4.
[12] *Ibid.*, pp. 12–13.

[13] Norman Thomas, *America's Way Out: A Program for Democracy* (New York: The Macmillan Company, 1931), p. 150.
[14] Norman Thomas, *A Socialist's Faith* (New York: W. W. Norton and Company, 1951), p. 300.

Socialists everywhere could agree with former Socialist Daniel Bell when he wrote of the fifties in *The End of Ideology:* [15]

One simple fact emerges: for the radical intelligentsia, the old ideologies have lost their "truth" and their power to persuade. . . . In the West, among the intellectuals, the old passions are spent. . . . The end of ideology closes the book, intellectually speaking, on an era, the one of easy 'left' formulae for social change.

It is difficult to estimate the contribution of socialism to American liberalism, because so many of the ideals of socialism became ideals of liberalism and vice versa that it was difficult to see just where America's uniquely pragmatic socialism left off and pragmatic liberalism began. Murray Seidler has called Thomas a "successful failure" and declared that the "key values of American liberalism have been incorporated into the socialist thought of Norman Thomas." [16] And Norman Thomas has observed that, although organized socialism failed in the United States, nevertheless we have "moved in the direction of a welfare state as far as any country in which democratic socialism is a first or second party in strength. It [the United States] has adopted a great many of the measures which in the United States, as elsewhere, were definitely socialist in origin." [17] But there can be no doubt that the drastic decline in significance of socialism in America further reduced the political spectrum on the left and, in effect, deprived liberalism of a vital source of ideas as well as a dedicated supportive following.

[15] Daniel Bell, *The End of Ideology* (New York: Collier Books, 1961), pp. 397, 398, 400.
[16] Murray Seidler, *Norman Thomas, Respectable Rebel* (Syracuse: Syracuse University Press, 1961), pp. 293, 316.
[17] Norman Thomas, "The Failure of Organized Socialism in America," *The Progressive*, January 1959, p. 29.

### Flagging labor movement

Finally, the labor movement itself lost much of its vitality in the postwar period. True, organized labor pushed for liberal political candidates and liberal political measures and, in its own immediate programs, such as the cost-of-living adjustments in wages and the guaranteed annual wage, it pushed for a more humane approach to industrial relations. Nevertheless, it was equally under the onus of the antiliberal consensus. Clearly, today, the Taft-Hartley Act is as settled in tradition as, for a brief period, the Wagner Labor Relations Act was before it, and labor is continually on the defensive against the euphemistically labeled "right-to-work" laws. The McClelland Committee hearings which exposed racketeering in the labor unions too often were used as a judgment on unions generally, and, unfortunately, many Americans forgot about the exemplary record of the Reuther brothers when they deplored the devious shenanigans of Jimmy Hoffa.

In all, the record of postwar America proved that liberalism had to struggle for damage control rather than advance in a society in which the fundamental values were "loyalty" and the preservation of the *status quo*. The atmosphere of hysteria over communism which prevailed in this period stifled, in effect, much wholesome criticism of society if that criticism might even remotely be considered something a Communist, or a fellow-traveler, or a former friend of a former fellow-traveler might have said. It was all too easy to disparage social or political criticism with the statement, "Sounds like a Communist to me." In many circles, arguments could not be examined on their merits until a suspicious check of the loyalty credentials of their adherents had been made. College students were reported to be reluctant to engage in public criticism of existing institutions for fear such actions might adversely affect their prospects for employment. It was charged, in at least one large state university, that the placement bureau kept a record of membership lists of the Young Socialist Club for reference of prospective employers. Too often, advocates of liberalism felt constrained to say in effect in their public pronouncements, "I am not a Communist but I believe along with Jefferson (or Lincoln or Roosevelt) . . ." in which the affirmation was in the anti-communism and the positive liberalism was the secondary and minor theme, subordinate always to the conjunction.

Full and frank interchange of ideas has always been an essential component of liberalism. This has been true not only because of the persuasive reasoning of Jefferson or the eloquent argument of John Stuart Mill on the utility of freedom of expression but because, by definition, a liberal society is a free society, in which the paramount freedom is freedom of the mind. Such freedom, however, is not only the goal of liberalism but equally the condition of existence of liberalism itself. In the postwar period, due to the combination of circumstances discussed above, liberalism, with its implicit criticism of the *status quo,* had to struggle for survival.

### LIBERALISM IN THE SIXTIES

It was with some reluctance in 1960 that many liberals accepted the presidential candidacy of John F. Kennedy; for, generally, they preferred Adlai Stevenson or Hubert Humphrey. For instance, *The Progressive* endorsed Stevenson until the Kennedy nomination, when it threw its support to him. Liberal journals generally checked candidates against a hypothetical liberal yardstick. An article in *The Progressive* stated: [18]

[18] Michael Armine, "Hubert Horatio Humphrey," *The Progressive,* April 1960, p. 13.

Humphrey's record in the Senate can best be summarized by reporting that he consistently achieves a 100 per cent voting score on the roll calls prepared by Americans for Democratic Action, the nation's labor unions, and liberal farm organizations and cooperatives. He is no radical, but rather accepts without apparent dissent the basic outlines of the moderate welfare state proposed by liberal Democrats.

James MacGregor Burns, a Kennedy political biographer and supporter, affirmed that Kennedy was a liberal. "History, indeed," he wrote, "may record that, until now, he is the most progressive candidate ever nominated by a major party," and he cited Kennedy's "plus" scores "on all major social welfare legislation on the scorecards of labor and liberal journals." [19]

Today, some two years after the close Kennedy election, there continues to be dispute over Kennedy's liberalism. In the eyes of the conservative journals, Kennedy's drastic policies are a less inhibited brand of Roosevelt's New Deal, and the President is called an "ultra liberal." In the eyes of the liberal journals, Kennedy has healthy liberal leanings but the area "left of Kennedy" is "rapidly becoming a vast area indeed." [20] This would seem to correspond with the judgment of a report in *Newsweek* that the peace between Kennedy and the liberals was "ill-fated from the beginning" for, in truth, "he never was *really* one of the visceral liberals." The same report quoted Joseph Rauh of the "all-out liberal, 50,000-member Americans for Democratic Action" as saying: "Compared to Ike or Nixon, Kennedy is OK. But compared to the 'high hopes' we had, he's a bitter disappointment." Kennedy himself was reported as saying, "Boy, when those

[19] James MacGregor Burns, "Kennedy's Liberalism," *The Progressive,* October 1960, p. 18.

[20] Robert Martinson, "State of the Campus: 1962," *The Nation,* May 19, 1962, p. 434.

liberals start mixing into policy, it's murder." [21]

In order to assess more accurately the current state of liberalism, a public-opinion survey was undertaken in the spring of 1962 at Michigan State University. Would college students, as might be expected, prove to espouse a natural liberalism of youth, or was Barry Goldwater correct in his finding that "The preponderant judgment of the American people, especially of the young people, is that the radical, or Liberal approach has not worked and is not working. They yearn for a return to Conservative principles"? [22] Was the judgment of the editors of *The Nation* supported when they found in their 1962 survey of American campus thought that, "except in the South, the 'rebellious' spirit seems to be spreading more rapidly among graduate students and faculty than among undergraduates"? [23] Although the survey could not deal with these large questions directly, the results are suggestive as to the current condition of liberalism on one large midwestern university campus.

Michigan State University may be considered quite typical of any large midwestern state university; it had, in the spring of 1962, some 20,546 students enrolled on campus. [24] The survey was designed to find out, among other things, the political attitudes of the students which might have bearing upon an understanding of contemporary liberalism. Students were asked whom they identified as liberals, whom as conservatives, and how they saw themselves, their friends, and the faculty. They were asked how they reacted to certain politically active groups in society,

whether they found themselves influenced by them, and, if so, whether favorably or unfavorably. They were asked how they identified certain national periodicals, whether they were liberal or conservative. Finally, they were asked whether they favored or opposed certain positions on public policy.

At the outset, it may be noted that 42 per cent of the students identified themselves as Democrats, or leaning in that direction, and 51 per cent identified themselves as being Republican, or having Republican leanings. However, 53 per cent said they were either very or moderately liberal, 20 per cent said they were middle-of-the-road, and only 20 per cent saw themselves as moderately or very conservative. [25] They saw their friends as slightly more conservative than themselves but still predominantly liberal; they saw the faculty as slightly more liberal than themselves. In an open-ended question, 64 per cent of them volunteered Goldwater as the most identifiable conservative, and nearly 62 per cent offered Kennedy as the most nationally known liberal. No other political figures came anywhere near these percentages in either category.

Of the various groups in American politics, the most salient was the American Medical Association (AMA). Some 71 per cent of the students indicated that they would be influenced by its position on an issue; 49 per cent said that they would be inclined to favor a political program sponsored by the AMA, and a fraction over 22 per cent said that they would be inclined to oppose such an AMA-sponsored political program. Next in salience was the House Committee on Un-American Activities (66 per cent); however, nearly 34 per cent were favorably influenced by it, and slightly over 32 per cent were unfavorably influenced by it. Next in salience

[21] *Newsweek,* April 16, 1962, pp. 29, 31.

[22] Goldwater, *op. cit.,* p. 3.

[23] *The Nation,* May 19, 1962, p. 431.

[24] The survey was undertaken by students of a political-science class in public opinion under the direction of Professor Joseph A. Schlesinger.

[25] For brevity's sake, those with no opinion are not included in the percentages.

(nearly 66 per cent) and most favorable in its influence was the Chamber of Commerce; nearly 56 per cent were favorably influenced by it with only a fraction over 10 per cent opposingly influenced. The fourth most salient group (nearly 60 per cent) was the American Federation of Labor and Congress of Industrial Organizations (AFL-CIO); here, however, 41 per cent were inclined to oppose what the AFL-CIO sponsored politically, and only 18 per cent were inclined to favor political programs with its sponsorship. The least salient (a fraction over 38 per cent) of the groups surveyed was the Americans for Democratic Action; 24 per cent indicated a favorable response to ADA, and slightly over 14 per cent were unfavorably impressed.

The survey revealed a rather astonishing ignorance on the part of students of political-opinion magazines. Over 75 per cent of the students indicated that they they knew so little about *The New Leader, The Progressive, The Nation, Commonweal,* or *The National Review* that they did not know what their political views were. Of those who ventured an opinion on *The Nation* more thought it was a conservative than a liberal magazine. Seven per cent of the students thought that the *National Geographic* was a liberal magazine; another seven per cent thought it was a conservative magazine.

On policy questions, there was a remarkable degree of consensus in favor of the Kennedy program, ranging from approval of the resumption of nuclear weapons testing to the Peace Corps. On domestic-policy issues, there was considerable disagreement, with the greatest support, however, falling consistently on the side of what would generally be called liberal social-welfare programs. The survey showed quite clearly that the ideological orientation of the students was generally liberal, yet their reference-group orientation was clearly conservative. Caught between these conflicting pressures, and generally ignorant of or indifferent to the persuasive appeal of politically oriented periodical literature, the students seemed unlikely to become decisively active in any political direction. Perhaps this dilemma of cross pressures, augmented by political ignorance and diffidence, was not confined to a university-student body but was the dilemma of much of America midway in 1962.

# IMAGES OF SOCIALISM

■ *Lewis Coser and Irving Howe*

"God," said Tolstoy, "is the name of my desire." This remarkable sentence could haunt one a lifetime, it reverberates in so many directions. Tolstoy may have intended partial assent to the idea that, life being insupportable without some straining toward "transcendence," a belief in God is a psychological necessity. But he must also have wanted to turn this rationalist criticism into a definition of his faith. He must have meant that precisely because his holiest desires met in the vision of God he was enabled to cope with the quite unholy

DISSENT, Spring, 1954, 122-138.

realities of human existence. That God should be seen as the symbolic objectification of his desire thus became both a glorification of God and a strengthening of man, a stake in the future and a radical criticism of the present.

Without sanctioning the facile identification that is frequently made between religion and socialist politics, we should like to twist Tolstoy's remark to our own ends: *socialism is the name of our desire.* And not merely in the sense that it is a vision which, for many people throughout the world, provides moral sustenance but also in the sense that it is a vision which objectifies and gives urgency to their criticism of the human condition in our time. It is the name of our desire because the desire arises from a conflict with, and an extension from, the world that is; nor could the desire survive in any meaningful way were it not for this complex relationship to the world that is.

At so late and unhappy a moment, however, can one still specify what the vision of socialism means or should mean? Is the idea of utopia itself still a tolerable one?

# I

The impulse to imagine "the good society" probably coincides with human history, and the manner of constructing it—to invert what exists—is an element binding together all pre-Marxist utopias. These dreamers and system makers have one thing in common: their desire to storm history.

The growth of the modern utopian idea accompanies the slow formation of the centralized state in Europe. Its imagery is rationalistic, far removed from the ecstatic visions that accompany the religiously inspired rebellions agitating feudal society in its last moments. As the traditional patchwork of autonomous social institutions in western Europe was replaced, in the interests of efficiency, by an increasingly centralized system of rule, men began to conceive of a society that would drive this tendency to its conclusion and be governed completely by rationality. But not only the increasing rationality of political power inspired the thinking of social philosophers; they were stirred by the growth of a new, bourgeois style of life that emphasized calculation, foresight, and efficiency and made regularity of work an almost religious obligation.

As soon as men began to look at the state as "a work of art," as "an artificial man, created for the protection and salvation of the natural man" (Hobbes, *Leviathan*), it took but one more step to imagine that this "work of art" could be rendered perfect through foresight and will. Thomas Campanella, a rebellious Calabrian monk of the seventeenth century, conceived in his *City of the Sun* of such a perfect work of art. In Campanella's utopia, unquestionably designed from the most idealistic of motives, one sees the traits of many pre-Marxist utopias. Salvation is *imposed,* delivered from above; there is an all-powerful ruler called the Great Metaphysicus (surely no more absurd than the Beloved Leader); only one book exists in the *City of the Sun,* which may be taken as an economical image of modern practice: naturally, a book called *Wisdom.* Sexual relations are organized by state administrators "according to philosophical rules," the race being "managed for the good of the commonwealth and not of private individuals. . . ." Education is conceived along entirely rationalistic lines, and indeed it must be, for Campanella felt that the Great Metaphysicus, as he forces perfection upon history, has to deal with recalcitrant materials: the people, he writes in a sentence that betrays both his bias and his pathos, is "a beast with a muddy brain."

And here we come upon a key to utopian thought: the galling sense of a chasm between the scheme and the subjects, between the plan, ready and perfect, and the people, mute and indifferent. (Poor Fourier, the salesman with phalanxes in his belfry, comes home daily at noon, to wait for the one capitalist—he needs no more than one—who will finance utopia.) Intellectuals who cannot shape history try to rape it, through either actual violence, like the Russian terrorists, or imagined violence, the sudden seizure of history by a utopian claw. In his *City of the Sun,* Campanella decrees—the utopian never hesitates to decree—that those sentenced to death for crimes against the Godhead, liberty and the higher magistrates are to be rationally enlightened, before execution, by special functionaries, so that in the end they will acquiesce in their own condemnation. Let no one say history is unforeseen.

Two centuries after Campanella, Etienne Cabot, a disciple of Robert Owen and Saint-Simon, envisaged the revolutionary dictatorship of Icar, an enlightened ruler who refuses to stay in power longer than necessary for establishing the new society; he no doubt means it to wither away. Meanwhile Icaria has only one newspaper, and the republic has "revised all useful books which showed imperfections and it has burned all those which we judged dangerous and useless."

The point need not be overstressed. The utopians were not—or not merely —the unconscious authoritarians that malicious critics have made them out to be. No doubt some did harbor strong streaks of authoritarian feeling which they vicariously released through utopian images; but this is far from the whole story. Robert Owen wanted a free co-operative society. Decentralization is stressed in Morelly's utopia, "Floating Islands." The phalanxes of Fourier are to function without any central authority, and if there must be one it should be located as far from France as possible, certainly no nearer than Constantinople.

The authoritarian element we find in the utopians is due far less to psychological malaise or power hunger (most of them were genuinely good people) than to the sense of desperation that frequently lies beneath the surface of their fantasying. All pre-Marxist utopian thinking tends to be ahistorical, to see neither possibility nor need for relating the image of the good society to the actual workings of society as it is. For Fourier it is simply a matter of discovering the "plan" of God, the ordained social order that in realizing God's will ensures man's happiness. (Socialism for Fourier is indeed the name of his desire—but in a very different sense from that which we urge!) The imagined construction of utopia occurs *outside* the order or flux of history: it comes through fiat. Once utopia is established, history grinds to a standstill and the rule of rationality replaces the conflict of class or, as the utopians might have preferred to say, the conflict of passions. Friedrich Engels describes this process with both sympathy and shrewdness:

82

Society presented nothing but wrongs; to remove these was the task of reason. It was necessary, then, to *impose this upon society from without* by propaganda and, whenever possible, by the example of model experiments. These new social systems were foredoomed as utopian; the more completely they were worked out in detail, the more they could not avoid drifting off into pure phantasies. . . .

We can leave it to the literary small fry to solemnly quibble over these phantasies, which today only make us smile, and to crow over the superiority of their own bald reasoning, as compared with such "insanity." As for us, we delight in the stupendously great thoughts and germs of thought that everywhere break out through their phantastic covering. . . . [Italics added.]

Given the desire to impose utopia upon an indifferent history, a desire which derives, in the main, from a deep sense of alienation from the flow of history, it follows logically enough that the utopians should for the most part think in terms of elite politics. Auguste Comte specifies that in the "State of Positive Science" society is to be ruled by an elite of intellectuals. The utopia to be inaugurated by the sudden triumph of reason over the vagaries and twists of history—what other recourse could a lonely, isolated utopian have but the elite, the small core of intellect that, like himself, controls and guides? Saint-Simon, living in the afterglow of the French Revolution, begins to perceive the mechanics of class relations and the appearance for the first time in modern history of the masses as a decisive force. But in the main our generalization holds: reformers who lack some organic relationship with major historical movements must almost always be tempted into a more or less benevolent theory of a ruling elite.

## II

Utopia without egalitarianism, utopia dominated by an aristocracy of mind, must quickly degenerate into a vision of useful slavery. Hence the importance of Marx's idea that socialism is to be brought about, in the first instance, by the activities of a major segment of the population, the workers. Having placed the drive toward utopia not beyond, but squarely—perhaps a little too squarely—within the course of history, and having found in the proletariat that active "realizing" force which the utopians could nowhere discern on the social horizon, Marx was enabled to avoid the two major difficulties of his predecessors: ahistoricism and the elite theory. He had, to be sure, difficulties of his own, but not these.

Marx was the first of the major socialist figures who saw the possibility of linking the utopian desire with the actual development of social life. By studying capitalism both as an "ideal" structure and a "real" dynamic, Marx found the sources of revolt within the self-expanding and self-destroying rhythms of the economy itself. The utopians had desired a revolt against history, but they could conduct it, so to speak, only from the space platform of the imaginary future; Marx gave new power to the revolt against history by locating it, "scientifically," within history.

The development of technology, he concluded, made possible a society in which men could "realize" their humanity, if only because the brutalizing

83

burden of fatigue, that sheer physical exhaustion from which the great masses of men had never been free, could now for the first time be removed. This was the historic option offered mankind by the Industrial Revolution, as it is now being offered again by the Atomic Revolution. Conceivably, though only conceivably, a society might have been established at any point in historical time which practiced an equalitarian distribution of goods; but there would have been neither goods nor leisure enough to dispense with the need for a struggle over their distribution; which means bureaucracy, police, an oppressive state, and in sum the destruction of equalitarianism. Now, after the Industrial Revolution, the machine might do for all humanity what the slaves had done for the Greek patriciate.

Marx was one of the first political thinkers to see that both industrialism and "the mass society" were here to stay, that all social schemes which ignored or tried to controvert this fact were not merely irrelevant; they weren't even interesting. It is true, of course, that he did not foresee—he could not—a good many consequences of this tremendous historical fact. He did not foresee that "mass culture" together with social atomization (Durkheim's anomie) would set off strong tendencies of demoralization acting in opposition to those tendencies that made for disciplined cohesion in the working class. He did not foresee that the rise of totalitarianism might present mankind with choices and problems that went beyond the capitalist/socialist formulation. He did not foresee that the nature of leisure would become, even under capitalism, as great a social and cultural problem as the nature of work. He did not foresee that industrialism would create problems which, while not necessarily insoluble, are likely to survive the span of capitalism. But what he did foresee was crucial: that the great decisions of history would now be made in a mass society, that the "stage" on which this struggle would take place had suddenly, dramatically been widened far beyond its previous dimensions.

And when Marx declared the proletariat to be the active social force that could lead the transition to socialism, he was neither sentimentalizing the lowly nor smuggling in a theory of the elite, as many of his critics have suggested. Anyone who has read the chapter in *Capital* on the working day or Engels' book on the conditions of the English workers knows that they measured the degradation of the workers to an extent precluding sentimentality. As for the idea of the proletariat as an elite, Marx made no special claim for its virtue or intelligence, which is the traditional mode of justifying an elite; he merely analyzed its peculiar *position* in society, as the class most driven by the workings of capitalism to both discipline and rebellion, the class that, come what may, utopia or barbarism, would always remain propertyless.

There is another indication that Marx did not mean to favor an elite theory by his special "placing" of the proletariat. His theory of "increasing misery"—be it right, wrong, or vulgarized—implied that the proletariat would soon include the overwhelming bulk of the population. The transition to socialism, far from being assigned to a "natural" elite or a power group, was seen by Marx as the task of the vast "proletarianized" majority. Correct or not, this was a fundamentally democratic point of view.

Concerned as he was with the mechanics of class power, the "laws of motion" of the existing society, and the strategy of social change, Marx paid very little attention to the description of socialism. The few remarks to be found in his early work and in such a later book as *The Critique of the Gotha Program* are mainly teasers, formulations so brief as to be cryptic, which did not prevent his disciples from making them into dogmas. An interesting division of labor took place. Marx's predecessors, those whom he called the "utopian socialists," had devoted themselves to summoning pictures of the ideal future, perhaps in lieu of activity in the detested present; Marx, partly as a reaction to their brilliant daydreaming, decided to focus on an analysis of those elements in the present that made possible a strategy for reaching the ideal future. And in the meantime, why worry about the face of the future, why create absurd blueprints? As a response to Fourier, Saint-Simon, and Owen there was much good sense in this attitude; given the state of the European labor movements in the mid-nineteenth century, it was indispensable to turn toward practical problems of national life (Germany) and class organization (England). But the Marxist movement, perhaps unavoidably, paid a price for this emphasis.

As the movement grew, the image of socialism kept becoming hazier and hazier, and soon the haziness came to seem a condition of perfection. The "revisionist" social democrat Eduard Bernstein could write that the goal is nothing, the movement everything; as if a means could be intelligently chosen without an end in view! In his *State and Revolution* Lenin, with far greater fullness than Marx, sketched a vision of socialism profoundly democratic, in which the mass of humanity would break out of its dumbness, so that cooks could become cabinet ministers, and even the "bourgeois principle of equality" would give way to the true freedom of nonmeasurement: "from each according to his ability and to each according to his need." But this democratic vision did not sufficiently affect his immediate views of political activity, so that in his crucial pamphlet "Will the Bolsheviks Retain State Power?" written in 1917, Lenin, as if to brush aside the traditional Marxist view that the socialist transformation requires a far greater popular base than any previous social change, could say, "After the 1905 Revolution Russia was ruled by 130,000 landowners. . . . And yet we are told that Russia will not be able to be governed by the 240,000 members of the Bolshevik Party—governing in the interests of the poor and against the rich."

What happened was that the vision of socialism—would it not be better to say the *problem* of socialism?—grew blurred in the minds of many Marxists because they were too ready to entrust it to history. The fetishistic use of the word "scientific," than which nothing could provide a greater sense of assurance, gave the Marxist movement a feeling that it had finally penetrated to the essence of history and found there once and for all its true meaning. The result was often a deification of history: what God had been to Fourier, history became to many Marxists—a certain force leading to a certain goal, And if indeed the goal was certain, or likely enough to be taken as certain, there was no need to draw up fanciful blueprints; the future would take care of itself and require no advice from us. True enough, in a way. But the point that soon came to be forgotten was that it is we, in the present, who need the image of the future, not those who may live in it. And the consequence of failing to imagine creatively the face of socialism—which is not at all the same as an absurd effort to paint it in detail—was that it tended to lapse into a conventional and lifeless "perfection."

## III

Perfection, in that the image of socialism held by many Marxists—the image which emerged at the level of implicit belief—was a society in which tension, conflict, and failure had largely disappeared. It would be easy enough to comb the works of the major Marxists in order to prove this statement, but we prefer to appeal to common experience, to our own knowledge and memories as well as to the knowledge and memories of others. In the socialist movement one did not worry about the society one wanted: innumerable and, indeed, inconceivable subjects were discussed, but almost never the idea of socialism itself, for history, strategy, and the Party (how easily the three melted into one!) had eliminated that need. Socialism was the future—and sometimes a future made curiously respectable, the middle-class values that the radicals had violently rejected now being reinstated, unwittingly, in their vision of the good society. There could hardly be a need to reply to those critics who wondered how some of the perennial human problems could be solved under socialism: one *knew* they would be. In effect, the vision of socialism had a way of declining into a regressive infantile fantasy—a fantasy of protection.

Our criticism is not that the Marxist movement held to a vision of utopia: that it did so was entirely to its credit, a life without some glimmer of a redeeming future being a life cut off from the distinctively human. Our complaint is rather that the vision of utopia grew slack and static. Sometimes it degenerated into what William Morris called "the cockney dream" by which efficiency becomes a universal solvent for all human problems; sometimes it slipped off, beyond human reach, to the equally repulsive vision of a society in which men become rational titans as well behaved and tedious as Swift's Houyhnhnms. Only occasionally was socialism envisaged as a society with its own rhythm of growth and tension, change and conflict.

Marx's contribution to human thought is immense, but except for some cryptic if pregnant phrases, neither he nor his disciples have told us very much about the society in behalf of which they called men into battle. This is not quite so fatal a criticism as it might seem, since what probably mattered most was that Marxism stirred millions of previously dormant people into historical action, gave expression to their claims and yearnings, and lent a certain form to their desire for a better life. But if we want sustained speculations on the shape of this better life we have to turn to radical mavericks, to the anarchists and libertarians, to the Guild Socialists. And to such a writer as Oscar Wilde, whose *The Soul of Man under Socialism* is a small masterpiece. In his paradoxical and unsystematic way Wilde quickly comes to a sense of what the desirable society might be like. The great advantage of socialism, he writes, is

86

that it "would relieve us from that sordid necessity of living for others which, in the present condition of things, presses so hard upon almost everybody." By focusing on "the unhealthy and exaggerated altruism" which capitalist society demands from people, and by showing how it saps individuality, Wilde arrives at the distinctive virtue of socialism: that it will make possible what he calls individualism.

## IV

We do not wish to succumb to that which we criticize. Blueprints, elaborate schemes, do not interest us. But we think it may be useful to suggest some of the qualities that can make the image of socialism a serious and mature goal, as well as some of the difficulties in that goal.

Socialism is not the end of human history, as the deeply held identification of it with perfection must mean. There is no total fulfillment, nor is there an "end to time." History is a process which throws up new problems, new conflicts, new questions; and socialism, being within history, cannot be expected to solve all these problems or, for that matter, to raise humanity at every point above the level of achievement of previous societies. As Engels remarked, there is no final synthesis, only continued clash. What socialists want is simply to do away with those sources of conflict which are the cause of material deprivation and which, in turn, help create psychological and moral suffering. Freedom may then mean that we can devote ourselves to the pursuit of more worth-while causes of conflict. The hope for a conflictless society is reactionary, as is a reliance on some abstract "historical force" that will conciliate all human strife.

The aim of socialism is to create a society of co-operation, but not necessarily, or at least not universally, of harmony. Co-operation is compatible with conflict, is indeed inconceivable without conflict, while harmony implies a stasis.

Even the "total abolition" of social classes, no small or easy matter, would not or need not mean the total abolition of social problems.

In a socialist society there would remain a whole variety of human difficulties that could not easily be categorized as social or nonsocial; difficulties that might well result from the sheer friction between the human being and society, *any* society— from, say, the process of "socializing" those recalcitrant creatures known as children. The mere existence of man is a difficulty, a problem, with birth, marriage, pain, and death being only among the more spectacular of his crises. To be sure, no intelligent radical has ever denied that *such* crises would last into a socialist society, but the point to be stressed is that, with the elimination of our major material troubles, these other problems might rise to a new urgency, so much so as to become *social* problems leading to new conflicts.

## V

But social problems as we conceive of them today would also be present in a socialist society.

Traditionally, Marxists have lumped all the difficulties posed by critics and reality into that "transitional" state that is to guide, or bump, us from capitalism to socialism, while socialism itself they have seen as the society that would transcend these difficulties. This has made it a little too easy to justify some of the doings of the "transitional" society, while making it easier still to avoid considering—not what socialism *will* be like—but what our image of it should be. Without pretending to "solve" these social problems as they might exist under socialism, but intending to suggest a bias or predisposition, we list here a few of them.

## Bureaucracy

Marxists have generally related the phenomenon of bureaucratism to social inequality and economic scarcity. Thus they have seen the rise of bureaucracy in Leninist Russia as a consequence of trying to establish a workers' state in an isolated and backward country which lacked the economic prerequisites for building socialism. Given scarcity, there arises a policeman to supervise the distribution of goods; given the policeman, there will be an unjust distribution. Similarly, bureaucratic formations of a more limited kind are seen as parasitic elites which batten upon a social class, yet, in some sense, "represent" it in political and economic conflicts. Thus bureaucratism signifies a deformation, though not necessarily a destruction, of democratic processes.

This view of bureaucratism seems to us invaluable. Yet it would be an error to suppose that because a class society is fertile ground for bureaucracy, a classless society would automatically be free of bureaucracy. There are other causes for this social deformation; and while in a socialist society these other causes might not be aggravated by economic inequality and the ethos of accumulation as they are under capitalism, they would very likely continue to operate. One need not accept Robert Michels' "Iron Law of Oligarchy" in order to see this. (Michels' theory is powerful, but it tends to boomerang: anyone convinced by it that socialism is impossible will have a hard time resisting the idea that democracy is impossible.) Thus the mere presence of equality of wealth in a society does not necessarily mean an equality of power or status: if Citizen A were more interested in the politics of his town or the functioning of his factory than Citizen B, he would probably accumulate more power and status; hence, the *possibility* of misusing them. (Socialists have often replied, But why should Citizen A want to misuse his power and status when there is no pressing economic motive for doing so? No one can answer this question definitely except by positing some theory of "human nature," which we do not propose to do; all we can urge is a certain wariness with regard to any theory which discounts in advance the possibility that noneconomic motives lead to human troubles.) Then again, the problem of sheer size in economic and political units is likely to burden a socialist society as much as it burdens any other society; and large political or economic units, because they require an ever increasing delegation of authority, often to "experts," obviously provide a setting in which bureaucracy can flourish. But most important of all is the sheer problem of representation: the fact that as soon as authority is delegated to a "representative" there must follow a loss of control and autonomy.

Certain institutional checks can, of course, be suggested for containing bureaucracy. The idea of a division of governmental powers, which many Marxists have dismissed as a bourgeois device for thwarting the popular will, would deserve careful attention in planning a socialist society, though one need not suppose that it would have to perpetuate those elements of present-day parliamentary structure which do in fact thwart the popular will. Similarly, the distinction made in English political theory, but neglected by Marxists, between democracy as an expression of popular sovereignty and democracy as a pattern of government in which the rights of minority groups are especially defended, needs to be taken seriously. In general, a society that is pluralist rather than unitary in emphasis, that recognizes the need for diversification of function rather than concentration of authority—this is the desired goal.

And here we have a good deal to learn from a neglected branch of the socialist movement, the Guild Socialists of England, who have given careful thought to these problems. G. D. H. Cole, for example, envisages the socialist society as one in which government policy is a resultant of an interplay among socioeconomic units that simultaneously co-operate and conflict. Cole also puts forward the provocative idea of "functional representation," somewhat similar to the original image of the Soviets. Because, he writes, "a human being, as an individual, is fundamentally incapable of being represented," a man should have "as many distinct, and separately exercised, votes, as he has distinct social purposes or interests," voting, that is, in his capacity of worker, consumer, artist, resident, and so on.

But such proposals can hardly be expected to bulk very large unless they are made in a culture where the motives for private accumulation and the values sanctioning it have significantly diminished. If, as we believe, the goal of socialism is to create the kind of man who, to a measurable degree, ceases to be a manipulated object and becomes a motivated subject, then the growth of socialist consciousness must prove an important bulwark against bureaucracy. A society that stresses co-operation can undercut those prestige factors that make for bureaucracy; a society that accepts conflict, and provides a means for modulating it, will encourage those who combat bureaucracy.

### Planning and Decentralization

Unavoidably, a great deal of traditional socialist thought has stressed economic centralization as a prerequisite for planning, especially in the "transitional" state between capitalism and socialism. Partly, this was an inheritance from the bourgeois revolution, which needed a centralized state; partly, it reflected the condition of technology in the nineteenth century, which required centralized units of production; partly, it is a consequence of the recent power of Leninism, which stressed centralism as a means of confronting the primitive chaos of the Russian economy, but allowed it to become a dogma in countries where it had no necessary relevance. Whatever the historical validity of these emphases on centralism, they must now be abandoned. According to the economist Colin Clark, the new forms of energy permit an economical employment of small decentralized industrial units. Certainly, every impulse of democratic socialism favors such a tendency. For if mass participation—by the workers, the citizens, the people as a whole—in the economic life of the society is to be meaningful, it must find its most immediate expression in relatively small economic units. Only in such small units is it possible for the nonexpert to exercise any real control.

From what we can learn about Stalinist "planning," we see that an economic plan does not work, but quickly breaks down, if arbitrarily imposed from above and hedged in with rigid specifications which allow for none of the flexibility, none of the economic *play,* that a democratic society requires. Social planning, if understood in democratic terms—and can there really be social planning, as distinct from economic regulation, without a democratic context?—requires only a loose guiding direction, a general pointer from above. The rest, the actual working out of variables, the arithmetic fullfillment of algebraic possibilities, must come from below, from the interaction, co-operation, and conflict of economic units participating in a democratic community.

All of this implies a considerable modification of the familiar socialist emphasis on nationalization of the means of production, increase of productivity, a master economic plan, and so on—a modification, but not a total rejection. To be sure, socialism still presupposes the abolition of private property in the basic industries, but there is hardly a branch of the socialist movement, except the more petrified forms of Trotskyism, which places any high valuation on nationalization of industry per se. Almost all socialists now feel impelled to add that what matters is the use to which nationalization is put and the degree of democratic control present in the nationalized industries. But more important, the idea of nationalization requires still greater modification: there is no reason to envisage, even in a "transitional" society, that all basic industries need be owned by the state. The emphasis of the Guild Socialists on separate guilds of workers, each owning and managing their own industries, summons no doubt a picture of possible struggles within and between industries; all the better! Guilds, co-operatives, call them what you will—these provide possible bulwarks against the monster Leviathan, the all-consuming state, which it is the sheerest fatuity to suppose would immediately cease being a threat to human liberty simply because "we" took it over. The presence of numerous political and economic units living together in a tension of co-operation-and-conflict, seems the best "guarantee" that power will not accumulate in the hands of a managerial oligarchy—namely, that the process already far advanced in capitalist society will not continue into socialism. Such autonomous units, serving as buffers between government and people, would allow for various, even contradictory, kinds of expression in social life. The conflicts that might break out among them would be a healthy social regulator; for while the suppression of conflict makes for an explosive accumulation of hostility, its normalization means that a society can be "sewn together" by noncumulative struggles between component groups. And even in terms of "efficiency," this may prove far more satisfactory than the bureaucratic state regulation of Communist Russia.

Only if an attempt is made to encompass the total personality of the individual into one or another group is conflict likely to lead to social breakdown. Only then would conflicts over relatively minor issues be elevated into "affairs of state." So long as the dogma of "total allegiance"—a dogma that has proven harmful in both its social democratic and Leninist versions—is not enforced, so long as the individual is able to participate in a variety of groupings without having to commit himself totally to any of them, society will be able to absorb a constant series of conflicts.

Nor would the criterion of efficiency be of decisive importance in such a society. At the beginning of the construction of socialism, efficiency is urgently required in order to provide the material possibility for a life of security and freedom. But efficiency is needed in order, so to speak, to transcend efficiency.

Between the abstract norms of efficiency and the living needs of human beings there may always be a clash. To speak in grandiose terms, as some anarchists do, of Efficiency vs. Democracy is not very valuable, since living experience always requires compromise and complication. All one can probably say is that socialists are not concerned with efficiency as such, but with that type of efficiency which does not go counter to key socialist values. Under socialism there are likely to be many situations in which efficiency will be consciously sacrificed, and indeed one of the measures of the success of a socialist society would be precisely how far it could afford to discard the criterion of efficiency. This might be one of the more glorious ideas latent in Engels' description of socialism as a "reign of freedom."

These remarks are, of course, scrappy and incomplete, as we intend them to be, for their usefulness has a certain correlation with their incompleteness; but part of what we have been trying to say has been so well put by R. H. S. Crossman that we feel impelled to quote him:

> The planned economy and the centralization of power are no longer socialist objectives. They are developing all over the world as the Political Revolution [the concentration of state powers] and the process is accelerated by the prevalence of war economy. The main task of socialism today is to prevent the concentration of power in the hands of *either* industrial management *or* the state bureaucracy—in brief, to distribute responsibility and so to enlarge freedom of choice. This task was not even begun by the Labour Government. On the contrary, in the nationalized industries old managements were preserved almost untouched. . . .
>
> In a world organized in ever larger and more inhuman units, the task of socialism is to prevent managerial responsibility degenerating into privilege. This can only be achieved by increasing, even at the cost of "efficiency," the citizen's right to participate in the control not only of government and industry, but of the party for which he voted. . . . After all, it is not the pursuit of happiness but the enlargement of freedom which is socialism's highest aim.

91

No Marxist concept has been more fruitful than that of "alienation." As used by Marx, it suggests the psychic price of living in a society where the worker's "deed becomes an alien power." The division of labor, he writes, makes the worker "a cripple . . . forcing him to develop some highly specialized dexterity at the cost of a world of productive impulses. . . ." The worker becomes estranged from his work, both as process and product; his major energies must be expended on tasks that have no organic or creative function within his life; the impersonality of the social relationships enforced by capitalism, together with the sense of incoherence and discontinuity induced by the modern factory, goes far toward making the worker a dehumanized part of the productive process rather than an autonomous human being. It is not, of course, to be supposed that this is a description of a given factory; it is a "lead" by which to examine a given factory. This theory is the starting point of much speculation on the nature of modern work, as well as on the social and psychological significance of the industrial city; and almost all the theorizing on "mass culture," not to mention many of the efforts to "engineer" human relations in the factory, implicitly acknowledges the relevance and power of Marx's idea.

But when Marx speaks of alienation and thereby implies the possibility of nonalienation, it is not always clear whether he has in mind some precapitalist society in which men were presumably not alienated or whether he employs it as a useful fiction derived by a process of abstraction from the observable state of society. If he means the former, he may occasionally be guilty of romanticizing, in common with many of his contemporaries, the life of pre-capitalist society; for most historians of feudalism and of that difficult-to-label era which spans the gap between feudalism and capitalism strongly imply that the peasant and even the artisan was not quite the unalienated man that some intellectuals like to suppose. Nonetheless, as an analytical tool and a reference to future possibilities, the concept of alienation remains indispensable.

So long as capitalism, in one form or another, continues to exist, it will be difficult to determine to what degree it is the social setting and to what degree the industrial process that makes so much of factory work dehumanizing. That a great deal of this dehumanization is the result of a social structure which deprives many men of an active sense of participation or decision making and tends to reduce them to the level of controlled objects can hardly be doubted at so late a moment.

We may consequently suppose that in a society where democratic ethos had been reinforced politically and had made a significant seepage into economic life, the problem of alienation would be alleviated. But not solved.

In his *Critique of the Gotha Program* Marx speaks of the highest stage of the new society as one in which "the enslaving subordination of individuals in the division of labor has disappeared, and with it also the antagonism between mental and physical labor; labor has become not only a means of living, but itself the first necessity of life. . . ." Remembering that Marx set this as a *limit* toward which to strive and not as a condition likely to be present even during the beginning of socialism, let us then suppose that a society resembling this unit has been reached. The crippling effects of the division of labor are now largely eliminated because people are capable of doing a large variety of social tasks; the division between physical and mental labor has been largely eliminated because the level of education has been very much raised; and— we confess here to being uncertain as to Marx's meaning—labor has become "the first necessity of life." But even now the problem of *the nature of work* remains. Given every conceivable improvement in the social context of work; given a free and healthy society; given, in short, all the desiderata Marx lists—even then there remains the uncreativeness, the tedium, what frequently must seem the meaninglessness, of the jobs many people have to perform in the modern factory.

It may be said that in a socialist society people could live creatively in their leisure; no doubt. Or that people would have to do very little work because new forms of energy would be developed; quite likely. But then the problem would be for men to find an outlet for their "productive impulses" not in the way Marx envisioned but in another way, not in work but in leisure. Except for certain obviously satisfying occupations—and by this we do *not* mean only intellectual occupations—work might now become a minor part of human life. The problem is whether in any society it would now be possible to create—given our irrevocable commitment to industrialism—the kind of "whole man" Marx envisaged, the man, that is, who realizes himself through and by his work.

It is not as a speculation about factory life in a socialist society that this problem intrigues us, but rather as an entry into another problem about which Marx wrote very little: what we now call "mass culture." Socialists have traditionally assumed that a solution to economic problems would be followed by a tremendous flowering of culture, and this may happen; we do not know. But another possible outcome might be a population of which large parts were complacent and self-satisfied, so that if hell is now conceived as a drawing room, utopia might soften into a suburb. In any case, we are hardly likely to feel as certain about the cultural consequences of social equality as Trotsky did when he wrote in *Literature and Revolution* that under socialism men might reach the level of Beethoven and Goethe. This seems implausibly romantic, since it is doubtful that the scarcity of Beethovens and Goethes can be related solely to social inequality; and what is more, it does not even seem very desirable to have a society of Beethovens and Goethes.

Between the two extreme forecasts there is the more likely possibility that under socialism a great many people would inevitably engage in work which could not release "a world of productive impulses," but would be brief and light enough to allow them a great deal of leisure. The true problem of socialism might then be to determine the nature, quality, and variety of leisure. Men, that is, would face the full and terrifying burden of human freedom, but they would be more prepared to shoulder it than ever before.

93

# VI

"The past and present," wrote Pascal, "are our means; the future alone our end." Taken with the elasticity that Pascal intended—he surely did not mean to undervalue the immediacy of experience—this is a useful motto for what we have called utopian thinking, the imaginative capacity for conceiving of a society that is qualitatively better than our own, yet no mere fantasy of static perfection.

Today, in an age of curdled realism, it is necessary to assert the utopian image. But this can be done meaningfully only if it is an image of social striving, tension, conflict; an image of a problem-creating and problem-solving society.

In his "Essay on Man" Ernst Cassirer has written almost all that remains to be said:

> A Utopia is not a portrait of the real world, or of the actual political or social order. It exists at no moment of time and at no point in space; it is a "nowhere." But just such a conception of a nowhere has stood the test and proved its strength in the development of the modern world. It follows from the nature and character of ethical thought that it can never condescend to accept the "given." The ethical world is never given; it is forever in the making.

Some time ago one could understandably make of socialism a consoling daydream. Now, when we live in the shadow of defeat, to retain, to will the image of socialism is a constant struggle for definition, almost an act of pain. But it is the kind of pain that makes creation possible.

# The Christian
# and modern Democracy

*by Dr. J. D. Dengerink*

The problem of democracy, especially when one is concerned with the modern democracy, is not an easy one. This is a result of the fact that the concept of democracy has attained an ever broader meaning in the course of history and that it has even received an ideological connotation. With this it has lost much of its clarity. In the Western World all well-intentioned people and parties are highly concerned about democracy. The adjective "un-democratic" implies a disqualification. But a closer analysis of the concept of democracy will reveal that there are a host of definitions involved in this term. And this becomes even more complex when we notice that the communist states in central and eastern Europe, where in our view not even the shadow of democracy is present, still present themselves explicitly as people's *democracies.* Similary, an Asiatic leader like Soekarno refers to Indonesia, the state which he rules in a rather dictatorial manner, as a democracy, even if he prefers to describe it as a "guided democracy."

In our view this confusion is a result of the fact that the concept of democracy has often been closely linked to the ideas of freedom and equality, whereby the emphasis fell at times on freedom, then again on equality, while it must be recalled that even these terms allow a variety of definitions. Confusion, more than clarity, thus marks the history of the concept of democracy.

This confusion, however, should not disconcert us. Rather, as Christians in the tradition of the Reformation we will have to find our own way in this jungle of ideas in the hope that thus we can make a valuable contribution to the political thought of our times.

## 1. The Origin of Modern Democracy

In the first place we will examine the origin of modern democracy, as it has developed in several countries in the western world but also in other continents. It is not my intention to present a phase of political or legal history but, instead, to discover which spiritual forces have led to the rise of modern democracies. These forces are the ones of Reformation and Humanism as they were first embodied in Renaissance-man.

It is no surprise that the Reformation of the sixteenth century greatly contributed to the development of the democratic idea. Contrary to the hierarchic idea which dominated the Middle Ages, the Reformation clearly stressed the general office of believers and the personal res-

INTERNATIONAL REFORMED BULLETIN, July, 1964, no. 18, 13-23.

ponsibility of every member of the church. This naturally affected the view of the relation between government and citizen within the framework of the emerging unified state characterized by its public-legal nature.

However, in the arena of Western European culture the Reformation surrendered an ever increasing area of human life to the forces of Humanism, affecting even the life of the church itself. This process already began in the second half of the seventeenth century and continued with forceful impetus in the following century. Modern democracy, as we know it in a variety of Western countries, must therefore by seen especially in connection with the rationalistic humanism of the seventeenth and eighteenth centuries. Our attention will first of all be focused on this phase.

A careful analysis of Humanism will reveal that it is driven by two central motives. On the one hand we detect the ideal of autonomous personality, bound in no way except by an order constituted by itself. On the other hand we discover the ideal of science, *viz.* the attempt to control the cosmos and human life in every respect by means of science, which, if consistently carried out, would destroy every form of autonomous self-determination. In Humanism, the ideal of personality and the ideal of science are thus ultimately in diametric opposition.

It is especially the idea of autonomous self-determination which has been the inspiration for modern democracy and the philosophies which have defended it. However, even then one must distinguish between two clearly different trends: the first of a more individualistic and liberal type (John Locke), the second tending more to political absolutism (Rousseau).


## 2. Democracy as a Universal Principle

In distinction from contemporary trends it must be clearly understood that the democracy defended by Locke and Rousseau was seen mainly in connection with the state and political life. This in itself is not surprising. For in the first phases of humanistic thought the state and the individual were the two poles determining the scope of human life. In all this there is a marked reaction to all sorts of privileges and guilds which greatly characterized the Middle Ages, and which could exist as more or less independent forces between the individual and the state. As a result of this reaction, for example, there was practically no recognition of the need for organizations of employers and employees in the last century. Labor unions, especially, were often contraband.

However, in due time this changed. There came an increasing recognition of the particular significance of diverse social relations and communities alongside of or at least apart from the state. And the idea took hold that the democratic principle should also be realized in these non-political relationships and communities. Terms such as industrial democracy, educational democracy and even family democracy came into vogue. In this connection one can think of the endeavor to grant employees a greater share in industrial life ("co-determination") and that not merely by means of trade-unions in general industrial relations but also in specific industries by means of industrial councils and company- directors appointed by the trade-unions. This idea of *industrial* democracy has been systematically elaborated by the famous Russian sociologist *Georges Gurvitch*, who claims that a political democracy cannot remain in existence without an "economic democracy."

Gurvitch defends an all-embracing anti-centralistic and anti-statist democratization of human life in its various expressions. Only in this manner can the most profound elements of the various communities find expression and only in this way can we arrive at a true synthesis between individualism and universalism. For Gurvitch the principle of democracy is not specifically political. It can serve as a principle of organization for both the state and society.

But this development did not stop with democracy viewed as only a principle of organization. In certain political circles democracy was connected with a striving for social reform. This implies that the idea of equality received greater stress in the definition of democracy. Dr. W. P. Berghuis, Chairman of the Central Committee of the Christian Anti-Revolutionary Party in the Netherlands and one of the Vice-Presidents of the International Union of Christian Democrats, in a publication about the nature of democracy, has made the observation that "democracy" was no longer in the first place confined to the administration and institution of the state with respect to the proper execution of the government's task but that "democracy" was also related to the material content and purposes of the state's administrative bodies. Democracy and the "law-state" (*Rechtsstaat*) are thus identified and, at a later stage, democracy and socialism are viewed as one and the same. Berghuis shows how the socialists were averse to democracy in their first marxistic phase since they viewed democracy as opposed to the revolutionary character of socialistic ideology but that they accepted the democratic form of the state in the first decades of our century and even made democracy one of their political slogans. And contemporary socialism, drifting away from its early marxistic foundations, has proclaimed democracy as its new basis, as its creed, as the sum-total, in form and content, of everything implied in a socialistic order of state and society. "Democracy" has thus become at once a view of life, a *Weltanschauung*, and a political program. As a fundamental political principle democracy has been absolutized. It has become a myth, says Berghuis, for many of our contemporaries, the indication of the highest political and social ideal. And as such democracy is no longer susceptible to rational description but is rendered absolute as a faith, as a creed only acceptable to those who accept the content of this political and social outlook. And thereby the idea of democracy has attained that vagueness which we have already referred to.

### 3. Authority and Freedom

Contrary to the development of the idea of democracy in modern times, we would prefer to maintain this idea as a principle of organization and, within the scope of this study, specifically as a principle of political organization, with reference to the relation between government and subjects.

It is undeniable that life confronts us constantly with relations of authority and subjection. The Bible presents a fundamental perspective here when, in several passages, it calls the believer to subject himself to those who are placed over him and to obey the rules, the ordinances instituted by those in authority. One can mention as an example the Fifth Commandment of the Decalogue and the explanation of this commandment in Lord's Day 39 of the Heidelberg Catechism.

In the community of the state one can also distinguish between rulers and subjects, between government and people. Romans 13 speaks of this relation in lucid language. The government is clothed with authority which is not based on or derived from the people (the doctrine of popular sovereignty). The government's authority is derived from God, and for this reason this authority must be exercised in accordance with His will, His law. The governmental authorities have a "right of their own," a right peculiar to themselves. Over against this it must be seen that the people also, as subjects, possess "rights" in a specific political sense. These rights, for instance, have found expression in the different democratic states in the right to free formation of political opinion, both active and passive; further, the right to establish political parties; right to franchise; right of petition, etc. By means of these rights the citizens, the subjects of the state, can effectuate their co-responsibility for the decisions to be made in the political process.

In all of this we are concerned with the central problem of *authority and freedom* with which, for that matter, we are confronted in every human community. The stress must lie on the proper balance between these two. Freedom without authority ends in chaos and licentiousness. Authority without freedom spells tyranny and ends, as if by a natural law, in totalitarian dictatorship, embracing the whole of human life. History presents ample evidence of this. A true balance between authority and freedom can only then be attained when government and people accept their respective responsibilities, each in its own way and in accordance with its specific place in the community of the state.

It is of utmost importance here to distinguish between the above-mentioned political rights of liberty (whose nature and breadth is wholly regulated by and dependent upon the legal order of the state itself) and the socalled non-political rights of liberty (which can be regulated in one way or another by the state's legislature, but which because of their very nature and essence escape the competence of the state-government). One can mention here the freedom of worship, the freedom of education, the freedom of association and private meeting, the freedom of the press, of speech, of vocation. These rights and liberties can be limited by the legislature in a certain way. As such, however, they are independent of the state. And as soon as the government infringes upon these rights and liberties and attempts to control them in their totality, by means of legislation or its executive power, it exceeds its proper competence.

## 4. The Meaning of Democracy from a Reformational Standpoint

How are we, in the light of the preceding, to view and evaluate democracy?

We have already seen that, within the state, government and people each occupies its own position, but they do so in an unbreakale corre-lation. As in the human body the head cannot say that it does not need the foot or hand, and the latter also cannot function properly without the head, so also government and people are dependent upon each other. For a sound development of political life close cooperation is essential. Although government and people each has its respective rights (and obligations!), they are jointly responsible for the course of political life. For this reason the government may never without ground declare the people politically immature. This joint responsibility of government and people is one of the fundamentals of democracy, as Dr. J. P. A. Mekkes has correctly taught us.

But this does not exhaust the meaning of modern democracy. Dr. Berghuis has brought to light another aspect of this question in the study mentioned above. In concurrence with Professor H. Dooyeweerd he shows that the *idea of law*, which must become valid in its own way also in the community of the state, is an "idea on the march," and the path for this "march" in the fulfilment of the idea of law is bound step by step to the historical development. And this idea, we may add, finds its ultimate realization only in the direction towards the King-dom of God. The application or positivization of legal principles is not possible without taking due account of the historical development of culture, including the ideas and convictions of the people. The government, in the fulfilment of its task, is also dependent upon the situation of the people. An example of the religious conditions is the hardness of hearts of which Christ speaks in Matt. 19 : 8 and Mark 10 : 5. The degree of knowledge of and obedience to God's law on the part of the people co-determines the degree to which the idea of law can be approached in political life. And in this connection it is important,

Berghuis claims, to achieve that form of government in which the stage of cultural development can immediately be detected as it were right in the very constellation of the organs and administration of the government. And that form of government is present in a well-functioning democracy. Democracy implies that form of government in which in the most simple and direct manner the policy of the government can be attuned to the social, economic, cultural, moral and religious situation of the people. The democratic method of government, so to say, has a built-in thermometer.

The foregoing implies that democracy is not universal as a political principle of organization in this sense that it can and must be applied everywhere under all circumstances.

A democratic system of government can only function properly where the people have attained a certain measure of political maturity, i.e., where they have been able to grasp and articulate definite political convictions. Democracy can flourish only where the people, by and large, have become conscious of their co-responsibility for the course of events and the decisions in the community of the state. Democracy presupposes a people possessed of a sense of citizenship. Without these conditions democracy cannot exist. The political development of various countries in South-America and Africa gives clear evidence of this.

### 5. Democracy and Spiritual Relativism

All of this confronts the Christian with this highly important problem: Does the assumption, that a democratic system of government can only function properly if its policy is at least in part attuned to the religious and political convictions of the people, not automatically lead to spiritual relativism? Or – to phrase the problem a bit differently – do we not, by accepting democracy in this sense, directly come into conflict with the absolute nature of the Christian faith, with the unconditional requisites of God's Word and His law which also pertain to the life of politics?

Hans Kelsen, the well-known Austrian-American legal philosopher, stresses the close affinity between democracy and relativism as a life-and world-view. Since democracy respects the political desires of each citizen equally, Kelsen asserts, it must also respect equally every political creed, every political opinion, of which the political desire is only the expression. The opposite opinion must also be considered a possibility when absolute values are abandoned. In Kelsen's view the democratic idea presupposes the *Weltanschauung*, the outlook of relativism. For this reason democracy allows the expression of every political conviction. The principle of majority-rule, so characteristic for democracy, distinguishes it from every other principle, and this logically does not merely imply the opposition of the minority, but in a democracy this minority is constitutionally recognized and protected by means of the fundamental rights of liberty and the principle of proportional representation. The relativity of every political creed and the impossibility of claiming absolute validity for a political program or a political ideal clearly require the rejection of political absolutism.

One cannot escape the impression that in this viewpoint of Kelsen truth and error are mixed in a critical fashion. We can agree with Kelsen when he states that no political principle has absolute validity in this sense that every practical political policy in a democratic régime more or less has the character of a compromise insofar as in such a policy the different convictions of the people and even the rights of minority-groups must be reckoned with. We are, however, radically opposed to Kelsen when he, on the basis of the limited possibility of the application of certain political principles, assumes the relativity and the relative value not merely of certain political convictions but of *every* political principle. For such a view involves the implicit denial of the radical and universal nature of the spiritual conflict which, according to the Word of God (cf. e.g., Gen. 3 : 17 and Eph. 6), is constantly waged between the Kingdom of God and that of satan. And the life of politics certainly does not escape this spiritual conflict.

Dr. A. M. Donner, formerly professor of political theory and constitutional law, at the Free University of Amsterdam and currently President of the Court of European Communities, has observed that the indication of relativism as the foundation of democracy has not failed to make an impression. The "fin-de-siecle" mentality, typical of this, has become common property in our day. But, Donner writes, as soon as man becomes fully conscious of this relativism and accepts it consistently, human life becomes a bare, monotonous desert and the human spirit becomes dull. For indeed, this relativism is miles apart from that spirit of toleration which arises out of respect for the convictions of one's fellows. This relativism is not a fruit of spiritual richness but of decadence and disillusion. And a democracy founded on such a relativism cannot recognize the continuity in the life of the state. There is no value which embraces the whole and authority is no longer acknowledged. Government no longer derives its authority from generally accepted legal norms but only from its origin: the people. And authority derived from that source, Donner claims, knows no bounds and limitations.

In our view, the recognition of the "specific rights" of the various views of life in the political order is indeed dependent upon the recognition of the limited competences and possibilities of the government in its relation to the people of the land and the balance of authority and freedom inherent in the community of the state. For we may not forget that the political activities of the citizens do not merely have an external character. These activities are a matter of the heart, and the government is given neither the competence nor the power to force the conscience of its subjects. Such a compulsion of conscience, even if executed by a Christian government, would not enhance the cause of the Kingdom of God. Still, it is precisely in democracy that Christians may find an acceptable form of government because this form makes it possible to effectuate divine ordinances for the life of the state in the activities of government and subjects without compulsion of conscience. The task of the Christian with respect to the state concerns the re-direction of the political conviction of both government and people through the power of the Word of God. But the execution of this task presupposes the existence of spiritual liberty in political life, also for those who do not want to subject themselves to this Word of God. In the spiritual struggle which unfolds itself also in the political arena the victory is not decided by the sword of the state but by the Sword of the Spirit.

We are fully conscious of the fact that this view entails the possibility that a governmental policy, directed in a Christian sense by means of democratic procedure, can also again be changed to another direction by means of the same democratic procedure. This, however, is a "risk" which the Christian must accept according to his own starting-point.


### 6. The Christian and Modern Democracy.

It should be evident by now that in our view politics is not a matter of impersonal, neutral, or purely technical affairs, that politics is not merely concerned with the striving for "practical ends." The battle of spirits (Gen. 3 : 17; Eph. 6 : 12) is also waged in the realm of the state, even if we are not always conscious of this and even if this does not constantly and expressly come to the foreground. The Christian community may not withdraw itself from this struggle because of Him Who tells us, "All authority in heaven and on earth has been given to Me" (Matt. 28 : 18). In politics, no less than in any other domain of human life, we are ultimately involved in religious decisions, confronted as we are with the question whether we will serve the Lord, the God of the Covenant, or call upon the idols of our time (Josh. 24 : 15). The political arena is also subject to the Word of God as a two-edged sword (Hebr. 4 : 12). The Christian community may not be passive in these matters, but must actively assume its responsibility.

This responsibility begins with the prayer of faith. The Apostle Paul urges us, first of all, that supplications, prayers, intercessions, and thanksgiving be made for all men, for kings and all who are in high positions, that we may lead a quiet and peaceable life, godly and respectful in every way. For this is good, and it is acceptable in the sight of God our Savior, who desires all men to be saved and to come to the knowledge of the truth (I Tim. 2 : 1-4).

However, the Christian community may not limit its activity to the inner room. It must engage the world, it must enter the political arena itself, to be a salting salt and to let its light shine (Matt. 5 : 13-16). This already is implied in the cultural mandate which the Creator gave to mankind (Gen. 1 : 28), for modern culture is not possible without a well-organized state-life. It is also implied in Christ's commission to make disciples of all nations, teaching them to observe *all* that He has commanded (Matt. 28 : 19, 20). Also in political life men must live in accordance with the divine mandates. Here lies a dimension of that spiritual service of which Paul speaks in Romans 12.

The question remains how the Christian community, wherever it is still given the freedom for this end, can make its influence felt on the specific policy of the state.

Here one must first point to the official proclamation of the church. As soon as the Word of God is proclaimed in the church with conviction in an integral, radical sense, it will make its power felt immediately as a two-edged sword to the world outside, and thus also in public life. The Spirit of God is our guarantee here.

This does not mean that the church in its official, institutional organization is clothed with a certain political authority. Nor does this imply that the church must orient its proclamation in a special way to political life. The highest authority for the state lies in the Word of God itself, regarding which the ecclesiastical offices only have a function of *service*. The proclamation of the Word of God is intended to equip the believer in a spiritual, centrally directive way so that the Christian can be molded to maturity.With this the general offices of all believers comes into view.

It was precisely the Protestant Reformation which posited with great emphasis the maturity of the regular, non-ordained member of the church, and that not only in the church but also for life outside of it. This had the consequence that wherever the Reformation made itself felt in the populace, a "democratic" form of government arose as it were automatically both in the church and in public life.

By means of the proclamation of the Word, as well as by personal and communal study of the Scriptures, the believer becomes a bearer of that Word, which directs him in his vocation, in his family and in his civic responsibilities. In all of these areas he will have to fight the battle with the Sword of the Spirit.

In the realm of political endeavor this implies that the Christian must renew and reform his view of the state and its life by the Word of God. And this does not imply merely incidental corrections or a limited number of special topics (such as, e.g., the relation between church and state, marriage-legislation or the consecration of the Lord's Day), no matter how important these may be in themselves. Instead, this renewal and reformation demands a radically altered view of the state itself. With less we cannot be satisfied. It is only too true, as Harry Blamires observes in his stimulating book, *The Christian Mind* (1963), that twentieth-century Christianity has chosen the way of compromise by making religion a private affair. It is exactly against this spiritual dualism, which permits "religion" the control of private life while public life is dominated by socalled commonly accepted "norms," that we must wage the battle.

It is clear that the task which this implies is not only one for Christians individually but for them communally. The initial step to be taken will involve the creation of study-centers where these problems can systematically be subjected to serious reflection.

But this study and reflection is not the end. For politics may indeed be determined by spiritual motives; it is nonetheless an extremely practical activity. Our purpose must be the reformation of political life itself. For this reason Christians, standing in the tradition of the Reformation, who have the capacity and the opportunity to do so, should not be afraid to accept public offices, especially because of their scriptural convictions. The possible influence of this may not be underestimated.

Furthermore, in a democratic state Christians can employ the opportunity to express their political opinions in freedom by means of the press and other available methods. Here especially one must point to the importance of the formation of a *political party* in which evangelical Christians can unite in order to influence political life in a reformational sense by means of cooperative effort. Such an influence ought to be exerted not to dominate but to serve, according to the Word of God.

Dr. H. Dooyeweerd points out, in the third volume of his *A New Critique of Theoretical Thought*, that a political party is precisely an organization in which the uniting force of a political conviction is expressed with respect to the principles which are to guide political life, the state and its administrative organs. One can rightly say that even those parties which claim to find a basis only in a "common goal for practical action" (this expression in used by G. N. Monsma Jr., "Christian Political Action," *The Reformed Journal*, July-August 1963, p. 18) are not devoid of certain principles or spiritual motives. For such political parties are controlled by the forces of modern pargmatism – a philosophy of life which is hardly in agreement with the fundamentals of the Christian life and which can spiritually affect political and social life in a disastrous manner.

We are conscious of the fact that the possibility for Christian political party-formation will depend to a great extent on the potentialities of reformational Christians in the respective countries. But we must not, with an eye to tradition and present fact, immediately think that this is impossible. There are situations in which even a small minority can exert great power. This also depends upon the power of faith, of conviction, and the competence of those involved.

One can also point to new opportunities which possibly may develop in the not too distant future. Here I am thinking of the voices of those Protestants, lost until now in largely Roman Catholic or non-Christian nations, which can become of fundamental importance if placed in a larger whole, for example, through the election of a European parliament. Our principle obliges us to follow such developments with great care.

However, no matter what the situation may be, the Lord calls us in Christ to be His witnesses and co-laborers also in the realm of the state. And for this reason Christians may not withdraw to the trenches and catacombs as long as He gives us the opportunity to fight as His soldiers in public, and that in steadfast faith in the Lordship and victory of Jesus Christ.

## Literature:

W. P. Berghuis, "Enkele Opmerkingen over Democratie," in *Rechtsgeleerde Opstellen*, Festschrift for Dr. H. Dooyeweerd, Kampen, 1951.

H. Blamires, *The Christian Mind*, London, 1963.

John Calvin, *Institutes*, Book IV, Chapter XX.

J. D. Dengerink, "A Christian Concept of Human Society," in *The Gordon Review*, Vol. VI (1961), pp. 82-91.

Idem, "The Power of the Reformation in Political Life," in *Intern. Ref. Bulletin*, No. 9 (April, 1962).

A. M. Donner, *Relativisme en Geestelijke Vrijheid*, Rotterdam 1945.

H. Dooyeweerd, *A New Critique of Theoretical Thought*, vol. III, Amsterdam – Philadelphia, 1957.

G. Gurvitch, *L'experience juridique et la philosophie pluraliste du droit*, Paris, 1935.

H. Kelsen, *Vom Wesen und Wert der Demokratie*, Tübingen, 1920.

John Locke, *Two Treatises on Government* (various editions).

J. P. A. Mekkes, *Ontwikkeling der Humanistische Rechtsstaatstheorieen*, Utrecht, 1940.

W. Stanford Reid, "The Reformation and the Layman," *Int. Ref. Bulletin*, No. 13 (April 1963).

J. J. Rousseau, *Le Contrat Social* (various editions).

H. E. Runner, "Scriptural Religion and Political Task," in: *Christian Perspectives* 1962, pp. 135-257, Hamilton, 1962.

# Revolution or Reformation: Which Heritage?

Philip C. Bom

L AST YEAR WE commemorated the 350th anniversary of the landing of the Pilgrims on our shores. This year plans are already under way for celebrating the 200th anniversary of the American Revolution.

It is popularly thought that these two dates go together—that the principles cherished by the freedom-seeking Pilgrims contributed directly to the revolutionary struggle of our founding fathers.

But is this so? I do not think it is. I believe that if we want to discuss intelligently the religious and political foundations of America, we must distinguish between these dates.

In 150 years a great deal can happen to the religious direction of a people. The spirit of 1620 was different from the spirit of 1776. The difference was as fundamental as the difference between reformation and revolution. That is why it is necessary to distinguish between our forefathers

ETERNITY, July, 1971, 14 ff.

(men of the Reformation) and our founding fathers (men of the Revolution). They were moved by an entirely different spirit. A better understanding of the underlying principles of reformation versus those of revolution is critical for Christian citizens today. For in the current confusion, disillusionment and breakdown of basic institutions in our nation, revolution (and its spirit) is *not* the answer. Reformation is.

## Who were our forefathers?

Who were our forefathers, the people who landed in New England? And what spirit guided their society? They were Protestants, men, women and children of the Reformation. They took their stand against a corrupt Christian state and church. As C. Gregg Singer has written in *A Theological Interpretation of American History* (1964), they confessed

106

the centrality of God's Word in all areas of life, in the world of labor and learning as well as of faith. They did not want to abandon education and economics to a "secular" sphere. God was to be honored in public service as well as the worship service. They understood the distinction between church and state, but believed that both were instituted by God. The Mayflower Compact beautifully expressed this belief:

> Haveing undertaken, for the glorie of God, and advancements of the Christian faith and honour of our king and countrie . . . doe . . . in the presence of God, and one of another, covenant & combine ourselves togeather into a civill body politick; for our better ordering, & preservation & furtherance of the ends aforesaid; . . . and frame shuch just & equall lawes . . . constitutions, & offices . . . for the general good of the Colonie; unto which we promise all due submission and obedience.

The Puritans who settled in Massachusetts based their legal and moral principles on the Judeo-Christian faith. In *A Body of Liberties,* a legal document, 46 of the 48 proposed laws were directly derived from the Old Testament. Their hopes and dreams were rooted in the Bible. They lived a God-centered life. One of their basic principles was civil obedience ("all due submission and obedience" to the laws they had drawn up), an integration of freedom and authority.

Unfortunately, the Puritans did tend to think of themselves as a Chosen People, rather than demonstrating the universality of the New Covenant which Christ established

for all mankind. But nevertheless, they showed in their community life the relevance of the Word of God to every area.

**Gradual decline**

During the next 150 years, however, we witness a gradual, but steady, spiritual and political decline. At the time of the troubles with England, revolutionary ideals were spreading rapidly through the colonies. In a letter to Hezekiah Niles, a Baltimore publisher, John Adams himself noted the change:

> The American Revolution was not a common Event. Its Effects and Consequences have already been Awful over a great Part of the Globe. And when and where are they to cease? . . . The Revolution was effected before the War commenced. The Revolution was in the Minds and Hearts of the People. A Change in their Religious Sentiments of their Duties and Obligations.

The change in the religious foundations of the political life of America is manifest in the principles of the Declaration of Independence: (1) that government is a human, not a divine contract; (2) that government exists to secure safety, freedom, and the pursuit of earthly happiness; (3) that when government becomes destructive of these goals, the people have the right to abolish it and establish a new form of government—a principle of civil disobedience.

The founding fathers were great politicians who made tremendous personal sacrifices. They were deeply religious men in the sense that they tended to deify Nature, even referring to the Creator as the Great Legislator. As men of the Enlightenment, however, they proclaimed a natural rights rather than a supernatural rights doctrine. Their ideal of a republic was mainly rooted in the Graeco-Roman tradition of law and order. They were members of the "Party of Humanity," not Christianity. Instead of acknowledging the centrality of the Word of God, they confessed to live by their own Reason, their "Oracle of Revelation." They believed in man's natural freedom, recognizing no higher or other authority than their own mind. They lived a man-centered life. Thus within 150 years a cultural transformation had taken place in this country. The former Christian colonies were now a humanist nation. According to historian Adrienne Koch, in *Power, Morals and the Founding Fathers* (1961), ". . . we may call the central vision of the founding fathers and the temper of the Enlightenment in America 'experimental humanism.' "

### Christianity retreats

Thus, in addition to the separation of church and state, we also witness in our early national history the separation of Christianity from public life. Christianity was relegated to the private life only. Formal education was no longer considered the responsibility of Christian parents or the church, but was under the jurisdiction of the state. The public school still permitted prayer and Bible reading, but not Christian education. Philip C. Friese, in *Essay on Party* (1856), wrote that this separation of the

"Kingdom of God from the republic of men" is at the heart of the American experiment in self-rule. Our form of government is historically known as republicanism, and wherever it has been tried—as in the French Revolution and its aftermath—republicanism has betrayed the stamp of dogged antisupernaturalism. This fact should at least put a brake on our uncritical acceptance of republicanism as a "Christian" institution.

It did not mean that the nation or the state's schools were without a religious foundation. They were not. But it was Deism, a *natural* religion. And this same natural religion was the basis for a *natural* rights political perspective. Deism and republicanism were integrally related. As G. Adolph Koch in *Republican Religion* (1964) has shown, republicanism in politics was integrated with republicanism in religion. Both theology and politics followed the cult of reason.

### Political religion

This has led, in our own time, to the rise of a political religion called Americanism. Our public schools have generally been the instrument of the state for indoctrinating our citizens in this life-style, the so-called American-democratic way of life.

The evangelical response to this fruit of the cult of reason has been two-fold. First, as a result of the early nineteenth century revivals, evangelical Protestants defeated deism in theology, but at the same time accommodated themselves to it in politics. They appear to have accepted the disestablishment of church and state and the separation of Christianity from public life as one and the same development.

Second, by becoming increasingly concerned with saving individual souls and nurturing personal piety, evangelicals withdrew from the world and, in a sense, limited the message of salvation. They no longer believed —as had the Puritan Protestants— that all areas of life and all societal institutions should be submitted to the judgment of Christ.

Thus, indirectly, they may have contributed to the impression that the Bible is irrelevant to the social, economic, and political ills of our society. And directly, they may have contributed to the impression that the evangelicals support one religion in private, but another in public, namely, the American Way of Life. In the course of time, the two have been integrated in the popular mind so that for many they are synonymous: Americanism has become identified with Christianity.

Addressing a conference of Christian black students, the well-known black evangelist, Tom Skinner, described the concept of Jesus Christ that he had inherited from evangelicals: "He was a man looking like an Anglo-Saxon, middle-class Protestant Republican. . . . They made Him the whole American system. They built a concept of Americanism around Jesus, so that a vote for Jesus was a vote for America. God's on our side."

Today America faces a fundamental crisis of confidence and direction. The affluent '50s made way for the over-confident '60s, which gave rise to despair in the '70s. At the 1970 annual convention of the American Psychiatric Association, Dr. Sheldon Wolin, one of America's most perceptive political theorists, said:

> The political life of the country is exhibiting unmistakable signs of derangement and systematic disorder. I would submit that the present crisis is the most profound one in our entire national history. . . . In contrast to previous crises, the present one finds the country not only divided, confused, embittered, frustrated and enraged, but lacking the one vital element of self-confidence.

The crisis has affected liberals in particular because their political humanism, which has been dominant for the past 200 years, is seriously questioned and found wanting.

The New Left and the Black Panthers want a new revolution, a radical humanism. Both justify their demands to abolish the political establishment by appealing to the principles embodied in the Declaration of Independence. They believe that the system no longer works toward the ideal of life and liberty for all. They rebel against Americanism, but maintain the tradition of revolution. Viewing the establishment as corrupt and tyrannical, they propose to abolish it, just as the Declaration of Independence provides.

### Leaders appeal

At the same time, ironically enough, the political establishment seeks to restore confidence by appealing to the same revolutionary ideals. During the 1968 campaign, Vice-President Humphrey unceasingly reminded us that the ideals of the

American Revolution are embodied in "the proud tradition of our party." And former Vice-President Nixon, speaking as his party's standard-bearer in Miami, turned to the same source of inspiration to bring us together again. "My friends," he said,

> We live in an age of revolution in America and in the world. And to find the answers to our problems, let us turn to a revolution that will never grow old, the world's greatest continuing revolution, the American Revolution. . . . And so it is time to apply the lessons of the American Revolution to our present problems.

In his 1971 State of the Union address, President Nixon again renewed his faith in the "New American Revolution" to end the "dark night of the American spirit."

Thus our national leaders face the dilemma of condemning violence by taking inspiration from the same revolutionary principles as does the New Left! But was the Revolution really such a glorious, inspiring event?

In the glorification of our past, we often forget the immoral, destructive aspects of the American Revolution. It was a lengthy revolutionary war with all the inevitable evil consequences of disease, starvation, dislocation, and destruction of property. Estimates of American battle deaths alone range as high as 12,000 (proportionately, 16 times the U.S. fatalities in Viet Nam). Out of a population of less than 3 million, approximately 100,000 Loyalists left the country as political refugees, their property confiscated.

After the War of Independence, the revolutionary leaders turned against each other, if not by terror tactics, at least by the stigma of treason. Dissent and opposition were considered subversive (Alien and Sedition Act of 1798). And the internal divisions were so deep that when the Jeffersonian Republicans gained preeminence, the Federalists seriously thought about secession, rather than support the Republicans (Hartford Convention of 1814). When all sides are considered, the Patriots paid rather dearly for their Revolution, probably more than they had originally anticipated.

These facts reinforce the question of how Christians can accept any appeal to the principles of revolution, whatever their source. As we have seen, revolution is the radical transformation of values, the substitution of humanistic for Christian values. As historian Carl Becker has carefully documented in *The Declaration of Independence* (1942), America tried to justify its rebellion by turning to the anti-Christian principles of the Enlightenment. And ever since then, humanistic values have permeated politics in America, in particular the political parties. Today there is a danger that evangelicals will uncritically accept the appearance that we are in an age of revolution; that they will feel compelled to re-dedicate themselves to the meaning of the American Revolution, and apply its principles to our society.

But, we must insist that revolutionary principles are not the answer. A society develops in accord with the religious direction of the heart of its people. Let us therefore break with the revolutionary principles of our founding fathers, and rediscover the reformation principles of our forefathers.

Many of us have accepted the American Way of Life without a searching analysis of its foundations. It is one thing to believe in democracy as a form of government. But it is quite another to believe in democracy as a social-political faith permeating all of life, all of man's institutions, including the church. This is what we have come to. The democratic way of life has become a political religion, like any other contemporary ism, and as such it is a real threat to Christianity. It is essential that we distinguish between Christianity and Americanism. Christ expects His followers to honor their nation-state, but not to glorify it on an untouchable pedestal.

Scripture does not demand that we defend the American Way of Life as over against the ideals of the new revolutionaries. Evangelicals need not choose between these apparent alternatives; it is a false dilemma. Even the "American Way," inasmuch as it is man-oriented, must lead to revolution. We should reject both the new and the old as revolutionary and humanistic. We should question, for example, one of the very basic articles of the American creed: that we are first-of-all Americans, irrespective of race or religion. We are Christians first, with our deepest and ultimate loyalties to Christ. Only after that are we Americans.

The only group of Americans who can hope to turn our country away from the inherent violence of revolution is our Christian minority. Christians are once again to become Pilgrims in America, a land estranged from God. With us lies the solution of reformation. By God's grace, we can avoid revolution.

But then, we must rediscover the meaning of the Reformation and also understand the spirit of the times in which we live. To this end, we must better understand the demands of God's Word and Christ's command in the world. As Harold O. J. Brown wrote in *Christianity and the Class Struggle* (1970):

> The reformation of a society by the Word of God does not involve . . . enforced conformation. . . . Instead, it must involve the leavening action of convinced and dedicated Christians and groups, dispersed throughout society like yeast in a mass of dough. To this end the Christians must be *genuine* . . . moving out from the Christ-centered core to encounter and influence the society that surrounds them. . . . The reforming power and authority of the Word of God for individuals and for social relationships must be *proclaimed* and exhibited.

Our big task, therefore, is two-fold: (1) to provide a Christian political education, and (2) to witness for Christ in the nation. A Christian political education is necessary because Christians are deeply divided on principles, let alone on particular policies. There is no unity of thought, no Christian mind. In our discussions we are not really thinking *as Christians* about issues. We are thinking as conservatives or as liberals.

Furthermore, such education would emphasize the need for joint endeavor. For too long we have gone our separate, individualistic ways. The agony of Christians in America is that they do not constitute a political movement so that they could stand together and encourage one another. Lacking unity, we cannot manifest the Body of Christ in the body politic.

Our options are not limited to joining some "activist" church or taking up a more vigorous, individualistic Christian witness. A more meaningful commitment for evangelical Christians would be to join a political-education organization such as the National Association for Christian Political Action, which is studying current issues and presenting briefs to legislatures. Such a movement could provide an avenue for evangelicals to effectively introduce a Christian perspective into the political debate and create an awareness of possible alternatives to reform the political structures. For instance, the need for a new Constitution is already being discussed. Are evangelical Christians going to let discussion and formulation of such a crucial document by-pass them and go to others by default?

We live in a troubled period of the nation's history. Yet it is a great time to be alive, with unprecedented opportunities for Christian witness. Americans, and evangelicals in particular, must rediscover the hope and vision of the men of the Reformation. Christians should be eager to participate in the public debate and confront the American people with the ultimate decisions they must make.

As the second centennial of our nation's founding draws near, Christians have a timely opportunity to re-examine critically the foundations of our country. The standard of evaluation for evangelicals should no longer be whether something is American or un-American, but whether it is Christian or unchristian. There is only one life style acceptable for Christians in America, namely, Christianity as a way of life.

Let us, therefore, reaffirm our Christian faith and choose for reformation. The way of revolution is a way of death and destruction.

# Trapped in a System

## Carl Oglesby

Seven months ago at the April [1965] March on Washington, Paul Potter, then President of Students for a Democratic Society, stood in approximately this spot in Washington and said that we must name the system that creates and sustains the war in Vietnam—name it, describe it, analyze it, understand it, and change it.

Today I will try to name it—to suggest an analysis which, to be quite frank, may disturb some of you—and to suggest what changing it may require of us.

We are here again to protest again a growing war. Since it is a very bad war, we acquire the habit of thinking that it must be caused by very bad men. But we only conceal reality, I think, by denouncing on such grounds the menacing coalition of industrial and military power, or the brutality of the blitzkrieg we are waging against Vietnam, or the ominous signs around us that heresy may soon no longer be permitted. We must simply observe, and quite plainly say, that this coalition, this blitzkrieg, and this demand for acquiescence are creatures, all of them, of a government that since 1932 has considered itself to be fundamentally *liberal*.

The original commitment in Vietnam was made by President Truman, a mainstream liberal. It was seconded by President Eisenhower, a moderate liberal. It was intensified by the late President Kennedy, a flaming liberal. Think of the men who now engineer that war—those who study the maps, give the commands, push the buttons, and tally the dead: Bundy, McNamara, Rusk, Lodge, Goldberg, the President himself.

They are not moral monsters.

They are all honorable men.

They are all liberals.

But so, I'm sure, are many of us who are here today in protest. To understand the war, then, it seems necessary to take a closer look at this American liberalism. Maybe we are in for some surprises. Maybe we have here two quite different liberalisms: one authentically humanist; the other not so human at all.

Not long ago, I considered myself a liberal. And if someone had asked me what I meant by that, I'd perhaps have quoted Thomas Jefferson or Thomas Paine, who first made plain our nation's unprovisional commitment to human rights. But what do you think would happen if these two heroes could sit down now for a chat with President Johnson and

Pamphlet issued by the Students for a Democratic Society.

McGeorge Bundy?

They would surely talk of the Vietnam war. Our dead revolutionaries would soon wonder why their country was fighting against what appeared to be a revolution. The living liberals would hotly deny that it is one: there are troops coming in from outside, the rebels get arms from other countries, most of the people are not on their side, and they practice terror against their own. Therefore, *not* a revolution.

What would our dead revolutionaries answer? They might say: "What fools and bandits, sirs, you make then of us. Outside help? Do you remember Lafayette? Or the 3,000 British freighters the French navy sunk for our side? Or the arms and men we got from France and Spain? And what's this about terror? Did you never hear what we did to our own loyalists? Or about the thousands of rich American Tories who fled for their lives to Canada? And as for popular support, do you not know that we had less than one-third of our people with us? That, in fact, the colony of New York recruited more troops for the British than for the revolution? Should we give it all back?"

Revolutions do not take place in velvet boxes. They never have. It is only the poets who make them lovely. What the National Liberation Front is fighting in Vietnam is a complex and vicious war. This war is also a revolution, as honest a revolution as you can find anywhere in history. And this is a fact which all our intricate official denials will never change.

But it doesn't make any difference to our leaders anyway. Their aim in Vietnam is really much simpler than this implies. It is to safeguard what they take to be American interests around the world against revolution or revolutionary change, which they always call Communism—as if that were that. In the case of Vietnam, this interest is, first, the principle that revolution shall not be tolerated anywhere, and second, that South Vietnam shall never sell its rice to China—or even to North Vietnam.

There is simply no such thing now, for us, as a just revolution—never mind that for two-thirds of the world's people the 20th Century might as well be the Stone Age; never mind the melting poverty and hopelessness that are the basic facts of life for most modern men; and never mind that for these millions there is now an increasingly perceptible relationship between their sorrow and our contentment.

Can we understand why the Negroes of Watts rebelled? Then why do we need a devil theory to explain the rebellion of the South Vietnamese? Can we understand the oppression in Mississippi, or the anguish that our Northern ghettoes make epidemic? Then why can't we see that our proper human struggle is not with Communism or revolutionaries, but with the social desperation that drives good men to violence, both here and abroad?

To be sure, we have been most generous with our aid, and in Western Europe, a mature industrial society, that aid worked. But there are always political and financial strings. And we have never shown ourselves capable of allowing others to make those traumatic institutional changes that are often the prerequisites of progress in colonial societies. For all our official feeling for the millions who are enslaved to what we so self-righteously call the yoke of Communist tyranny, we make no real effort at all to crack through the much more vicious right-wing tyrannies that our businessmen traffic with and our nation profits from every day. And for all our cries about the international Red conspiracy to take over the world, we take only pride in the fact of our 6,000 military bases on foreign soil.

We gave Rhodesia a grave look just now—but we keep on buying her chromium, which is cheap because black slave labor mines it.

We deplore the racism of Verwoerd's fascist South Africa—but our banks make big loans to that country and our private technology makes it a nuclear power.

We are saddened and puzzled by random back-page stories of revolt in this or that Latin American state—but are convinced by a few pretty photos in the Sunday supplement that things are getting better, that the world is coming our way, that change from disorder can be orderly, that our benevolence will pacify the distressed, that our might will intimidate the angry.

Optimists, may I suggest that these are quite unlikely fantasies. They are fantasies because we have lost that mysterious social desire for human equity that from time to time has given us genuine moral drive. We have become a nation of young, bright-eyed, hard-hearted, slim-waisted, bullet-headed make-out artists. A nation—may I say it?—of beardless liberals.

You say I am being hard? Only think.

**This country, with its thirty-some years of liberalism, can send 200,000 young men to Vietnam to kill and die in the most dubious of wars, but it cannot get 100 voter registrars to go into Mississippi.**

What do you make of it?

The financial burden of the war obliges us to cut millions from an already pathetic War on Poverty budget. But in almost the same breath, Congress appropriates $140 million for the Lockheed and Boeing companies to compete with each other on the supersonic transport project—that Disneyland creation that will cost us all about $2 billion before it's done.

What do you make of it?

Many of us have been earnestly resisting for some years now the idea of putting atomic weapons into West German hands, an action that would perpetuate the division of Europe and thus the Cold War. Now just this week we find out that, with the meagerest of security systems, West Germany has had nuclear weapons in her hands for the past six years.

What do you make of it?

**Some will make of it that I overdraw the matter. Many will ask: What about the other side? To be sure, there is the bitter ugliness of Czechoslovakia, Poland, those infamous Russian tanks in the streets**

of Budapest. But my anger only rises to hear some say that sorrow cancels sorrow, or that *this* one's shame deposits in *that* one's account the right to shamefulness.

And others will make of it that I sound mighty anti-American. To these, I say: Don't blame *me* for *that!* Blame those who mouthed my liberal values and broke my American heart.

Just who might they be, by the way? Let's take a brief factual inventory of the latter-day Cold War.

In 1953 our Central Intelligence Agency managed to overthrow Mossadegh in Iran, the complaint being his neutralism in the Cold War and his plans to nationalize the country's oil resources to improve his people's lives. Most evil aims, most evil man. In his place we put in General Zahedi, a World War II Nazi collaborator. New arrangements on Iran's oil gave 25-year leases on 40 percent of it to three U.S. firms, one of which was Gulf Oil. The CIA's leader for this coup was Kermit Roosevelt. In 1960 Kermit Roosevelt became a vice president of Gulf Oil.

In 1954, the democratically elected Arbenz of Guatemala wanted to nationalize a portion of United Fruit Company's plantations in his country, land he needed badly for a modest program of agrarian reform. His government was overthrown in a CIA-supported right-wing coup. The following year, Gen. Walter Bedell Smith, director of the CIA when the Guatemala venture was being planned, joined the board of directors of the United Fruit Company.

Comes 1960 and Castro cries we are about to invade Cuba. The Administration sneers "poppycock," and we Americans believe it. Comes 1961 and the invasion. Comes with it the awful realization that the United States Government had lied.

Comes 1962 and the missile crisis, and our Administration stands prepared to fight global atomic war on the curious principle that another state does not have the right to its own foreign policy.

Comes 1963 and British Guiana, where Cheddi Jagan wants independence from England and a labor law modeled on the Wagner Act. And Jay Lovestone, the AFL-CIO foreign policy chief, acting, as always, quite independently of labor's rank and file, arranges with our Government to finance an eleven-week dock strike that brings Jagan down, ensuring that the state will remain *British* Guiana, and that any workingman who wants a wage better than 50¢ a day is a dupe of Communism.

Comes 1964. Two weeks after Under Secretary Thomas Mann announces that we have abandoned the *Alianza's* principle of no aid to tyrants, Brazil's Goulart is overthrown by the vicious right-winger, Ademar Barros, supported by a show of American gunboats at Rio de Janeiro. Within 24 hours, the new head of state, Mazzilli, receives a congratulatory wire from our President.

116

Comes 1965. The Dominican Republic. Rebellion in the streets. We scurry to the spot with 20,000 neutral Marines and our neutral peacemakers—like Ellsworth Bunker, Jr., Ambassador to the Organization of American States. Most of us know that our neutral Marines fought openly on the side of the junta, a fact that the Administration still denies. But how many also know that what was at stake was our new Caribbean Sugar Bowl? That this same neutral peace-making Bunker is a board member and stock owner of the National Sugar Refining Company, a firm his father founded in the good old days, and one which has a major interest in maintaining the status quo in the Dominican Republic? Or that the President's close personal friend and advisor, our new Supreme Court Justice Abe Fortas, has sat for the past 19 years on the board of the Sucrest Company, which imports black-strap molasses from the Dominican Republic? Or that the rhetorician of corporate liberalism and the late President Kennedy's close friend Adolf Berle, was chairman of that same board? Or that our roving ambassador Averell Harriman's brother Roland is on the board of National Sugar? Or that our former ambassador to the Dominican Republic, Joseph Farland, is a board member of the South Puerto Rico Sugar Co., which owns 275,000 acres of rich land in the Dominican Republic and is the largest employer on the island—at about one dollar a day?

Neutralists! God save the hungry people of the world from such neutralists!

We do not say these men are evil. We say, rather, that good men can be divided from their compassion by the institutional system that inherits us all. Generation in and out, we are put to use. People become instruments. Generals do not hear the screams of the bombed; sugar executives do not see the misery of the cane cutters—for to do so is to be that much *less* the general, that much *less* the executive.

The foregoing facts of recent history describe one main aspect of the estate of Western liberalism. Where is our American humanism here? What went wrong?

Let's stare our situation coldly in the face. All of us are born to the colossus of history, our American corporate system—in many ways, an awesome organism. There is one fact that describes it: With about 5 percent of the world's people, we consume about half the world's goods. We take a richness that is in good part not our own, and we put it in our pockets, our garages, our split-levels, our bellies, and our futures.

On the *face* of it, it is a crime that so few should have so much at the expense of so many. Where is the moral imagination so abused as to call this just? Perhaps many of us feel a bit uneasy in our sleep. We are not, after all, a cruel people. And perhaps we don't really need this super-dominance that deforms others. But what can we do? The investments are made. The financial ties are established. The plants abroad are built. Our system *exists*. One is swept up into it. How intolerable—to be born moral, but addicted to a stolen and maybe surplus luxury. Our goodness threatens to become counterfeit before our eyes—unless we change. But change threatens us with uncertainty—at least.

Our problem, then, is to justify this system and give its theft another name—to make kind and moral what is neither, to perform some alchemy with language that will make this injustice seem to be a most magnanimous gift.

A hard problem. But the Western democracies, in the heyday of their colonial expansionism, produced a hero worthy of the task.

Its name was free enterprise, and its partner was an *illiberal liberalism* that said to the poor and the dispossessed: What we acquire of your resources we repay in civilization. The white man's burden. But this was too poetic. So a much more hard-headed theory was produced. This theory said that colonial status is in fact a *boon* to the colonized. We give them technology and bring them into modern times.

But this deceived no one but ourselves. We were delighted with this new theory. The poor saw in it merely an admission that their claims were irrefutable. They stood up to us, without gratitude. We were shocked—but also confused, for the poor seemed again to be right. How long is it going to be the case, we wondered, that the poor will be right and the rich will be wrong?

Liberalism faced a crisis. In the face of the collapse of the European empires, how could it continue to hold together our twin need for richness and righteousness? How can we continue to sack the ports of Asia and still dream of Jesus?

The challenge was met with a most ingenious solution: the ideology of anti-Communism. This was the bind: we cannot call revolution bad, because we started that way ourselves, and because it is all too easy to see why the dispossessed should rebel. So we will call revolution *Communism*. And we will reserve for ourselves the right to say what Communism means. We take note of revolution's enormities, wrenching them where necessary from their historical context and often exaggerating them, and say: Behold, Communism is a bloodbath. We take note of those reactionaries who stole the revolution, and say: Behold, Communism is a betrayal of the people. We take note of the revolution's need to consolidate itself, and say: Behold, Communism is a tyranny.

It has been all these things, and it will be these things again, and we will never be at a loss for those tales of atrocity that comfort us so in our self-righteousness. Nuns will be raped and bureaucrats will be disembowelled. Indeed, revolution is a fury. For it is a letting loose of outrages pent up sometimes over centuries. But the more brutal and longer-lasting the suppression of this energy, all the more ferocious will be its explosive release.

Far from helping Americans deal with this truth, the anti-Communist ideology merely tries to disguise it so that things may stay the way they are.

Thus, it depicts our presence in other lands not as a coercion, but a protection. It allows us even to say that the napalm in Vietnam is only another aspect of our humanitarian love—like those exorcisms in the Middle Ages that so often killed the patient. So we say to the Vietnamese peasant, the Cuban intellectual, the Peruvian worker: "You are better dead than Red. If it hurts or if you don't understand why—sorry about that."

This is the action of *corporate liberalism*. It performs for the corporate state a function quite like what the Church once performed for the feudal state. It seeks to justify its burdens and protect it from change. As the Church exaggerated this office in the Inquisition, so with liberalism in the [Joseph] McCarthy time—which, if it was a reactionary phenomenon, was still made possible by our anti-Communist corporate liberalism.

Let me then speak directly to humanist liberals. If my facts are wrong, I will soon be corrected. But if they are right, then you may face a crisis of conscience. Corporatism or humanism: which? For it has come to that. Will you let your dreams be used? Will you be a grudging apologist for the corporate state? Or will you help try to change it—not in the name of this or that blueprint or "ism," but in the name of simple human decency and democracy and the vision that wise and brave men saw in the time of our own Revolution?

And if your commitment to human value is unconditional, then disabuse yourselves of the notion that statements will bring change, if only the right statements can be written, or that interviews with the mighty will bring change if only the mighty can be reached, or that marches will bring change if only we can make them massive enough, or that policy proposals will bring change if only we can make them responsible enough.

We are dealing now with a colossus that does not want to be changed. It will not change itself. It will not cooperate with those who want to change it. Those allies of ours in the Government—are they really our allies? If they *are,* then they don't need advice, they need *constituencies;* they don't need study groups, they need a *movement.* And if they are *not,* then all the more reason for building that movement with a most relentless conviction.

There are people in this country today who are trying to build that movement, who aim at nothing less than a humanist reformation. And the humanist liberals must understand that it is this movement with which their own best hopes are most in tune. We radicals know the same history that you liberals know, and we can understand your occasional cynicism, exasperation, and even distrust. But we ask you to put these aside and help us risk a leap. Help us find enough time for the enormous work that needs doing here. Help us build. Help us shake the future in the name of plain human hope.

Richard Flacks

# ON THE USES OF PARTICIPATORY DEMOCRACY

## I

The most frequently heard phrase used for defining participatory democracy is that "men must share in the decisions which affect their lives." In other words, participatory democrats take very seriously a vision of man as citizen; and by taking seriously such a vision, they seek to extend the conception of citizenship beyond the conventional political sphere to all institutions. Other ways of stating the core values are to assert the following: each man has responsibility for the action of the institutions in which he is embedded; all authority ought to be responsible to those "under" it; each man can and should be a center of power and initiative in society.

## II

The first priority for the achievement of a democracy of participation is to win full political rights and representation for all sectors of the population. Democracy, in fact, is an issue for this generation of radicals largely because their political experience has been shaped by the Negroes' elemental struggle for a political voice in the United States. This struggle has not been simply for the right to vote—though even this right has not yet been guaranteed—but, more broadly, it has been an effort to win a share of political power by poor Negroes. It has been the experience of Negroes in the North, where voting rights have been formally guaranteed, that Negroes as a group have remained systematically underrepresented in the political process and that, where Negro representation exists, it operates in behalf of Negro middle-class interests

DISSENT, November/December, 1966, vol. 13, 701-708.

and is highly dependent on the beneficence of white-dominated political machines. The results of this situation are plain to see in every Northern city. Thus the main thrust of radicals in the civil rights movement has to do less with breaking the barriers of legal segregation and formal exclusion than with attempting to build viable grass-roots organizations of poor Negroes, which would actually represent the needs of the poor and remain independent of white and middle-class domination. The ideology of "participatory democracy" has been useful in this effort, since it provides a rationale for avoiding premature "coalition" of grass-roots groups with more powerful white or middle-class organizations, for effectively criticizing "charismatic" styles of leadership which prevent rank-and-file people from learning political skills, for criticizing tendencies toward bureaucratism, demagoguery, and elitism which are predictable in mass movements. Moreover, "participatory democracy," unlike black nationalist ideology, which also helps to mobilize grass-roots Negroes, offers a possible bridge between Negroes and other groups of poor or voiceless people. Thus we find much of the same rhetoric and organizing technique being used by SNCC workers in Southern Negro communities, SDS organizers among poor whites in Chicago and Cleveland, and farm labor organizers among the multi-national grape workers in California.

Just how is participatory democracy being applied to the organization of economically disadvantaged groups? It has influenced the analysis of the problem of poverty in an affluent society, by stressing political voicelessness and lack of organization as a root cause of deprivation. This analysis leads to an emphasis on grass-roots organization and mobilization of the poor as the main way of ending poverty. Since the people involved lack political skill, organization requires a full-time staff, initially composed of students and ex-students, but soon involving "indigenous" leadership This staff has the problem of allaying the fear, suspicion, and sense of inadequacy of the community—hence there has been a strong emphasis on building a sense of community between staff and rank-and-file, and of finding techniques which will facilitate self-expression, enable new leadership to emerge, enable people to gain dignity by participation, and the organization to become self-sustaining. Such techniques include: rotation of leadership, eschewing by staff of opportunities to "speak for" the organization, the use of "consensus" to foster expression by the less-articulate.

More important than such procedural techniques has been the attempt to generate institutions which help to bind people to the organization, to see immediate benefits from participation. Thus, in Mississippi, alongside the political organization (the Freedom Democratic party), a variety of related "projects" have grown up—community centers, freedom schools, a Poor People's Corporation to help finance small business enterprise, cooperatives, and the like. In Newark, the Newark Community Union has established its own radio station. In California, the Farm Worker Association established a credit union. In Cleveland, the SDS Community Project established a traveling street theater. Although these new institutions are sometimes viewed as alternatives to participation in "organized society" (vide Staughton Lynd in DISSENT—Summer, 1965), in practice, they are a very important way of sustaining a developing organization. They enable people to participate in an organization in a continuing fashion, help develop organizational resources, train people for leadership, and give people a sense of the possibilities for social change. But they are in no sense a *substitute* for political activity, direct action, and the development of a program. These, and not the development of "parallel institutions," constitute the main functions of the local political parties, community unions, etc., which are developing in many urban slum and rural areas.

The emphasis on participatory democracy has helped these developing grass-roots organizations formulate and articulate *issues and programs*. Although the constituencies of these organizations include the most impoverished sectors of society, it is remarkable that—particularly in the northern cities—the main activity of these organizations has not been focused on economic issues. They have rather, been struggling over issues of *control, self-determination,* and *independence*: Shall the poor have a voice in the allocation of War on Poverty funds? Shall urban renewal be shaped by the people whose neighborhood is being renewed? Shall the police be held accountable by the community? Who is to decide the dispensation of welfare payments? Who makes the rules in the welfare bureaucracies? Who controls the ghetto?

The outcome of these grass-roots organizing efforts, of course, cannot be predicted. The civil rights movement, in its direct action phase, began the process of bringing Negroes and the poor into the political arena—and the results, in terms of political alignments and issues, have already been substantial. The more recent efforts of political organization initiated by the participatory democrats will certainly increase the degree of Negro representation in the political process. These efforts are now being emulated by more established and less insurgent agencies—Martin Luther King's Southern Christian Leadership Conference, for example, in the massive organizing campaign in Chicago, used many of the techniques and rhetorical devices developed by SNCC and SDS.

It seems clear, then, that the poor are being organized and mobilized. But such mobilization can lead in two directions. On the one hand, there is the strong probability that the newly developed constituencies will take their place alongside other ethnic and interest groups, bargaining for benefits within the framework of the Democratic party. An alternative to this path is embodied in the vision of participatory democracy—the development of community-based, self-determining organizations, having the following functions:

Achieving community control over previously centralized functions, through local election of school and police administrators; by forming community-run co-operatives in housing, social services, retail distribution, and the like; by establishing community-run foundations and corporations.

Maintaining close control over elected representatives; running and electing poor people to public office; ensuring direct participation of the community in framing political platforms and in shaping the behavior of representatives.

Acting like a trade-union in protecting the poor against exploitative and callous practices of public and private bureaucracies, landlords, businessmen, and others.

## III

The values underlying participatory democracy have, so far, achieved their fullest expression in efforts to organize and mobilize communities of disenfranchised people, but such democratizing trends and potentialities also exist in other sectors of society. The most obvious example is the nationwide effort by university students to change the authority structure in American higher education. For the most part, this activity has been directed at protest against arbitrary restrictions of student political expression and against paternalistic regulations limiting students' rights to privacy and self-expression. The most dramatic and widely known instance of this activity was that of the civil disobedience and student strikes at Berkeley in the fall of 1964. But the Berkeley situation has been repeated in less intense form on scores of campuses across the country. Student reform efforts have increasingly shifted from protest and direct action to demands for a continuing voice in the shaping of university policy. Some students now have demanded representation on administrative committees. Others have looked to the formation of organizations along the trade-union model—organizations which would be independent of and could bargain with university administrators, rather than becoming participants in administration. Thus far, the impact of the student protest has been to generate a considerable degree of ferment, of re-examination and experimentation among college faculties and administrators, as well as efforts coercively to repress the protest.

Student protest has spread from the elite, liberal campuses to Catholic schools and from there to other clerical bodies. The talk at Catholic seminaries now prominently includes "participatory democracy," and "New Left" clergymen have gone so far as to propose the establishment of a trade-union for priests. But the university and the church are not the only institutions witnessing challenges to existing authority structures. In recent years, there has been an enormous growth of unionization among schoolteachers and other white-collar workers, particularly among employees in the welfare bureaucracies. Now one can also observe ferment in the professions: young doctors and young lawyers are developing organizations dedicated to challenging the authority of the highly conservative professional societies and to bringing an active sense of social responsibility to their professions.

It is not farfetched to predict that the idea of "workers' control" will soon become a highly relevant issue in American life. American industrial unions have largely had to sacrifice the struggle for control in the workplace for higher wages and fringe benefits; but at union conventions, control over working conditions is repeatedly urged as a high-priority bargaining demand. The impetus for making such a demand paramount, however, may first come from the ranks of white-collar and professional employees. The authority structure of the modern bureaucratic organization is plainly unsuited for a work force which is highly educated and fully aware of its competence to participate in decision making. The first impulse of modern managers faced with threats to authority has been to make small concessions ("improve channels of communications"). But the exciting time will come when such insurgency turns from protest over small grievances to a full-fledged realization of the possibilities for first-class citizenship in public bureaucracies and private corporations. The forms of such democratization could include further unionization of the unorganized, worker representation in management, young-turk overthrows of entrenched leaderships in the professions, and, ultimately, demands for elections and recall of managers and administrators and for employee participation in the shaping of policies and regulations.

## IV

The most authoritarian sector of public decision making in the United States is in the area of foreign policy. The American Constitution gives enormous power to the President to make foreign policy without substantial built-in checks from Congress. The scope of Presidential power has, of course, been greatly expanded by the technology of modern war; the unchecked power of the government to mobilize support for its policies has been greatly enhanced by the invention of conscription, by the mass media and their centralization, by covert intelligence operations, and so forth. It is not surprising that foreign policy has been the special province of elites in America and, since World War II, has been carried on within a framework of almost total popular acquiescence.

The simultaneous occurrence of the Vietnam War and the emergence of a New Left in America may generate change in this situation. Due largely to student initiative, we are witnessing more protest during time of war than in any other comparable period in United States history. Not only does this protest begin to shatter the foreign policy consensus but it also shows signs of bringing about more permanent change in the structure of foreign policy decision making.

First, the teach-ins and similar initiatives mark the emergence of an *independent public* in the foreign policy area—a body of people, satisfied neither with official policy nor with official justifications of policy, determined to formulate alternatives, stimulate debate and criticism, and obtain independent sources of information. This public is to be found largely in universities, but now spills over to include much of the intellectual community in the country. Moreover, the teach-in, as a technique for disseminating information suggests, at least symbolically, a significant breakthrough in the effort to find alternatives to the propaganda media controlled or manipulated by the state.

Second, the emerging foreign policy public has plainly had an at least transitory impact on Congress. The revival of congressional independence with respect to foreign policy would be a signal advance of democracy in America.

Third, the attempts to find a nonreligious moral ground for conscientious objection in time of war has led to a rediscovery of the Allied case at the Nuremberg Trials—a case which argued in essence that individuals were responsible for the actions of institutions taken in their name. This principle, taken seriously, is revolutionary in its implications for individual-state relations; and it converges, interestingly enough, with "participatory democracy." The Nuremberg principle is now being used as a basis for legal defense of draft refusal and civil disobedience at draft boards; it inspires professors to refuse to grade their students and become thereby accomplices to Selective Service; it inspires intellectuals and artists to acts of public defiance and witness. In fact, it is possible that one positive outcome of the war in Vietnam will have been its impact on the moral sensibility of many members of the intellectual and religious communities—forcing them to rethink their relationship to the state and to the institutions of war.

It is possible, then, that an unforeseen by-product of the highly developed society is the emergence of potential publics that are (1) competent to evaluate the propaganda of elites and (2) impatient with chauvinistic definitions of loyalty. The organization of such publics in the United States may be a significant outcome of the war in Vietnam. These publics do not have the power to change the course of this war, but the spread of their influence may be a factor in transforming the issues and alignments of American politics in the coming period. Moreover, the strength of these publics on the campus is now being reflected in the growing conflict over the role of the universities in national mobilization. The current campaign to prevent university participation in the Selective Service induction process may portend a more profound effort to make universities centers of resistance to encroaching militarization. The outcome of this particular struggle could be important in democratizing the structure of foreign policy decision making.

## V

The development of democratic consciousness in communities, organizations, and foreign policy decision making will mean little if the national distribution of power remains undisturbed. This means that the social theory of the New Left must be centrally concerned with the development of relevant models for democratic control over public decisions at the national level.

It is clear that implicit in the New Left's vision is the notion that participatory democracy is not possible without some version of public control over the allocation of resources, economic planning, and the operation of large corporations. Such control is, of course, not missing in the United States. The federal government has taken responsibility for national planning to avoid slump, to control wages and prices, and to avoid inflation. Moreover, the postwar period has seen a tremendous increase in public subsidy of the corporate economy—through the defense budget, urban redevelopment, investment in research and education, transportation and communication, and so on. In many ways the "two governments"—political and corporate—are merged, and this merger approximates an elitist corporatist model (hence breaking down even the modest pluralism which once characterized the system). The further development of this trend will foreclose any possibility for the achievement of democratic participation.

The demand for more national planning, once the major plank of American socialism, is now decidedly on the agenda of American political and corporate elites. The question for the Left has become how to *democratize* that planning. There are as yet no answers to this or to the question of how to bring the large corporations under democratic control.

## VI

Thus the main intellectual problem for the new radicals is to suggest how patterns of decentralized decision making in city administrations, and democratized authority structures in bureaucracies, can be meshed with a situation of greatly broadened national planning and co-ordination in the economy.

That no such programs and models now exist is, of course, a consequence of the disintegration of the socialist tradition in America and of the continuing fragmentation of American intellectual life. Unless the New Left consciously accepts the task of restoring that tradition and of establishing a new political community, the democratizing revolts which it now catalyzes are likely to be abortive.

## VII

These tasks were, less than a generation ago, declared by many American intellectuals to be no longer relevant. Ideology, it was argued, had no place in highly developed societies where problems of resource allocation had become technical matters. But the reverse may be true: that ideological questions—that is, questions about the structure and distribution of power—are *especially* pertinent when societies have the capacity to solve the merely technical problems.

It seems clear that the issue in a highly developed society is not simply economic exploitation; it is the question of the relationship of the individual to institutional and state authority which assumes paramount importance. In America, today, the familiar mechanisms of social control—money, status, patriotic and religious symbols—are losing their force for a population (particularly the new generation) which has learned to be intensely self-conscious and simultaneously worldly; to expect love and self-fulfillment; to quest for freedom and autonomy. All this learning is a consequence of increasingly sophisticated educational opportunities, of increasingly liberated standards in family and interpersonal relations, of affluence itself. Against this learning, the classic patterns of elite rule, bureaucratic authority, managerial manipulation, and class domination will have a difficult time sustaining themselves.

The virtue of "participatory democracy," as a basis for a new politics, is that it enables these new sources of social tension to achieve political expression. Participatory democracy symbolizes the restoration of personal freedom and interpersonal community as central political and social issues. It is not the end of ideology; it is a new beginning.

# COMING TOGETHER IN GARY

**ERWIN A. JAFFE**

The National Black Political Convention, which met in Gary, Ind. from March 10 to 12, marked, however uncertainly, a new beginning for American blacks. Its meaning was aptly expressed by the Rev. Jesse L. Jackson:

> I don't care how much confusion we have here today. This is a beautiful occasion. . . . We are pregnant. We are ready for change, and whether a doctor is there or not, the water has broke, the blood has spilled. A new black baby is going to be born.

The collective parents of this baby were the approximately 3,500 delegates and alternates, and several thousand observers, who in turn claimed proxy for the 23-to-25 million black Americans not present. By simply being there, by coming together, they joined with Jackson to make the point: this was a public birth, the coming into existence of a black child who is, or whose parents intend him to be, visible to all.

Logistically, the convention was a near disaster. Located in a high school impressively mammoth but ill-designed for the occasion, subjected to interminable delays and interruptions (some apparently contrived), inconvenienced by a shortage of housing facilities that scattered delegates (the Illinois delegation protested that it had been placed in a motel 31 miles away—and with no arrangements for transportation), financially destitute by comparison with a Republican or Democratic gathering (and certainly the recipient of no large endowment from public-spirited corporations), the convention operated in an atmosphere approaching chaos.

THE NATION, April 3, 1972, 422-426.

These difficulties were magnified by decisions seemingly forced on the conveners. Delegates, though younger and poorer than their counterparts at traditional political conventions, were incongruously charged $25 to register (a resolution from the floor finally did order special consideration for hardship cases). And while denunciations of the values and concerns of a white, money-oriented society were commonplace, interspersed with demands to "cut us in," the arrangements could readily convince observers that they were witnessing a replica of the typical American convention. Concessionaires lined the walls, trading vigorously and at high prices in pennants and celebrations of folk heroes, many of them martyred. Appropriate buttons and books were on sale everywhere. The convention floor, with its familiar arrangement by states, in apparent acknowledgement of the priority of the ongoing federal system, looked ilke an imitation of the "real" thing—that is, it gave the impression that **a candidate was being selected and a platform being written in the customary style.**

Nor was the echo of white politics dimmed by the kind of "news" that did emerge. Reports circulated, and were printed, of splits between "nationalists" and "integrationists"; between those who favored endorsement of Shirley Chisholm and those who didn't; between those who spoke for a new black political party *now* (Reverend Jackson) or in the immediate future (Mayor Richard G. Hatcher of Gary); between those who favored or opposed bussing (resolutions were passed condemning bussing and integration but not, so it was claimed, rejecting the principle of desegregation and supporting the CORE plan for "Unitary Community Controlled School Districts"); between opponents and supporters of the executive committee's decision to let white reporters cover the convention. But even bad management, deliberate delays and internal conflict could not hide what delegates from forty-three states and ten national black organizations succeeded in doing. They not only came to Gary, they came together in Gary; they sustained the first contemporary, nationwide effort to drive off the curse of black invisibility.

The invisibility that afflicts black men and women is not synonymous with lack of celebrity or achievement. There are indeed obstacles to blacks in these respects, but black invisibility is more fundamental. It is a denial of and obstruction to humanness. The black man in a white world has been unseen because his presence as a singular human being has not been acknowledged. The white world attaches pre-established images to him, iden-

129

tifies him accordingly as "a Negro," sees then only the stereotype and thus loses sight of the man. Regarded only as representatives of a category fixed in the mind of the beholder, he is invisible. The world deals with him *as if* he weren't there.

This nonexistence (from the world's point of view) would mean little if it did not in addition threaten the invisible man's own sense of individuality and presence. But it does. He is incapable of identifying with those around him, those who matter most to him, because, being black, they are similarly afflicted. Denied his uniqueness, denied the presence of those other individuals who can confirm his individuality, the invisible man is doomed to an existence in which he measures himself and is measured against stereotypes, a life without the possibility of authentic identity. Black men, as long as their world is white, are therefore lost not only to whites but also to themselves.

How then can a black man achieve visibility? How is he to be seen as *somebody*, not as a large or small, dark or light pebble on the beach? The black answer began to be given in this country in the drive to wipe out the shame inculcated among blacks by millions of white-sponsored humiliations. By stressing black pride, black pan-nationalism, black identity, black power—terms now used to describe a sense of black brotherhood that had been aroused at last—black consciousness began to emerge. The simple gesture implied by the words "brother" and "sister," now commonplace, reinforces *connectedness*, makes possible a self-generated group identity that simultaneously opens the possibility to individual identity. The Gary convention, by moving one step further, by openly displaying community and consensus, by certifying the existence of a "black nation," also reasserted the right of each black man to his manhood, each black woman to her womanhood.

What happened in Gary, then, to quote a comment by Hannah Arendt about a very different movement, was that the men and women who came there "had become 'challengers,' had taken the initiative upon themselves, and therefore . . . had begun to create that public space between themselves where freedom could appear." The "freedom" sought in Gary is precisely that condition that people achieve when they inject themselves into or create a public arena or forum, a place in which they can meaningfully act together to shape out, insofar as human beings can, their destinies. And this kind of coming together, rather than the means by which men get their

cut or share of society's pie, rather than the pressures
they develop to push and pull at one another, is the underlying realm without which they can never act and never
be free, the realm of "power."

That sense of power was understood and expressed
by the men and women at the National Black Political
Convention. It was evident in the bearing, the faces, the
words of the men and women who testified before the
Resolutions and Platform Committees. It was evident in
the attitudes of members of a small Western delegation,
who admitted to some doubts as the convention opened,
who were bothered by the "troubled looks" on the faces
of "the people around here," but who within the few
days found themselves happily joined in an important
undertaking with their brothers.

It was evident in the behavior of convention leaders:
Hatcher, Reps. Charles Diggs and Walter Fauntroy, the
latter an impressive and able chairman of the convention's platform committee, all moderates moving into more
militant stances; Imamu Amiri Baraka (LeRoi Jones), a
militant who presided over the final and crucial session
and who, however confused and occasionally dictatorial
his chairmanship, nonetheless clearly adopted a relatively
moderate position and repeatedly urged the delegates to
maintain "unity without uniformity;" and the Reverend
Jackson, at some points eager for quick action to form
a new party, at others seemingly ready to endorse Shirley
Chisholm, but, publicly at least, calling on the delegates
to honor those leaders who had called them "home to
Gary." Internal struggles undoubtedly took place, but the
entire leadership, none of them yet with the influence
of the late Martin Luther King or Malcolm X, knew what
this meeting was about, knew the importance of black
visibility.

And it was evident in the decisions reached: to "move
forward" with a national Steering Committee and National Black Assembly; to adopt a National Black Political Agenda and its preamble, the Gary Declaration. Despite inconsistencies within the agenda and between it
and the declaration, both were written in the spirit of initiation:

> We may choose in 1972 to slip back into the decadent
> white politics of American life, or we may press for-
> ward, moving relentlessly from Gary to the creation
> of our own Black life. . . . We begin here and now in
> Gary. We begin with an independent Black Political
> Agenda, an independent Black spirit. Nothing less will
> do. . . .
> *(Quoted from the printed, preliminary version.)*

American blacks had reached a crucial moment in the long march which began with their emigration to the North in the 1920s. In the thirties they had moved into the Democratic Party as a significant voting bloc, now possibly 20 per cent of that party's voters, strategically located in the larger states. By the fifties, they were involved in joint civil rights demonstrations with whites. By the sixties, they had put together organizations no longer dependent on white support or leadership. They had been moving from "passion," in the old meaning of suffering the acts of others, toward action and initiation. Now they were trying to erect the spirit and substance of a political shell within which to work together. To be able to display that much, to make it clear beyond speculation that black men and women were now visible and were consequently going to be heard, was an extraordinary achievement.

On March 10, before the convention officially opened, the NAACP issued a statement rejecting the Gary declaration, the preamble to the National Black Political Agenda:

> It is clear that in fundamental tone and thrust, as well as in numerous of its specific references, it is not an acceptable document to the NAACP. If the "agenda" adopted by the Convention turns out to be consistent with the draft preamble, the agenda will also be impossible for the NAACP to endorse.
>
> The draft preamble is rooted in the concept of separate nationhood for black Americans. . . . It proclaims a doctrine of black racial superiority in that it holds that only persons of African descent are capable of spearheading movements toward desirable change in the society.

The NAACP correctly noted that the preamble did not follow its own logic and opt for complete separation of blacks and whites, but it could not know at that time that the agenda, not yet released, was to have a thrust very different from that of the preamble. It calls for "reshaping of American institutions that currently exploit black America and threaten the whole society," demands proportional black representation in the economy and political system, urges home rule for the District of Columbia —in sum, is largely reformist in character, despite rhetorical flourishes.

The agenda's discussion of "economic empowerment" takes a similar line, demanding reparations, forced allocation of funds from private foundations to the black community, termination of racist union practices or encouragement of parallel black unions by the federal government, a guaranteed annual income of $6,500 for families of four, curtailment of defense spending, revamping of the mass transit system, etc. In sum, the original agenda chooses neither separation nor integration, but leans toward black involvement within the system in cooperation with the national government *and* with black community control. It straddles, and it does so because of difficulties that cannot be glossed over.

No talk about ethnic politics can hide the differences between the black movement and the "characteristic" immigrant pattern. Sons and daughters of immigrants penetrated the society, at first individually and then in clusters. They eventually converted municipal politics into an aspect of this societal penetration, using city hall as an economic as well as political directorate, thereby making "politics" a vehicle for general upward social mobility. They either "Americanized" themselves or built new ladders of social prestige for hyphenated (Irish-American, Italian-American, et al.) groups. This process was set in motion while the country, however ambivalently, still welcomed strangers. Whatever the tensions produced, much of the conflict was absorbed and localized over a long period by adjustment and assimilation within the society.

But while ethnic groups adjusted to or were being adjusted by America, blacks were rejected, isolated and shut out of society. Their *current* effort comes well after the promise of upward mobility had weakened and is late precisely because of racism. The old tension absorbing devices, even if they could be relied upon, will simply not work fast enough in the current context to suit anyone. To complicate matters further, every issue is now quickly nationalized by the media: local disputes and confrontations are transformed into national crises. The integrationist notion, modeled after the experience of immigrants, is therefore at best only moderately applicable to the current problems of blacks.

The alternative approach, though forced on some blacks by persistent white racism, possesses its own logic. Stressing a black heritage and history, rather than seeing the black man as a reflex of the European experience, it reinforces the self-identity that was so much in the air at Gary. But it creates serious problems and dangers.

Modern American (internal) political experience is largely geographical; it is not hooked to political connectedness based on race. Our political space is a given; our political involvement is an accident of place and placement. We have been citizens because we live within an already defined boundary. The only experience the United States has had with groups that "make" their own boundaries has been with classes and occupational groupings—workers, farmers, businessmen—defined by interests; it is a form of political "coming together" particularly congenial to the American outlook, that is, congenial to an almost exclusive concentration on economic gains and losses.

The black movement, to the degree that it identifies as a separate nation culturally linked to Africa, is not rooted in class—despite the impoverishment of blacks—but in skin color, race and "history." This represents a dynamic which, despite American experience with white racism and with hardened, hysterical world views and ideologies, our own and others', threatens the myths that have propped up the American political dialogue for some time. That threat in turn gives rise to a fear of an inverted white racism or Nazism.

Since human affairs are unpredictable, the fear cannot simply be brushed aside. There is no evidence that the American black movement, despite bitterness toward whites, is committed to race war. It represents not a majority turning on a minority but a minority trying to get itself together. Its first, and undoubtedly long-term, orientation is internal. "Love thyself," "respect thyself," are its primary mottos. The implications of black American nationalism are, at least for the time being, remote from the racism that has plagued human affairs. Yet the long-term consequences of the separatist or nationalist impulses of American blacks, particularly as the society continues to demonstrate an inability to face acute problems and particularly as blacks feel driven to disrespect "law and order" —that is, the boundaries white society lays down for them —could be a hardening of blind race hatred and the eventual emergence of a yet more vicious white racism and accompanying black racism.

This possibility becomes even more foreboding when, stepping away from the black movement per se, one glances at the general societal situation, particularly as it affects the current election campaign. What is observable is increasing fragmentation. American society looks like an array of disconnected groups, each struggling with "its" problems, each increasingly angered by the imposition of "others'" problems. As this tendency escalates, the capacity to resolve any problem weakens (for no one difficulty in the society is in fact disconnected from any other), and a general political malaise intensifies. The fabric of American life, in short, is simply coming apart.

Recent electoral history demonstrates this. The 1964 election, a Johnson landslide, obscured but did not bury these tendencies. The Goldwater "movement" and candidacy was unlike previous campaigns within or by a major political party in the United States. Born in the suburb-cities of the New West, Goldwaterism was largely a rebellion against "sameness," that is, the relative lack of sharp class differentiation previously characteristic of that part of American society above the poverty level. It responded to discontent among the middle- and upper-middle classes with a style of life that did not produce traditional status rewards. The Goldwater campaign therefore followed ideological patterns relatively novel in American politics: voting blocs were built around an inner core of the already persuaded; individuals and groups with apparently similar discontents were appealed to; and an effort was made to build an alliance among professionals who no longer felt the status gratifications of their antecedents, the relatively well-to-do among the retired, the new rich and the young, struggling middle-class families. Above all, little energy was wasted on pulling together the typical American electoral alliance, which cuts across as many lines as possible. Fragmentation was treated as inevitable *and* desirable, given the widely proclaimed loss of traditional values. The plan worked well enough among the believers, it developed strong support among those who attributed the rise of blacks to big government, it gave Goldwater and the Republicans the South, but otherwise produced what appeared to be a crushing defeat.

In 1968, the third party Wallace candidacy produced a sometimes overlapping but essentially different constituency. Wallace spoke (and speaks) directly to those who fear the blacks, who equate their rise with decisions of the Supreme Court and the bureaucracy, who associate the tensions in the society with the fat cats in government and business and with radicals on the campus. He appeals to the many who can barely conceal their rage, as he put it in 1968, at the "smart folks who look down their noses at you and me." He can thus, with plain talk that is strikingly different from the flabby rhetoric of most other politicians, appeal to rural Southern voters, to lower-middle-class concerns over schooling, high prices and heavy taxes, and to laborers who might be willing to concede "equal education" to blacks but who resent bitterly their presence on welfare rolls and accept them neither as neighbors nor as competitors for jobs. He addresses himself, in sum, to the sense of societal stasis and degeneration manifest in the anger of the lower and lower-middle classes, and he does so with obvious success—10 million votes in 1968 and a possibly serious threat to the Democratic Party in 1972.

The 1968 anti-war movement was yet another exercise in fragmentation, representing disenchanted youngsters, mostly white and largely of middle-class background allied with an assortment of academic and other middle-class allies. While this group found itself shut out of or chose to remove itself, at least in part, from the 1968 election, and while its core issue, the war, is less viable, it was also a protest against the banality and injustices of the great society. And the McCarthy campaign in important respects followed tactics similar to those of Goldwater and Wallace. No alliances or concessions were to be made to "hard hats" or, for that matter, to blacks. There is good reason to believe that disenchantment persists and that a reasonable percentage of new young voters feel similarly, though thus far at least this group is divided and without a candidate in 1972.

If the new black movement is added into the mixture, the possibilities are obvious. The electoral strategy adopted at Gary is entirely negative. Democrats will either learn to give blacks their due or black voters will be urged to sit on their hands. Republicans may be appealed to if the Democrats fail, but realistically that threat means little. Furthermore, the decision to endorse no candidate, not even Shirley Chisholm, makes it certain that her constituency at the Democratic convention will consist exclusively of uncommitted black delegates.

**Overlooked is the possibility that even the Gary leadership cannot deliver the black votes. Overlooked is the** opportunity to come to Miami with an organized black delegation armed with platform proposals and candidate. But what other strategy fits a perspective that regards Humphrey, Wallace and Nixon—momentarily the strongest Presidential possibilities—as identical by virtue of their "whiteness"? Ironically, that conviction plays directly into Wallace's hands, as the Florida primary suggests. While he may well wind up with enough votes, or at least enough "prestige" to create havoc at the Democratic convention, the new black political movement has apparently decided to arrive there as an interested bystander.

That may be what the disenchanted in the United States would like to see. However, those who fear a move to the right, and who suspect that Wallace victories in Democratic primaries will make only less likely any Republican disposition to offer blacks and other disenfranchised groups more than empty gestures, have good reason to be anxious. And everyone must wonder when good liberals will take any of these tensions seriously, when they will concede that this is not the best of all possible worlds and begin to address themselves to the legitimate complaints, and they are many, of each of these groups.

In any event, the new black baby is going to be very busy indeed. While many whites, in spite of what some blacks believe, wish it well and even wonder how they can help, others will watch in contempt and fear. The ultimate irony is that blacks, who have been the victims of a cruel racism, will now also feel the burden of monitoring and attenuating that racism—lest they become the victims of a violent black/white confrontation. But that kind of responsibility is, after all, what authentic political movements seek to achieve. And it was a political movement, however immature, that finally came together in Gary.

# WALKING THE WAY OF THE WASP

## By James Olthuis

An eerie quiet hovers over the land. No longer does every day generate another student riot of protest. And black rhetoric seems to have mellowed along with the militancy it fostered. Some of us are even pretending to do business as usual — as if the American ship of state has again weathered the most recent storm. Perhaps a new era of peaceful domesticity is just around the corner.

Let us not fool ourselves. The quiet on the North American front is eerie — it is foreboding. It is calm without serenity; the pause before the bomb bursts. Black-white confrontation in America is still as explosive as it ever was. Absence of present smoke does not cancel out the threat of future fires. Since the basic contours of the racial landscape remain unchanged, all the elements for outright racial conflagration are still in the kindling stage. It is only a matter of moments, days, perhaps months before the flames of ever greater holocausts engulf us.

In these days or months of respite we cannot afford to sit idly by, nurturing the false hope that the worst is past. The reprieve must be used for profound reflection on the fundamental issues involved in the situation.

### The future course is uncharted

In times of trouble and transition it is difficult to tell time. New clocks are in the process of construction. The clocks of the past have a habit of running too

VANGUARD, July/August, 1971, 7 ff.

slow or too fast in the present. This makes it impossible to pinpoint precisely where black-white relations are today.

This unnerves us; it makes us uneasy — far too uneasy I believe. What should strike us cold — and does not as we lose ourselves in trying to time immediacies — is the general temper and direction of these relations. About this there can be little doubt. The exact time nobody knows, but even the blind and deaf know the hour is late and the road of black-white relations is increasingly rocky and potholed.

Blacks and whites are now entering critical uncharted stretches of the road. The romantic stage à la Booker T. Washington is past; the assimilation section of the NAACP and the National Urban League has been travelled; the non-violent miles of Martin Luther King et al have passed under foot. Even the "black is beautiful" nationalistic strip appears to have ended. What is ahead?

### Black-white confrontation in world perspective

But we are getting ahead of ourselves. It is first necessary to go back and place the whole matter of black-white racial confrontation in the U.S.A. in world perspective. Generally speaking the history of the non-white races has been a history of white exploitation. Today the non-white races are overwhelmed by common problems of poverty, ignorance, disease and usually political instability. These non-racial factors tie together the Asian yellow race, the South American brown people, and the African black people into what has become known as the "Third World." These non-white peoples, who comprise more than 80% of the world's population, watch the white man feed his pets sophisticated, scientific meat diets — while their own people suffer malnutrition and slowly die. They observe that the white race enjoys 75% of the world's circulating wealth. They remember that the white race has exploited their wealth, dragged them through two world wars, and is threatening them with a third.

It is this convergence of non-racial factors with the racial which complicates the issue dangerously, and which as we shall see, makes the matter of black-white confrontation much more than racial. Racial tensions have distinct international dimensions. The third-world non-white races are frustrated, and their frustration has grown into anger and indignation. Aside from their own intramural conflicts (in themselves also often tragically based on matters of race), they unanimously conclude that the white man has had his day. They must take over and redirect civilization.

In this desperate international situation there is one group of people who have a unique place. They form the bridge between Africa and the West. They are the non-whites who could with the greatest degree of authority speak for the white race. They have their ethnic roots in Africa, but they are also an authentic segment of American society. Our relationship to this community will in all likelihood play a crucial role not only in America, but in the history of the world. I refer of course to the American Black community.

## In the United States

When American industry mobilized during World War II, the glow of the Northern blast furnaces was like a pillar of fire in the sky. Thousands of southern blacks left for the Promised Land. Industry was somewhat prepared; the cities were not. Ghettos developed. Soon after the war, the black man discovered that the North was not Canaan — but only another exit to more homeless wandering. Everything in the ghetto reminded him that he was not a full-fledged citizen.

Meanwhile his distant blood brothers were finding their place in the world and were sending their ambassadors to the United Nations. However, since the American black man was still homeless, he did not as a rule attempt to bridge the West and the developing nations. Instead, he increasingly identified himself with the aspirations of the struggling nations. In so doing the American civil rights movement became a part of the global revolution of the Third World.

In other words, insofar as White America has meaningful relationships with Black America, insofar can she meaningfully relate to the non-white peoples of the world. This situation makes it all the more serious that white-black relations in America are on such a low level. It would appear that through a combination of ignorance, indifference, not to speak of prejudice, and unwillingness, White America is fast undermining her position of world leadership. For the fact is that she seldom deals Christianly, that is, according to the Biblical norms of justice and love, with her black compatriots.

Daily, it is fair to say, the chasm between black and white grows. "Every three years Whitey strikes and threatens violence to get higher wages," cries the black. "Violence and money are the

139

only languages the white man understands. Violence is as American as cherry pie and we're catching on. The white man is getting the message, but he doesn't like it. He preaches law and order — it's a real laugh — in order to protect his economic interests and continue to exploit us."

Bewildered White America cries, "What's eating the Negroes anyway? They've never had it so good. It must be the work of Communists. We just have to keep the Negro in place; he obviously cannot be trusted."

Despite the growth and success of the civil rights movement as such, the Black situation is deteriorating. As Kenneth Clark puts it in *The Dark Ghetto* (p. 34), "The Negro has been left out of the swelling prosperity and social program of the nation as a whole." The Black is sensing, certainly his more articulate leaders are proclaiming, that although he is constitutionally free, he is still in more important ways a slave. He is still under the hegemony of white-dominated structures. He still must fit in or starve. The law has only been oppression for him, yet he is told that he must obey or be punished. The same law has been unable to make good its written pledges of equality in employment, education, housing, or even simple protection. Whereas the white man preaches law and order to the rioters, it is not only the rioters who are law breakers. The white community, we, in resisting implementation of relevant legislation are just as guilty. "Negroes today are in worse economic shape, live in worse slums, and attend more highly segregated schools than in 1954," so said the black moderate leader Bayard Rustin in 1966. The day to day existence of the ghetto Negro has not been improved by the various juridical and legislative measures of the past decade. Economic deprivation is still a reality.

The economic control strings run from the white man's hands through all strata of ghetto society right to its garbage cans.

## Black goals are shifting

The present struggle is no longer a battle for civil rights, but the more difficult matter of socio-economic and political conditions and more basically of religious, moral attitudes. The riots of the past years were not simply race riots: they were the aggressive explosions of the "have-not" class in an affluent society. The riots took on the macabre form they did because in an increasingly disastrous way the "have-nots" and the "black race" are converging.

The black goal has shifted from racial integration to economic and cultural independence.

This motive has crystallized especially in the Black Power movement. No longer do the blacks desire to be imitation, carbon-copy whites. No longer are they impressed by white do-gooders who wish to ease their moral guilt for past crimes — without a change of heart.

The veils of illusion — education, litigation, integration — have been ripped away. These "solutions" proved only to touch the fringes of the problems. There are deeper structural problems besetting America. The Black Panther ideology, nondescript and obscure as it is in some ways, nevertheless serves today to bind together white as well as black radicals in initial efforts to restructure American society pluralistically and in the process to replace capitalism with socialism.

## The American Proposition

This evolving problematics, whether we like it or not, has pointed out the extreme superficiality of the usual approaches to the race problem. Not only does the average white American have a non-Christian, immoral, condescending, bordering on racist attitude towards the black, but he tends to see the problem of black-white relations largely in terms of interrupting business, shattering peace, protecting his family and preventing future riots. All of us are indebted to the blacks for revealing the fatuity of such analyses.

There are deep structural problems involved in the American Experiment. In fact, the present complex of events reveals as never before a basic contradiction or antinomy in the American proposition "that all men are created equal, that they are endowed by their creator with certain unalienable rights, that among these are life, liberty and the pursuit of happiness." The assumption is that the American community is founded on and centered in the supposed commonness of Reason. In this view everyone is reason in his core, and in this sense, free and equal. A man can be a *free* individual and at the same time an equal member of the American community because everyone without exception is reasonable.

However, this view of man is schizophrenic. It suffers from a split-personality: "free" is Dr. Jekyll and "equal" is Mr. Hyde. The two concepts free and equal are unalterably opposed to one another, even as they are inexorably tied to one another. On the one hand, the concepts negate each other. If everyone is free, anarchy results. To fend off anarchy, it is necessary to deny the equality of all men: the privileged few are the self-appointed elite who set up rules; the remainder are the masses who obey the rules. If everyone is considered equal in the usual sense of similarity or even sameness, there is a levelling process which restricts individual freedom and self-expression. On the other hand, the concepts depend on each other. Since there is no Biblical awareness of sin, freedom cannot be conceived as freedom from the power of sin; in terms of this situation it must be freedom from levelling, freedom-negating equality. Similarly, equality means nothing in this context unless there is the possibility of inequality, of being free.

Due to the inherent tensions in this humanistic mould in which the American constitution was poured, it is not surprising but rather to be expected that all men in the American experience are not in fact free and equal. Rather, an "elite" group comes to power and determines how everyone is allowed to be free and equal. The result has been called *the* American Way of Life. In reality it is only the way of life of a certain faith-community, a faith-community which is in power and which acts as if its vision is normative for all. This group absolves itself from accounting for its way of life by pretending as if it were the common, neutral, possession of every American. This is a bald untruth. What passes as *the* Community, as the American Way of Life, is really the ideals and values of the White-Anglo-Saxon-Protestants, the W A S P S. (*Time Magazine* of Jan. 17, 1969 had an interesting essay in this connection entitled: "Are the WASPS coming back? Have they been away?")

This levelling tendency which characterizes the American way of life, that is, the attempt to forget basic differences of faith in the central areas of human culture, must come to our attention in spite of its complexity because of the light it sheds on the problem at issue. The American melting-pot ideal, the trend to colorless uniformity, explains as simply as possible why the separate-but-equal principle is unjust in the United States. According to the WASP-formed American Way of Life there must be one monolithic community. Not to be part of that community is something less than desirable, it is anti-normative, sub-standard and abnormal. To be separated from *the* community is to be second-class.

## Assimilation — not integration

This melting-pot ideal which characterizes the American Way of Life also explains what integration has meant. In simple terms it implies that the black man must become a carbon-copy of the white man. Integration is actually a misnomer for this situation. As practised and taught in the USA, integration has been in fact assimilation. Blacks are to be absorbed into a supposedly color-blind society. This is the kind of integration which is the goal of both liberal white organizations and black organizations such as NAACP and the National Urban League.

Inasmuch as possible the differences between races are played down as being negligible and of little importance. The white man, it is true, must in this view give up his prejudice—but the black man is asked to give up his identity and integrity as a black man. In the assimilation view of integration—the view characteristic of the USA and of most Christians—it is the WASP stereotype which serves as norm. Thus, anxious to integrate, many Negroes are in a panic to straighten their hair, to bleach their dark color, and even to thin their nostrils. Each year a few blacks toe the white line, move into white neighborhoods, and live undetected as blacks in a white world. They have become imitation whites; they have been "integrated;" but in the process they have denied their culture and history and lost even more of their identity and heritage.

The integration of the races must proceed towards a "new type of society," as Whitney Young stated it in *To Be Equal*, combining the positive elements of both blacks and whites and eliminating the negative. The best qualities from each group will be saved. But which qualities are "best"? How does one decide? By what criterion? The qualities most useful to American society, is the usual answer. What is good for General Motors is also presumably good for the black man.

## "Black is Beautiful"

Black Power is the reactionary and inevitable response of the black man to this forced and degrading type of integration. Today the black man is fighting to regain his identity. Black is beautiful, wonderful; Black is soul. We ought not to underestimate the importance of this renewed search for identity. After all, the white man too came to America largely to preserve his religious and cultural identity. The black, on the other hand, was torn brutally out of his African motherland and borne across the Atlantic in chains. His identity, his history, culture, family life, religion, and even often his original name were blotted out. The X, for example, in Malcolm X stands for the lost, tribal name. The leading black writer, LeRoi Jones, prefers his adopted Arabic name "Ameer Baraka" along with the Swahili title "Imamu," meaning spiritual leader. Along with his adoption of the Moslem faith basketball star Lew Alcindor has also adopted a new name: Kareem Abdul Jabbar.

The barriers which white men erected against the rediscovery of black identity are only today being overcome. The black search for meaning in life, especially since it is coupled with an effort at a Black Power-New Left power alliance, has shaken American life to its roots. A right wing law-and-order backlash has emerged in reaction, and growing groups of white Americans are also engaging in renewed searches for meaning and relevance.

I have been told that along 47th Street on Chicago's South Side the going prices for men's clothes are outrageous: an ordinary pair of shoes, $35; a short-sleeved knit shirt, $20, etc. Yet, the blacks are willing to pay such prices, even though they can go downtown and buy the same item at a fraction of the cost in the chain stores. For the black man wearing a new suit of clothes or a new pair of shoes is one means by which he can convince himself that he is still a man. He pays the high prices because he can buy, for example, $150 worth of merchandise on the credit of his $50 a week pay cheque. This he cannot do downtown. By the end of the year the clothes have no doubt cost another $100, but the search for self-respect is so desperate that he is unable to think of the future.

We have now seen some of the background for the Black Power movement. In reaction to the white demand that the black act as if he is colorless (as if black is any more a color than white!), the black is intent today on emphasizing the difference, and the beauty of the difference. Consequently, since assimilation type integration is not a real answer, various black leaders have openly advocated segregation, the development of separate black kingdoms within America. Others push for an open pluralistic society in which blacks have their own place alongside other ethnic groupings. Again there are others who call for a complete abolition of the capitalistic system and the introduction of socialism.

### The unity of mankind in Christ

What should be the Christian community's reaction? What should we do?

The Christian community finds its direction and its perspective in the Scriptures. There is one Word of God calling to obedience, there is one creation subject to the Word, and one mankind entrusted with ruling the world in the Lord's name.

This fundamental unity of the human race is not a colorless uniformity, either all black or all white, but a unity in diversity (all the colors in the rainbow). Christ is the Root of the New Humanity, in Him there is no black and white, male or female. Before Christ and in Christ mankind, all of mankind, are equal and can be free. In Christ these terms receive their basic meaning.

As parts of the One Body of Christ, each member is to show how great it is to obey the laws of the Lord. But each member does this in its own way: each member has a diversified task even as it serves the Body as a whole. Individuals, groups, races and nations must in accord with their own gifts, culture, history and land, work out their salvation in obedience to the Word of God. The diversity enriches the unity, and the unity gives purpose and direction to the diversity.

A Christian must, therefore, accept all men as fellow human beings, and treat them with the respect, concern and love which fellow image-bearers of the Lord deserve. This concern and love must be motivated by the knowledge that all men need to be re-created in the image of the Son. There is clearly a major line of division, of demarcation, in the world. But it is not that of black-white, or even that of "have not's"-"haves," or oppressed-oppressor. The opposition in life, the antithesis, is between the Kingdom of Light centered in Jesus Christ and the Kingdom of Darkness championed by Satan. In the end all that counts is whether we are co-workers with Christ in the ministry of world reconcilation, or are agents of the Devil living the Lie. The all-encompassing distinction is between obedience to the

Word and disobedience to the Word.

All other distinctions, in spite of their importance, are relative. They only find meaning in the context of obedience-disobedience and may never be granted absolute status. Difference in color is real and is not to be overlooked. But, not only is this difference virtually the least of all considerations in any situation, it loses all significance when examined in full scope of the Kingdom of God. Before God and his people, it is not race or color or whatever, but the actions which flow from the heart which are judged.

All men, whatever their color or pedigree, are equal before the Lord. No race is inherently inferior or superior to any other. We are to do good to all men; and thus also to the black, red and white. The way we do good depends on the nature and type of relationship pertaining at the moment. It depends, to put it simply but perhaps helpfully, in which "room" in God's creation one is.

Since the Word of God is a multi-dimensioned unity, obedience to the Word in the heart involves obedience to the Word in all its dimensions. Bowing before the Word leads one to obey every word of the Lord. One acts, regardless of the color of the persons involved, in accord with the particular word of God which norms and structures the "room" or sphere in question, in accord with the structural norm of the various life-zones—state, church, school, family, marriage, industry, friendship, art, music, etc. A person is always treated as a person; dependent on the situation he is treated as a fellow worker, a friend, a fellow citizen, a classmate, a fellow worshipper and so on. Skin pigmentation is one of the last considerations if not *the* last consideration, which enters in.

## Racism

Racism is basically the attempt to supplant the antithesis between obedience and disobedience with the black-white or some other racial contrast. Racism is an "ism," exaggeration or absolutization of the matter of race. And as happens wherever a relative thing is made absolute, everything else becomes distorted. This means the loss of true perspective.

Racist doctrine judges mankind according to hereditary bio-physical characteristics (shape of head, color of skin, nose form, hair texture, color of eyes, etc.) instead of according to whether there is Obedience or Disobedience to the Word of the Lord. Racism is a false religion; it is essentially a pretentious way of saying, "I belong to the Elect, you don't."

Our rejection of racism as such implies that not only white racism but also black racism is to be condemned. The danger inherent in the Black Power movement is not in its fight for black dignity, integrity and identity as such, but in its tendency to accomplish this within a racist framework of reference. Caught within this un-Biblical framework, black identity can only be asserted at the expense of the White. Black Power is white racism—in reverse. And in this context it too must be condemned.

But here, too, it is really impossible to blame the black man. He is just catching on to the American game, a game we Christians have played just as well, although usually not as successfully, as our non-Christian neighbors. We have taught him that the majority is assumed to be right, and can lord it over minorities. We have taught him to consider the dollar almighty and all persuasive here below (the Christians among us at the same time paying lip service to some "private" almighty God above). We have condoned a society in which basic faith differences are regarded as matters of private concern, in which making money and consuming what money can purchase are the highest values (in practice, if not in theory). We have let the black know unmistakably that we are on top, and that on the top we enjoy the good life which he can only envy, out of reach, on the TV screen. Is it any wonder that the black man wants to taste, rather than only drool?

The difficulty is not simply white or black racism. As we have already noticed, it lies much deeper. The American way of life which encourages such developments must be critiqued.

### Assimilation too is wrong

The Christian community must not only reject racism and its concomitant segregation, but also the assimilation or homogenized view of integration which is customarily championed. As we already noted, this type of integration is also based on the humanistic myth of the great American community. The goal is not the integration of the black race, but the absorption of the black race into a homogenous, bland, uniform amalgam. Is it right to assume that the characteristics of the WASP establishment should be the supreme criterion for the give and take of integration? One should even go farther: What about the legitimacy of elevating the WASP-way-of-looking-at-things to the norm by which all other faith communities, black as well as white, must live? And now we are close to the heart of the problem. The blacks are not the only second-class citizens in the United States. Any faith community, be it Jewish, Catholic, agnostic or Christian, which does not buy the WASPish model is discriminated against. This is because the Way of the WASPS has been elevated to the place where it now is supposed to hold for all Americans regardless of their cardinal beliefs. For example: the American Way (read: the Way of the WASP) recognizes only one public school system. Citizens who wish to educate their children in a way that differs from the way of the WASPS are not free and equal. They have to support the American school and at the same time finance their own schools. And all who in spite of the pressures still seek to educate their children in accord with their own beliefs are further accused of being unpatriotic and dividing the nation. Example two: Operating on the unproven assumption that every American basically agrees as to the direction of life, the American way knows only two main political wings: the fast (Democrat) and the slow (Republican). These in turn divide up into the fast-fast, the fast-slow, the slow-fast, the slow-slow, etc. Any real difference of opinion is simply not entertained.

In actual fact the matter of color has been used as a convenient scapegoat to hide this appalling state of affairs. But, as we have already seen, the blacks themselves have pointed out to all who can see that there are basic inequalities built into the American system. Discrimination on the basis of color can only really be solved when attention is paid to all forms of discrimination.

There is no one homogenous community in America. This is the great American myth. To anyone who looks at all beneath the surface veneer, it is clear that America is in reality a society composed of many differing faith-communities. When told to integrate into white society, the blacks could rightly ask: into which group of white Americans, the WASPS?, the Italian-Americans?, the Jewish-Americans, the Polish-Americans? etc.

Integration as assimilation ought to be

rejected by the Christian community. In spite of its high sound, it enables the white American, especially the WASP, to retain his superiority. It assumes that white is not a color, and that a colorless society is a white society. This view reeks of white hypocrisy. In such a situation, in which blackness is regarded as an economic, physical and moral burden, "integration" is as degrading and as God-dishonoring as segregation. There is no recognition of the fact that God has so ordained that races of mankind must in their own way, with their own unique talents, gifts and history, show forth the glory of God. God desires a symphonic poem of praise, not monotonous prose.

The black race has its own unique contribution to make to the Kingdom of the Lord. But in order to do this the black community must rediscover its individual and communal identity. Without such a sense of pride in themselves as blacks, they will be unable to contribute meaningfully to the welfare of the American nation. Without such self-consciousness they will continue to be a drag on the nation, and will never develop into responsible citizens. America should not try to assimilate or absorb the black man — this is impossible in any event—but encourage him to recover his identity. For the other side of the coin of identity is responsibility. The white man often stands aghast at the lack of responsibility shown by the black race, often forgetting that the mark of inferiority which he has engrained on the black is not conducive to exercise of personal responsibility. Recovery of identity will simultaneously lead to a recovery of a sense of responsibility. This is the first step towards a healthy integration. True integration can only take place when the parties involved integrate without loss of individual or communal identity.

Just as the arm belongs to the body as much as the leg, so the various races belong to Mankind. Just as all the members have a common task to serve the body as a whole, but then as arm or leg or eye, so each race, in its own way, must serve the Body of Christ as a whole and is part of the Body of Christ. This is integration. It is as wrong to sever the arm or the leg (segregation) as it is to desire to make all arms into legs (assimilation). Integration as assimilation (artficial unity denying diversity) is just as wrong as segregation (isolation for the wrong reasons).

**Integration requires identity**

A Biblically-alive view of integration is a process of interweaving of different structures and of various societal relations, each having its own structure, without loss of identity. There is no erasure of structures, boundaries, races or colors, but a growing consciousness that the different "elements" or "members" with their diverse make-ups together have a common purpose and together form one kingdom. Integration and segregation are not to be played off against each other in the customary way. Rather, even as the various structures interweave or integrate, life within these structures can take on more individual character in accord with the diversity of gifts, races, etc. of the people concerned. Integration takes place without a loss of identity; indeed the diverse structures come into their own more and more as history unfolds.

*Integration without loss of identity,* racial integration as well as political, economic, social and moral, must be seen as a norm of obedience which will usher in the Coming Kingdom.

At this moment the fight should not be for the abolition of the black community through a false ideology of assimilation, nor for the isolation of the black community in ghettoes or even kingdoms, but for its cultural and socio-economic rehabilitation. In this way the blacks, along with other ethnic groups, can take their own responsible place in the building of the nation. The question is how the black race granted its civil rights can make use of its unique qualities for the welfare of the American nation. In broader perspective: how can our society be rescued from its false belief in the one American community, a belief which excommunicates all Americans who do not adhere to this ideology? How can our society be made more liveable and more just for all regardless of color, race, or creed?

**The Crisis**

Must the black continue to seek assimilation into mainstream America? This is not only difficult (one cannot shake his culture, skin or belief); it is downright degrading. One point is becoming increasingly clear: it is illusory for Americans to close their eyes and canonize the American way of life. The melting-pot is at best a bland least-common denominator potpourri, a hodge-podge without a real pinch of strength or cummin of conviction.

Must we have black supremacy then? That would be just as bad as white supremacy. And as it would mean about 11% of the people ruling 89%, it appears unrealistic.

What about black separation? In the America of today, this would always mean inequality and thus would be unsatisfactory.

What then?

Today the black man stands at the crossroads, just as he did after slavery was abolished, and he must choose. The choices are impossible, yet he must choose. Black militants and black moderates are urging the black masses to choose, respectively, for their positions. Will the black masses decide for assimilation or for black supremacy?

Upon their decision — and that is terrifying — upon the decision of poorly educated, oppressed blacks rests the question whether our country will be cast into a second civil war or not. What choice will they make, can they make? Need I say that it seems that more and more would rather die fighting for their cause rather than succumb any longer to white exploitation?

**A New America must be born!**

Before it is too late, and with the help of God, let us raise a Christian voice. Let us present black and white alike with an option, a viable option, which will work for the good of all men. Stokely Carmichael has gone on record as stating that for "racism to die, a totally new America must be born." ("What We Want", *The New York Review of Books*, Sept. 22, 1966, p. 6). He is absolutely right. Only he does not know that his position is only another variety, be it colored, of Humanism — and Humanism already has America within its clutches. A new America can only be brought in by the total commitment of Christ-believers who are not willing to relegate their faith commitment to the private, inner chamber, but who work so that all of society can be structured according to the demands of the all-encompassing Kingdom of God.

**Needed: structural pluralization**

A Christian approach to the race problem demands a Christian view of society. North American society must first be reformed, restructured along Biblical lines before the major issues of our day can be solved, including the matter of black-white confrontation.

Humanism has a levelled view of society. This is also true in the United States. The democratic way of life is only pluralistic in the realm of grace, church, the sacred, and private. In

147

every other area of life America purports to be one monolithic community. However, it is not as Americans, also unfortunately most Christian Americans, assume, that pluralism is undesirable, unhealthy and dangerous in all the so-called natural regions of life. Recognizing that a man's heart commitment guides his every life expression, and recognizing that there are diverse spheres or rooms in the Lord's creation none of which have the authority to rule it over the others (such totalitarian authority is the Lord's), society ought to be structured pluralistically. The various faith communities ought to be free to work out their faith in all the areas of society according to the nature of the area involved.

American Humanism in elevating democracy as a political conception to an all-encompassing pseudo-Kingdom of **God consequently does injustice to the** various differently structured segments of society.

A Christian view of society, which we can only mention here, but which will no doubt receive much attention in the VANGUARD, would work to the healing of the nation as a whole. In such a view the state as the universal integrator of public justice would recognize and guarantee the equal civil rights of all citizens regardless of color. The state, however, always acts as state, as a public legal community, and does not interfere with other societal associations except insofar as public justice is concerned. It must see to it that all obstacles in the way of a free exercise of God-given rights are removed; in this way public justice is served. The state cannot discriminate in favor of any faith-community. All barriers to interracial marriages must be prohibited. Black education must be upgraded.

At the same time it is necessary to build up the black view of marriage and the family. The disintegration of black families is also largely due to white masters outlawing any real kind of family life. Often slaves could not even have last names. Since mother raised the family, the matriarchal family has been carried over to the black community even today.

Another factor abetting the situation is the high rate of unemployment among black men. Black women can more easily find work — usually in the traditional role as domestic servant.

Until there comes a pluralist restructuration — and this demands basic changes — North America will never know integration in the true sense of the word. It will always be caught in the ricochet between separatism and assimilation.

Without a structural pluralism which allows every faith community its identity even as it pools resources with other communities in certain common projects, it is impossible for the various existent faith groupings to play their integrated role in North American life.

As long as the WASP mentality is granted superior status in America, so long must every other way of looking at things be considered second-rate. And as being "white" is part and parcel of being a WASP, no matter how zealously the government guarantees the civil liberties of every citizen, everyone who is not white, everyone who is not WASPish is simply second-class, inferior. Such persons or communities must constantly guard themselves against being co-opted or assimilated by the establishment, and at the same time they can only separate or oppose at the threat of persecution and even expulsion. That, starkly put, is the present unhappy situation.

Today it is necessary from the Christian point of view to point the black man as well the white man to the various "rooms" which make up creation. The rehabilitation of the black must not take place individualistically — by large government hand-outs to individual persons. Rather, in every area of society the black man should see the peculiar structure of freedom and authority which holds, and he must be taught how to live in accord with the demands of the various rooms.

Every man regardless of race or color, must be taught that only in Christ can he escape his slave-status and be truly "free." And that obedience to the demands of the various "rooms" is not obedience first of all to any human authority but to the only King and High Priest Jesus Christ — who died that all men might be free.

Any view of integration, even if it begins from the unity of the human race, is bound to fail if this unity is conceived outside of a common submission to the Word of the Lord. Only in Christ does a man come to know himself integrally. Only in Christ is mankind able to experience its unity and oneness. Only in Christ is there no male or female, black or white. . . . This is the message Christ-confessors must live today.

### Two Kingdoms and three Worlds

*There is only one history of the world. That is the history of the tension and antithesis between the City of God and the City of Man as cultures march and unfold throughout time.* Remarkably enough, Yahweh has chosen to accomplish His purposes through a "chosen People", a "new humanity", "His Body". But His People have to *know* that they are a People, a flesh-and-blood bound and gathered People, owing allegiance to One Lord (not many). His People must *know* they are called to one battle in three worlds.

Brotherhood of Radical Christians. The flow of "religious expertise" is a one-way flow, unless we invite some Third World choir or speaker to North America for propaganda purposes (our mission society is doing a fine job, isn't it?) In the dust-and-ashes of our sin, we must repent of misdirecting the cosmos, of offering the Third World only Coca-Cola when we should have offered them the explosive new wine of Jesus Christ. **One Lord: toward the expulsion of all fake gods from our life together in Christ.**

Another impelling theme in the Scrip-

# where are the christians hiding ?

A communal position paper by students of the international Institute for Christian Studies.

**One People: towards an international brotherhood of radical Christians**

Seldom have we met face to face as strugglers in the common task of subjecting all things to Jesus Christ. A smugness has pervaded our missionary labours overseas and we have served up racist pap in our missionary propaganda films that would make Kipling feel quite happy. There exist only Japanese Christians, African Christians, American Christians but no International

tures is that Yahweh's People constantly forget that they are called to serve ONE God with an undivided heart; that they have ONE Lord, not many. The struggle for Canaan (see Judges) is illustrative of this fundamental theme: Yahweh versus Baal, or, will God's People divide their allegiance between Yahweh (He is a great help in military crises) and Baal (he is a great help in agricultural production). But the People must be gathered; they must hear the Word of God as One Man, expose the false spirits and then

INSIDE, March, 1971, 18-21.

get busy together — holding hands, standing side by side, building a Nehemiah wall, symbol of God's presence and the People's unity on earth, not in heaven.

This is also the fundamental message of the New Testament: that Jesus Christ is the Lord of *all* of culture, and that His People are called to witness as a People (1 Peter, 1 Corinthians, Ephesians) to the Word of God which holds for all of creation; that the "new humanity" should be an International Brotherhood of Radical Christians who cannot have any depth-level religious fellowship with Baal (11 Cor. 6: 14-18).

But we, as God's International Brotherhood, have served racist gods, nationalistic gods, rationalistic gods in our theoretical lives, capitalistic or socialistic gods in our economic lives, pragmatic gods in politics (why is there no distinctive *Christian* politics in the US?), moralistic gods in our personal lives and ascetic gods in our churchly lives. We have become a Sunday-gathering collection of monads and a Monday-scattering and secularly-absorbed non-Peoplehood. We are in bondage throughout the three worlds. Who will deliver our imprisoned in Communist countries, our despised in Islamic countries, our ignored in Europe and North America?

**One Struggle in Three worlds: towards a genuine Christian contribution to the needs of all mankind.**

The modern mission era is over. It is dying in our preoccupation with techniques of evangelism. Hovering over the gigantic attempts to rally interest in "missions" at the World Congress of Evangelism and other satellite congresses in the US, West Africa, Asia, and Canada is the smell of death. Evangelism has been reduced to the *verbalizing* of a codified message and the primary concern of "Missions" has become a technical one, how to maximize the efficiency of the church and sustain her growth through the utilization of all the media possible such as art, film, public parades, cell groups, door-to-door visitation, etc. *The fundamental purpose that the churches in North America serve is to socialize their adherents into the American Way of Death. But where there is a commitment to Jesus Christ, a speck of light remains. Only a speck of light, because as soon as the individuals leave the doors of their churches they scatter in order to exercise a "moral" influence.* But our "moral" influence doesn't make a bit of difference and merely oils the Christ-hating System!

More and more secularization is correlative with more and more revival meetings. Evangelism-in-Depth doesn't go very deep and the public mass demonstrations are hollow, be it ever so sincere, efforts in futility because in actuality Christians so gathering have absolutely no structural impact on the public sectors of life. Once the large collection of individuals, temporarily united for a "public" witness disperses, so does the "witness". This is a serious matter because the organizers of these gatherings think this is very radically Christian. It isn't. For our "witness" is peripheral to the central culture areas because we cannot believe that we are a People, and that God has called us as a People, to witness to politics as politics, education as education, economics as economics . . . Thus evangelism is a kind of last-spark effort to fire a moribund Christianity. Without a reformation more incisive than the one in the 16th century, Evangelicalism will continue to die its slow death as thousands evacuate the churches in search of wholeness, not splitness, searching for a Way that embraces the totality of man's cultural Life. *Evangelicalism drives people to other than Christian ways of life.*

The nature of our global struggle for Jesus Christ cannot be reduced to an other-worldly "soul-winning" with a bit of individualistic social concern tacked on as an afterthought (Here we are aware of the serious thinking going on in evangelical circles by men around the globe: Escobar, Dr. Frank Epp, Skinner . . .). It is only as our lives are seen as one-piece, as rooted in Jesus Christ, (Why do we always want to place ourselves outside of history?) that we can even begin to sense the *nature* and scope of our task in the world. If we *were* living integral, radically Christian lives, we would never place evangelism over against social concern for we would reject the implications and dualism *inherent* in this formulation.

We would see that evangelism can never be isolated from the total communal Life of the International Brotherhood of Radical Christians. We would not want to speak of "getting the gospel in" as if the mere announcing of a Bible verse is "witness". *We would want to speak of "evangelism" as the magnetic Life-Way of a People who are compellingly attractive because they are engaged as a Shalom-bringing People in politics, education, economics, the arts . . . engaged in everything as a distinctive People, drunk on the New Wine of Jesus Christ!* This means that the Inter-national Peoplehood would be engaged as an independent force in the state-life of their particular countries, a radical vanguard prophetically subverting (where necessary) an anti-normative and justice-excluding. and pragmatic political system, calling men to obey God's norm for the state.

### Vanguard in three Worlds

In the "First World" (the US and Canada), *our basic fight is for a structurally pluralistic society*, i.e., a society that allows the various religious communities to express the totality of their Way in every part of culture. That this is not happening in the US and Canada is obvious! *Where are the millions of Christians hiding?* If God's International Peoplehood were witnessing-as-a-community in this manner, it would mean that *Christians would be known not as reactionaries, as racists, as other-worldly-oriented people, as Birchers, as Nixon-ites, as Capitalists, or as Socialists, but as "Christians."*

We must see the International Peoplehood as *the* vanguard in the three worlds. As an International Brotherhood of Radical Christians we would be an independent culture-forming religion "competing" in the global marketplace alongside other Visions — Americanism and Marxism or some "Mix". Home and foreign missions would disappear as categories and instead we would see the world in terms of two kingdoms. We would see ourselves as a global Peoplehood battling the forces of darkness in all societies, in all nations. And, by the grace of God, we would be able to "speak" to the "wretched of the earth", for we would have earned that right— as Paul did—by performing our earthshaking task: upsetting kings and governments, economic orders based on idolatry, false philosophies. We would be known as the "offscouring" of the earth, a lowly, loving, joyous, suffering, and subversive People.

### The battle rages on

The battles for the direction of the three worlds are being fought most intensively in the universities. Here the radical Christians' struggle is three-fold (1) To create a Christian mind among Evangelicals (2) To create parallel *Christian* universities where possible and to win a place within the existing public university systems for a christian infra-structure. In both ways the new wine of Jesus Christ *can explode the old structures* to fight for the "social room" to educate our children, according to our vision of God's world. If we do not, our children will be gobbled up by scientistic gods and Christianity will be strangled before it gets its cultural breath.

And, shifting to Africa, it is obvious to us that *the mission-school educated kids are getting drunk on the bad wine of the science-ideal and not on the wine of the King!* If Christians are alert they can capture the imagination of the students who are being short-changed with a humanistic learning that provides no lasting or satisfying answers to theoretical questions. And, maybe, maybe, Islamic and Buddhist students are the crack in the monolithic traditional structures. If they could only be shown that there is a distinctive Christian Way of theorizing about the cosmos! Can we not see? This is God's world! There is only one structure of reality! And Christ—our King—holds the key that unlocks its meaning!

Another important arena where one can see the contesting of the spirits is in the industrial sector. Marxist spirits are there. Numerous trade union leaders have been trained at Patrice Lumumba University in Moscow. The Marxists know where the battle is and what fronts they should be engaged on. Christians in the Third World must struggle against Marxist dominated trade unions. Christians must organize where they are not organized. This is urgent. Christians must bring the healing power of the gospel in a society with tensions between the elite and the masses, urban and rural.

If we cannot demonstrate communally what difference it makes to confess Jesus Christ for labour and business, then we are radically disobedient stewards of the creation! The Peoplehood of Christ in the US and Canada are under the judgment of God right now because we have not driven the wedge of the Word of God into the heart of the secular trade union movement and the result has been that the blue-collared man with the bucket scarcely ever darkens the door of a church or even gets offered a taste of the New Wine of Jesus Christ.

O God, we hope that there is a stirring in the ranks of those who should be your International Brotherhood! In many parts of the world a consciousness of your International Brotherhood has yet to come; in other parts it has "come" into many hearts but lies there dormant.

A new sense of hilarity in doing God's will must tingle our hearts, and push us into the swirl of life, into oneness with radical Christians everywhere.

# Government Support of Nonpublic Education: Development and Issues

JOHN   VANDENBERG

One of the most crucial domestic issues facing the citizens of the United States is the question of government support of nonpublic education. Although aspects of the question have been under discussion for many decades, surely going back to the Pierce case,[1] the current debate over the question probably began with the decision of the United States Supreme Court in the Everson case.[2]

One of the direct consequences of the decision in the Everson case was the formation of Protestants and Other Americans United for the Separation of Church and State (POAU). As the name of this organization indicates, it was established to maintain separation of church and state, and for POAU separation was to be absolute, for "any permitted encroachment, no matter how slight, upon the separation of church and state causes subsequent encroachments merely of degree, not of kind. Ultimately, there will be no wall of separation." In the field of education this meant opposition to any government aid, direct or indirect, to nonpublic education.

Protestants and Other Americans United were joined by the American Civil Liberties Union and the American Jewish Congress in opposition to government aid of nonpublic education. For almost a decade these groups were the only public voice speaking to the issue of government support of nonpublic education.[3] Very little, consequently, was accomplished by way of increasing such support.

It was not until more than a decade after the Everson case that a public voice began to be heard in support of government aid to nonpublic education. That voice was Citizens for Educational Freedom (CEF), which was

REFORMED JOURNAL, February, 1970, 9-12.

organized in St. Louis, Missouri in 1959. CEF was organized by a group of parents who were concerned with their rights to choose the kind of education they wanted for the children, without economic penality. Today CEF is composed of citizens, mostly Christian and Jewish parents and educators, who are interested in promoting the intellectual and moral development of every American child and who claim "that freedom of choice in education for parents and students is an inalienable right any infringement of which is a violation of the First and Fourteenth Amendments to the Constitution." CEF is positively dedicated to using the democratic process, including supporting friendly legislators and opposing contrary ones, in shaping legislation which will promote freedom of choice in education, either for parents or students.

In the past half dozen years other groups have organized and joined CEF in the promotion of government aid of nonpublic education. These include the National Association for Personal Rights in Education (NAPRE), a citizens group which has been active, particularly in the State of Illinois. Another citizens group, composed chiefly of members of the Reformed faith, The Christian Action Foundation, has recently begun action in Iowa, New Jersey, Illinois, and Michigan. On an institutional level the Michigan Association of Nonpublic Schools (MANS) has been very active in the past two years. It should also be noted that associations of independent colleges, particularly through their presidents, have been highly successful in some states in promoting government aid to students attending nonpublic colleges and universities.

That the proponents of government aid have been successful in moving toward their goals is evidenced by the large number of government programs supporting nonpublic education which have been passed in the last ten years, particularly within the last five.

According to a survey, dated March 5, 1969, undertaken by Dr. William A. Kramer, Secretary of Schools for the Lutheran Church (Missouri Synod), twenty-seven states provided some form of financial assistance for the education of children attending nonpublic schools. Rev. Blum, writing in *America*,[4] notes that the following benefits have been gained, mostly within the past five or six years, for students attending nonpublic schools and colleges: (1) tuition grants for college students in Wisconsin, Michigan, Illinois, and Iowa; (2) freedom-of-choice college scholarships, useable at public or nonpublic colleges, in Minnesota, Wisconsin, Michigan, and Indiana; (3) bus transportation in Wisconsin, Michigan, Ohio, Pennsylvania, New Jersey, and Ohio; (4) auxiliary services in Michigan and Ohio; (5) textbooks in New York, Pennsylvania, and Rhode Island; and (6) supplementary grants for nonpublic elementary and secondary school teachers' salaries under purchase-of-service agreements in Pennsylvania, Rhode Island, Ohio, and Connecticut.

The grants for payment of salaries of nonpublic school teachers are of particular significance, for they could lead to the payment of substantial amounts of money in support of nonpublic education. The Connecticut and Rhode Island laws provide for the payment of 20 percent and 15 percent, respectively, of the salaries of the teachers teaching secular subjects in nonpublic schools. Ohio will pay salary supplements of up to $3,000 per year to lay teachers teaching secular subjects. And Pennsylvania, the first state to pass a purchase-of-service bill (1968), allows the state to pay nonpublic schools the "actual cost" of teachers' salaries, textbooks, and teaching aids in four secular fields: mathematics, modern foreign languages, physical sciences, and physical education.[5]

Much of the legislation that has been passed in the various states is being or has been tested in the courts. Until now, however, in the judgment of this writer, no clear-cut case pertaining to government support of nonpublic education has been decided by the U. S. Supreme Court. Perhaps that decision may soon be forthcoming, for the Pennsylvania purchase-of-service bill was upheld by a panel of three federal judges and this decision has been appealed to the U. S. Supreme Court.

The Pennsylvania law was upheld (November 28, 1969) by a 2-to-1 vote of a panel of three federal judges. Judges E. Mac Troutman and Alfred Luongo of the Federal District Court said in the majority opinion that the First Amendment does not require "an absolute separation between necessarily overlapping interests in the secular education of school-age children. To require such a standard would assume that the state and religion exist in mutually exclusive and sharply defined spheres having no common material interests in the education of our youth," they ruled.[6]

Opponents of the Pennsylvania bill will appeal the decision, and since the members of the special panel hearing the case were all federal judges, the appeal will go directly to the United States Supreme Court.[7]

Before concluding this brief survey of the developments in the field of government aid to nonpublic education, two additional items should be noted. First, is the organization, in 1968, of Parents' Rights Incorporated, an organization founded to help parents obtain equal rights in education through court action, rather than through the legislative process. On November 19, 1969, in San Diego, California, a suit was filed by a group of parents seeking the protection of their civil rights by the federal courts. On November 20, 1969, a similar suit was filed in St. Louis, Missouri. In each case, parents of children attending nonpublic schools have filed suit to seek relief from discriminatory state laws that deny them any educational benefits unless their children attend the public schools.

An unusual development, announced in late December, 1969, is the funding by the Office of Economic Opportunity of a study to determine the feasibility of giving low income parents vouchers for the education of their children. According to the Associated Press release, the study will be made by the Center for the Study of Public Policy in Cambridge, Massachusetts under a $196,313 grant announced by the OEO.

The OEO envisions the planning grant leading to a five-year pilot project, funded at an annual level of $1.2 million, in a major city, yet to be selected. Under the project parents would receive a $600 voucher or tuition grant and could send their children to any school they wished, public or nonpublic, by using the voucher.

Legislative action and court decisions are not effected in a vacuum; they are the results of many variables, which, in turn, are exceedingly complex and interrelated. Two kinds of variables seem to have shaped the development of government aid to nonpublic education in the last two decades: (1) the practical, more immediate circumstances and consequences of action and (2) the theoretical or philosophical grounds for supporting or opposing such aid. Of these two the practical issues seem to have played a more significant part than the theoretical issues in determining the course of action in the field of government aid.

Four practical factors were especially important: (1) the political activity of Citizens for Educational Freedom, (2) the economic crisis in the nonpublic school systems, particularly in the Catholic school system, (3) the American preference for a pluralistic school system, rather than a monolithic system, and (4) dissatisfaction with the performance of the public schools.

Although the justness and rightness of a cause are normally a necessary condition of achieving the goals of the cause, they are not a sufficient condition. Achievement also requires effective political action and public education.[8] It was CEF that provided the leadership in developing political action, without which any discussion of government aid would be purely academic.

Despite CEF's political activities, substantial progress in obtaining government aid for nonpublic education was made only after the public and elected officials saw that the nonpublic schools were in an economic crisis. This crisis was most apparent in the decreasing enrollments in nonpublic schools.[9] The nonpublic schools were in trouble and something had to be done to save them from extinction, and that something was substantial financial assistance.

In addition to the economic crisis facing nonpublic schools there was the fact that Americans favor the continued existence of a pluralistic education system. A 1969 Gallup survey clearly reveals this preference. Thus, in reply to a question dealing with whether there should be nonpublic schools in addition to public schools in a hypothetical new community, 72 percent of the respondents answered "Yes," 23 percent "No," and 5 percent had no opinion or did not answer. The vote for nonpublic schools was even higher, 84 percent, in those communities where such schools are actually found.

The same Gallup survey also indicated that 59 percent of the respondents living in areas where nonpublic schools existed would send their children to nonpublic schools if they had the money or if their children could go tuition free. On a national level 40 percent would choose nonpublic schools given these options.

Not only was the public desirous of maintaining a pluralistic education system but there was considerable discontent with the performance of the public schools. Some critics of the public school system went so far as to say that the system should be broken up or radically changed.[10] Positively, it was argued that nonpublic schools must be supported and promoted as a means of providing competition to the public schools, and thus promote excellence in education.[11]

Government aid has developed and been discussed largely in the context of immediate, practical circumstances. Although the economic plight and the continued existence of the nonpublic schools, the dissatisfaction with the public schools, the continuation of a pluralistic system of education, and the promotion of competition in education are all important and legitimate considerations, they are not the essential ones in the issue of government aid. Rather, the fundamental issue is that of the relationship between the government and its citizens in the crucial area of forming and shaping the hearts and minds of their children. At issue is the question of whether the government may establish in the field of education the religious and philosophical views of some of its citizens over the views of other citizens. Ultimately, the question of government aid deals with the issue of religious liberty.

The logic of this position can be stated quite simply: education is compulsory and is always religiously or philosophically oriented.[12] If this is true, then the government forces children into contact with some religious or philosophical outlook on life and it has no business giving preference to one of these views over all other views. But this is precisely what happens when government support of education is confined almost entirely to the public schools, schools whose philosophy of education is unacceptable to millions of American citizens. If parents object to the education provided in the

159

state schools, they cannot simply forego having their children educated; they must either accept the state philosophy of education or provide expensive alternatives. Parents have a right to send their children to a nonpublic school but when they exercise this right they are deprived of all public educational benefits. Liberty at a price — this is not liberty. This is the suppression of liberty.

The position of the public school in American life is succinctly stated in a letter to the editor of the *Saturday Review*, appearing in the issue of December 17, 1966. Here is the letter:

> The public school today holds a position in American life similar to that held by the State Church in earlier times, in that one school system instead of one church receives favored treatment and tax support. Such an official establishment of education imposes exactly the same restrictions on the liberties of minorities as an established church. When parents are forced by law to have their children exposed to teachings that are alien and inimical to their own beliefs, it doesn't really matter to them whether that teaching takes place in a church or a school, whether it comes from a state-approved preacher or a state-approved teacher. (Philomene Di Giacomo)

The issue of government support is, indeed, more than a matter of preserving the nonpublic schools, of stimulating competition in education, of dissatisfaction with the public schools. For it is the very survival of a free, pluralistic society that is at stake in this issue. Until Americans see this fact and actively seek to change the present financing of schools, public policy will continue to be determined by circumstances rather than principle, and aid will be less than adequate to preserve freedom.

---

[1] Pierce vs. Society of Sisters, 268 U.S. 510 (1925). In this case a statute of the State of Oregon requiring all children between the ages of 8 and 16 to be sent to a public school was declared unconstitutional by the U.S. Supreme Court.

[2] Everson vs. Board of Education, 330 U.S. 1 (1947). The Supreme Court ruled in this case that the government could reimburse parents for the cost of sending their children to nonpublic schools on buses regularly used in the public transportation system.

[3] Rev. Virgil Blum, S.J., a leading proponent of government aid

to nonpublic education, recently observed that "What I had to say was considered so radical that editors who love controversy printed my articles by the score."

[4]Virgil Blum, "Tax Funds for Nonpublic Education," *America*, September 27, 1969.

[5]It should be noted that a purchase-of-service bill is pending in the Michigan legislature. The bill would permit the state to pay a portion of the salaries of teachers who were teaching secular subjects in nonpublic schools.

[6]The quotations from the decision were quoted in the *New York Times*, Sunday, November 30, 1969, p. 82.

[7]One can only conjecture as to how the Supreme Court will rule in this case (assuming the court will accept the case). Something may be learned, however, from fifty-two articles dealing with government aid to nonpublic education which appeared in leading law journals from September, 1964 to December, 1968. Of these, thirty-five are favorable to the constitutionality of aid, nine are uncommitted, and only eight are unfavorable. Cf. "The Constitution and Aid to Church Related Education," *Educational Freedom*, Autumn-Winter, 1968-9, pp. 39-42.

[8]This position is clearly stated by Missouri's State Senator T. D. McNeal. Speaking of tax funds for nonpublic education, he said: "In order that our cause may prevail, we must face up to the cold fact that in the political arena one does *not* win because he is right — that a legislative proposal is *not* adopted because it is just. Legislation is adopted or defeated because *somebody* put together *enough* votes to get the end result!"

[9]In Michigan nonpublic school enrollment reached its peak of 361,000 in September, 1964 and then declined by approximately 82,000 from September, 1964 to September, 1969. In the five school years enrollment dropped by 3,000 from 1964 to 1965, by 11,000 from 1965 to 1966, by 12,000 from 1966 to 1967, and then by 28,000 in each of the next two years. On the national level enrollments in nonpublic elementary schools declined by 300,000 in the decade of the 1960's according to the U.S. Office of Education. Most of the decline took place since 1964, for enrollment in Catholic elementary schools decreased by 500,000 between 1966 and 1968 according to Bishop Joseph Bernandin, General Secretary of the U.S. Catholic Conference.

[10]Cf. "Harmful Monopoly," *Barrons*, September 11, 1967 and Christopher Jencks, "The Public Schools Are Failing," *Saturday Evening Post*, April 23, 1966, p. 14.

[11]A leading proponent of this position was the U.S. Chamber of Commerce's Task Force on Economic Growth and Opportunity. The position is set forth in a report entitled *The Disadvantaged Poor: Education and Employment*, published in 1967. Milton Friedman of the University of Chicago is another leading exponent of this approach. Cf. particularly his article "On Decentralizing Schools," *Newsweek*, November 18, 1968.

[12]It is not necessary to verify the compulsory nature of education, and space does not permit extensive substantiation of the position that all education is religiously or philosophically oriented. It should be noted. however, that most nonpublic schools are avowedly religiously oriented and that public school officials acknowledge spiritual and moral values as giving purpose to the public schools. Thus. in a National Education Association publication, *Moral and Spiritual Values in the Public Schools,* published in 1951, the following is stated: "The development of moral and spiritual values is basic to all other educational objectives. Education uninspired by moral and spiritual values is directionless."

# McGovern at Wheaton

Nicholas P. Wolterstorff

The secular press scarcely mentioned it. But on October 11, after holding a private discussion with leaders of the evangelical community, presidential candidate George McGovern made a historic speech at Wheaton College. He discussed how his Christian conviction has shaped his politics. One has to go very far back to find anything comparable in American politics. To say openly and publicly on the American scene today that one's Christian faith has shaped one's politics is nothing less than an act of courage.

The standard practice of presidents and presidential candidates is to bring God in at the end of their speeches, invoking his blessing on the values of the speaker and on the residual beliefs of the American people. But here was a man saying instead that American life must be judged by God's design. Here was a man expressing the unity of his politics with his Christian faith. One thought fleetingly of John Kennedy's talk to Protestant pastors in Dallas in 1960. The brunt of that talk, though, was just the opposite. Kennedy insisted that in political matters he would act as a good American and would not submit to the discipline of his magisterium.

So far as I can tell George McGovern's theology is close to that of the classic social gospelers, minus some of their utopianism. Accordingly I think he fails fully to discern the radicalness and the realism of the gospel. He comes too close to reducing the Scripture to a moral message and a social program. Yet we evangelicals had better balance our criticism of McGovern's theology with a strong sense of guilt and embarrassment. The gospel calls for a right theology. But also it calls for a politics shaped by

REFORMED JOURNAL, November, 1972, 3-5.

our Christian commitment. How many of us can show that? It calls for an equitable society. How many of us have taken that yoke upon our shoulders? It calls for peace among races and nations. How many of us have borne the scorn of working for that?

There are indeed stirrings of change. The very fact that McGovern was invited to speak at Wheaton College, that he was introduced and endorsed by Tom Skinner, that representatives of the evangelical community were willing to confer with him, is a sign of change. Yet in this election, as in all others, most evangelical Christians will have voted for the preservation of the American way under the incredible illusion either that it is God's will or that it has nothing to do with God's will. Confronted with the chance to vote for someone who has heard the radical social message of the prophets, they will have voted for cynical, power-hungry, sanctimonious manipulators who promise to do nothing to disturb American values.

George McGovern was raised in a fundamentalist evangelical family and church. He departed from that tradition because it neglected social structures and concentrated all its attention on the salvation of individual souls. He found that he could not square that with what he heard the Bible saying. He was right. The Bible knows nothing of that selfish human concern for one's individual soul. It knows of the coming of God's Kingdom. It issues the call for workers. One wonders: for how much of the heretical liberalism of the social gospel must one blame the heretical escapism of fundamentalism?

But enough of my words. Here is some of what McGovern said on that historic occasion. He began by quoting from a radio sermon of Rev. Joel Nederhood on the "Back to God Hour," in which Nederhood said: "To suggest that one's faith might influence a person in his discharge of public office, apparently, is akin to suggesting that the man is guilty of dishonorable conflict of interest. Thus,

164

while candidates for public office often claim some kind of membership in a religious body, they ordinarily disavow any connection between their faith and their views of public policy."

In response to this McGovern said: "I believe this is wrong for a nation whose founders were so deeply motivated by religious conviction. We all stand for the Constitutional principle of separation of church and state. But we should all stand against the distortion of this principle into the practice of separating faith from politics, and morality from government . . . .

"The Bible teaches that government is to serve man, not that men are the servants of government. When the New Testament speaks of 'honoring those in authority,' for instance, it points out that power is ordained by God for the purpose of doing good for the people. In this light, I have come to understand the responsibility of political office, and the opportunities for service which it holds.

"But we must also recognize a central fact: All that we seek in our society will not come solely from government. The greatest challenges of our age defy purely political answers . . . . The war in Indochina could be ended at any moment by the President of the United States. As I pointed out last night, it can be ended by the simple choice of different policies. But what about the attitudes that brought us to this war? . . . We can change our course, and make peace, as I am committed to do. But we must also change those things in our national character which turned us astray, away from the truth that the people of Vietnam are, like us, children of God. As President, I could not resolve all the problems of this land. No President and no political leader can. For our deepest problems are within us . . . .

"So Christians have a responsibility to speak to the questions of the spirit which ultimately determine the state of the material world. Most Americans yearn for meaning and value in life. This is a pre-eminent task for those who are in the church—but it cannot be separated from what happens outside the church.

"Some Christians believe that we are condemned to live with man's inhumanity to man—with poverty, war, and injustice—and that we cannot end these evils because they are inevitable. But I have not found that view in the Bible. Changed men can change society, and the words of Scripture clearly assign to us the ministry and the mission of change.

"While we know that the Kingdom of God will not come from a political party's platform, we also know if someone is hungry, we should give him food; if he is thirsty, we should give him drink; if he is a stranger, we should take him in; if he is naked, we should clothe him; if he is sick, we should care for him; and if he is in prison, we should visit him. 'For inasmuch as you have done it unto the least of these my brethren, you have done it unto me.' That is what Scripture says. None of us can be content until all of us are made whole . . . .

"Today the conscience of our nation must be touched anew . . . . We must have a fundamental stirring of our moral and spiritual values if we are to reclaim our true destiny. That kind of awakening can free us from a relentless devotion to material affluence, with too much for some citizens and too little for others. It can free us from a blind trust in armed might. It can free us from a dogmatic faith in salvation through technology . . . . We must look into our souls to find the way out of the crisis of our society. As was so often true for the people of God in biblical days, we must heed the words of the prophets. The New Testament tells us, 'Be not conformed to the world, but be you transformed by the renewing of your minds.' Some Christians have misused this passage as a pretext for isolation from the existence around us. But the point is that our thinking, our perspectives, and our actions should not be molded by the world's view, and its tides of opinion; rather, they are to be rooted in God's vision. And

166

we must carry the good news of that vision into the world . . . .

"Because spiritual currents are moving across our land, I am hopeful for our future. I believe that these currents must reach into our public life as well as our own souls. The President can exercise a profound influence to this end. I believe that it is his most serious responsibility. The President can be the moral leader of the nation. He can ask us to face issues, not merely from a political standpoint, but in our conscience and our souls. By his words and deeds, the President must witness to the values that should endure among our people . . . .

"Power cannot be his only purpose. There is no virtue in simply 'being President.' A candidate should seek the presidency to serve the nation, and call it to a higher standard. This is the meaning of true leadership. It is not expressed in power, fame, and honor, but in the washing of dusty feet. We know that 'he who saves his life shall lose it.' And he who seeks the presidency should not be willing to pay any price. He must do so in allegiance to his principles and his faith. 'For what shall it profit a man if he should gain the whole world, but lose his own soul?' . . .

"The prophet gives us God's promise: 'If my people, which are called by my name, shall humble themselves, and pray, and seek my face, and turn from their wicked ways, then will I hear from heaven, and will forgive their sins, and will heal their land.' So what then do we do? What is your responsibility, and what is mine? Micah asked and answered the same question in a verse I have remembered since my childhood, and turned back to ever since: 'What doth the Lord require of thee, but to do justly, and to love mercy, and to walk humbly with thy God.' "

# The American Party

# A Christian Option?

by Dr. William A. Harper

In the April issue of POLITIKON I undertook an evaluation of the way of looking at
politics known as political conservatism.
This month I want to focus on a concrete
manifestation of political conservatism:    the
American party.   As I mentioned in my previous
article, any critical comments are not to be
taken as a boosting of political liberalism.
Liberalism is another false political option,
and must be equally critiqued.
The first national convention of the
American party met in August 1972 and nominated
John G. Schmitz for president and Thomas J.
Anderson for vice president.   Many evangelical
Christians were attracted to the party, apparently because they felt it was in some sense
"Christian" or at least "more Christian" than
the existing major parties.   This article is an
attempt to discover whether such an evaluation
was justified or misplaced.

## EXAMINE THE PROGRAM

I begin with the assumption that the
supporters and candidates of a party do not
in themselves provide decisive information as
to the true character of a party.   Specifically
whether there were evangelical (orthodox,
reformed, etc.) Christians involved with the
American party is irrelevant if they were not
operating as Christians and if in such a role
they failed to make a decisive impact.   A
case in point would be the Republican party's
Committee to Re-Elect the President.   I personally know one staff member who was an evangelical, but he rejects a distinctively

POLITIKON, May, 1973, vol. 3, no. 1, 1,6.

Christian approach to politics and was hardly decisive in shaping the actions of the committee as the Watergate hearings have made clear. In the case of the American party, there is evidence indicating that the candidate for vice president was an evangelical Christian. There is (as I hope to make clear) little evidence to suggest, however, that this fact made much of a difference for his or his party's political views.

Since personalities are a poor guide, and the party has no record of governing, it is necessary to examine the program of the American party in order to determine its basic direction and character. Such an examination provides some, though not convincing, evidence that the party constitutes a "Christian" option.

First, the opening paragraph of the preamble to the party's platform contains the following statement:

> The American party...gratefully acknowledges the Lord God as the Creator, Preserver, and Ruler of the Universe and of the Nation, hereby appeals to Him for aid, comfort, and continuing guidance....

Unfortunately, this fine declaration is not followed up elsewhere in the document, thus reducing it to the kind of "thing-to-do" invocation common in American civic life.

Second, the party evidenced a genuine concern for justice in the areas of employment, tax policy, health care, and preservation of life.

Third, the party rightly criticized the practise of pressure group politics--politics that implicitly reject the guidance of principial norms for making public policy and accept the relentless power struggle among competing groups. Such a judgment to me seems justified by a Christian view of the state and society.

But, unfortunately--and I say that as one convinced of the bankruptcy of our two party system--much evidence exists to suggest that the American party is no more "Christian" than the Democratic or Republican parties.

### "THE PEOPLE" AND "THE AMERICAN WAY"

If the American party were Christian in any significant sense one could expect to find it committed to the Scriptures as the basic

authority for its evaluations and proposals.
No such commitment was to be found, explicitly
or implicitly, in the documents which I had
access to.  Instead, the party fell back on
two typically American bases of authority:
"the people" and "the American way."  In the
paragraph of the preamble quoted above the
final words are "...to preserve this nation as
a government of the people, by the people,
and for the people."  Let us recognize that
familiar statement for what it is: an oath
of a faith in man (collectively, the people)
and his ability to conduct his affairs apart
from God and His norms for human existence.
This choice is made clear in the next to last
paragraph of the preamble:  "...the little
people are right....The people will ultimately
have their way" (emphasis mine).
    The party's reliance on the "American
way" as an authority for action is illus-
trated by this quote from the platform:
"The American party is totally committed to
the governmental framework embodied in the
constitution of the United States...."
(emphasis mine).  I am prepared to take that
statement at face value, i.e. the party
derives its sense of direction from America.
Does the Word of God allow us to absolutize
one country's historical experience for guidance?

## SPOKESMAN FOR "MIDDLE AMERICA"

    Another place where the American party's
character and direction are revealed are its
objectives.  To what does it give priority?
The platform makes clear that its chief
concern is a particular section of the population:

> The American party speaks for the
> majority of Americans, the hard-working,
> tax-paying citizens....
> No other party today speaks for the
> average American or expresses his
> concepts, hopes, and goals....
> The platform of the American party is
> a response to his desires....
> (emphasis mine)

In short, the American party is a self-
designated spokesman for the interests of
"Middle America."  While it is true that
"Middle America" has legitimate grievances,
the American party, in so far as it aspires
to be Christian, errs in making such grievances its central concern.  Surely there

are ends more Biblical in their derivation,
e.g. justice--economic, racial, legal, social—
for all persons, especially those least able
to secure it for themselves. A party tied so
rigidly to one socio-economic class is really
just angling for a bigger piece of the pie,
hardly a change from the usual pattern.

Finally, let me mention two positions
of the party which I think are especially
revealing. First, the party stands for an
undiluted, laissez-faire version of individualism when it is thought to be advantageous
for "Middle America;" e.g. the (apparently)
absolute right to dispose of property and own
guns. Second, a strong strain of anti-govern-
mental sentiment permeates the American party.
An editorial in Choice: 1972 promoting the
party claims "that the only real threat to
a man's life, liberty, and property is the
government under which he lives..." and
that "...all governments will, if permitted,
waste and...enslave the people...."

Neither of these two positions, typical
of political conservatism in this country,
deserve to be supported by Christians.
Individuals are important and actions by
governments are often repressive, but that
leaves no room to set up the individual against
the communal needs of society or to condemn
government in principle.

Though parties and ideologies cannot be
equated exactly, many of the same misgivings
that I expressed last time about political
conservatism apply to the American party.
They both ignore Scripture as a source of
norms, reject the role of government in
securing justice, absolutize the rights of
the individual, and make the American way of
life an idol.

The American party is expressive of a gut
feeling on the part of many Americans (including Christians) that something is radically
wrong with America. They are right, but the
reason is our national ignorance of Biblical
norms for social existence and not our
rejection of political conservatism.

In my opinion, therefore, the American
party is neither intrinsically "Christian"
nor, as an interim solution, "more Christian."
It is simply another example of man, apart
from God, trying to grope his way through the
darkness. Frankly, I think the Christians
of America can do better than that. We
must muster the patience and make the sacrifice that an authentic Christian witness in
politics requires.

# DO CHRISTIANS HAVE A POLITICAL FUTURE?

## Part II. Developing a Policy for Christian Political Action

by Bernard Zylstra

In the first part of this series of explorations (VANGUARD March/April) I discussed the immense scope of politics. How can Christ's disciples today become vessels of reconciliation in this vast arena? Politics has been described as the art of the possible. What is politically possible for Christians in the national, state or provincial, metropolitan, and local settings? At present, very little that is authentically Christian. By "Christian" I mean the pursuit of a biblically directed policy in the resolution of issues that require settlement by the state and its organs. Such a policy hardly exists. Today there is no significant body of citizens that would support such a policy. And the avenues of bringing such a policy effectively to bear on the actual political decision-making process are not to be found. In view of these inadequacies our problem can be more precisely formulated: How can the conditions be created to make possible a scripturally directed contribution in politics? The major avenue that I propose is the organization of a Christian political movement in both Canada and the United States. The central tasks of such a movement must be (1) the development of a Christian social and political policy; (2) the development of Christian political maturity and consciousness among citizens; and (3) the development of an action front relating Christian policy to political decisions.

### Links with the Past and Present

In this essay I will focus mainly on the first of these tasks. Before doing so, however, I want to point out certain group efforts among evangelical Christians that can be meaningfully used as stepping stones to broader political witness and action.

### The Christian Government Movement (CGM)

Especially during the last decade small groups of Christians have joined hands to form a common front for a variety of social and political purposes. Among the Covenanters, spiritual heirs of John Knox and ecclesiastically gathered together mainly in the Reformed Presbyterian Church, there is still the conviction that Christ is not only Saviour of men but also Lord of the state. The Reformed Presbyterian Church, which sponsors Geneva College in Beaver Falls, Pennsylvania, has supported the Christian Amendment Movement for many years. The reflection behind the endeavor to obtain a recognition of Christ's Lordship in the US Constitution has deep historical roots, as Dr. Samuel E. Boyle, long-time director of the Christian Amendment Movement (CAM) and at present a missionary in Japan, has shown in *The Christian Nation*. Recently the interest in political affairs in RP circles broadened to

VANGUARD, August/September, 1972, 13-19.

transform the Christian Amendment Movement into the Christian Government Movement. (804 Penn Avenue, Pittsburgh, Pa. 15221). The CGM, under the direction of Robert Milliken, can play an important role in reviving John Knox's convictions among the North American sons and daughters of the Scottish and British Reformation by directing these biblical convictions to the problems of the modern state. Many Convenanters died for precisely these convictions in the seventeenth century, and they are still worth fighting for today. It should help us all in reviving the best of the Christian political tradition in the Anglo-Saxon experience. *The Christian Patriot*, CGM's monthly, is already beginning to become a voice for renewal by republishing a wide variety of articles, including the politically relevant parts of William Symington's *Messiah The Prince*. This book, first published in Glasgow in 1838, is a remarkable dogmatic-exegetical treatise on the universality of Christ's office as mediator between God and man where the individualistic evangelical understanding of salvation is radically rejected. *Messiah The Prince* deserves renewed attention by all evangelicals who want to come to grips with the relevance of Christ's redemptive work for men *and* nations.

### The National Association for Christian Political Action (NACPA)

Canadian Christians with a European Calvinian heritage established the Christian Action Foundation in Edmonton, Alberta, during the early sixties. Rev. Louis Tamminga was instrumental in setting up a US branch of the CAF when he became pastor of a church in Sioux Center, Iowa, the home of Dordt College. By now this former branch has become a political movement with sub-divisions in Chicago, the home

of Trinity Christian College, and in Philadelphia, one of the main centers of Presbyterianism. The organization is known as the National Association for Christian Political Action (NACPA), and publishes *The NACPA Politikon* (Box 185, Sioux Center, Iowa 51250) eight times annually. Jim and Glenda Vanden Bosch, its dynamic husband-wife development team, have introduced NACPA to numerous Christians in the Midwest and lately in several southern and eastern states. In the US the NACPA programme deserves wide support. Its aims are:

1. To bring together into a national political movement all those who accept the principles of NACPA.
2. To develop a unified Christian political mind and a deepening understanding of our Christian political task.
3. To articulate through communal reflection and analysis a responsible Christian political programme.
4. To rally around certain issues and present Christian political alternatives in local, state, and national levels.
5. To develop and promote ways and means of implementing a united Christian political platform.

The promotion and realization of these aims require, I think, the relocation of NACPA headquarters in a national cultural centre, such as Chicago, Pittsburgh, or Philadelphia. Moreover, the informal links with the Christian Government Movement should be intensified, not on the basis of a common denominator of present positions, but on the foundation of a growing awareness on both sides of the meaning of biblically directed social and political action.

### New US Evangelical Developments

A number of additional phenomena on the US evangelical scene which indicate a growing social conciousness. A few of these should be mentioned here. The

Evangelical Committee for Urban Ministries in Boston (ECUMB, 387 Shawmut Avenue, Boston, Mass. 02118) is "an association of evangelicals concerned about the oppressed people in our cities, the forces maintaining the conditions in which they live and the general lack of positive and effective Christian response." It supports black Christian schools and assists students from oppressed minority groups at Christian colleges like Gordon. It has moved into other urban centres where its name undergoes a slight change; for instance, ECUMP operates in Paterson, New Jersey. In this way local initiatives dovetail into a common concern sharing mutual insight. The entire project is stimulated by the bimonthly publication of *Inside*: a Forum for Progressive Evangelical Thought, edited by Roger Dewey, which publishes some excellent theme issues, notably the proceedings of the Conference on Race Relations held in Chicago in 1971 under sponsorship of the Reformed Ecumenical Synod and just recently an in-depth analysis of race relations in South Africa. The announcement of future issues indicates the ECUMB is moving from an orientation on race to the entire problematics of Christian social and political concern.

The work of ECUMB in New England is linked to the work of evangelicals around Wheaton College (and in the Midwest) who issue *The Other Side* magazine. Fred Alexander, a philosophy teacher at Wheaton, has fought racism and bigotry in conservative evangelical circles, and today *The Other Side* is an effective new white evangelical voice for social justice linked to the prophetic and redemptive themes of liberation found in the biblical record. *The Other Side* has allied itself closely with *The Inside*, forming a major part of the alternative evangelical press that focuses a growing evangelical movement for social justice.

The greater Chicago area is also the home base for the quickly spreading People's Christian Coalition, first initiated by students and staff at Trinity Evangelical Divinity School in suburban Bannockburn. It has published *The Post-American* (Box 132, Deerfield, Illinois 60015) since 1971 on a quarterly basis and fills it with incisive analysis of certain facets of the American way of life. Led by former New Leftist Jim Wallis, this emerging coalition describes itself in these words: "The People's Christian Coalition is a non-membership alliance of people and communities working together to build radical Christian consciousness, commitment, and action in our time. We wish to serve the people by proclaiming the gospel of liberation in Christ, by articulating the ethical implications of that gospel, by working for peace, justice and freedom and by serving you — you who are interested in organizing others in your universities, seminaries, churches and communities to work for these objectives. We are convinced that strength will never lie in bureaucratic structures but in the dedication of people willing to organize locally . . . . We are a grassroots coalition calling for people committed to the Christian message that is distinctively Post-American, that changes men's lives and generates an active commitment to social justice which serves as the basis for social liberation."

It is interesting to note that each of these organizations or alliances is engaged in journalistic activity. As a matter of fact, new journalism efforts that support Christian social reflection and action without themselves being involved in action programmes have been initiated in various areas of the US. Two examples of this trend are *New Reformation:* The

Magazine of Campus Missions (Box 13850, University of California, Santa Barbara, Calif. 93107). It is edited by journalist-campus missionary Jon Reid Kennedy at the Institute for Christian Communication in Isla Vista, and is made available free in bulk to students on campuses throughout the nation. Its purpose is evident from its statement of policy: "As the publication of a Christian community dedicated to the reformation of mass communication, *New Reformation* will seek to demonstrate in every article in each issue the journalistic practice necessary to a reformational, reformed journalism. A major effort to this end will be the treatment in each issue of a major development, event, or trend in current events having implications for all people and life in general in the era we live in. Such articles may be a new Christian critique of news events based on reports appearing in other major media, or original Christian research into current historical phenomena."

While *New Reformation* is written for Christians, and aims to develop an integral Christian cultural conscious, Kennedy also publishes *Renaissance Review*, an attempt to reach modern pagan students on their own cultural turf with the life-transforming Good News of Jesus. *Renaissance Review* features film, record and book reviews, as well as cultural analyses. Because of his sensitivity to the non-Christian public of *Renaissance Review*, and because of his keen gifts as a reviewer and stylist, Kennedy is a leader in a core group of radical Christian journalists.

## Canada: The Committee for Justice and Liberty (CJL)

In Canada, unlike the United States, one cannot find nearly as much evidence of an incipient Christian social conscience among younger evangelicals. Is this perhaps a result of the fact that traditional evangelical leadership in Canada looks for direction from *mainline* evangelicalism in the US? Is it because there are few outstanding Christian liberal arts colleges and evangelical theological schools in this nation? Is it because English-speaking Canada has so long depended first upon Great Britain and now upon its southern neighbour for cultural direction that it lacks the vigour to come to grips with its problems on its own account?

In this rather bleak setting the Committee for Justice and Liberty (CJL) (Box 151, Rexdale, Ontario) is now struggling to mold itself into a national political movement. The CJL has two main roots. It was incorporated ten years ago as an organization to defend the rights of workers to join a union of their choice before the courts and administrative tribunals of the province of Ontario. In cooperation with its spiritual ally, the Christian Labour Association of Canada, it fought and won several legal battles dealing with the pluralism of religio-economic conviction and the monolithic adversary structure of the collective bargaining process. Thus through action in labour relations the CJL called attention to one of the key legal problems of a religiously divided citizenry.

The second root of the CJL lies in the Christian Action Foundation (CAF), which originated in Alberta. The CAF acted on a number of fronts, notably in the area of equal treatment of children in the educational system. After several years of struggle in the 60's, it won a limited but significant victory: children educated in Albertan so-called "non-public" schools receive $150 per year as the province's contribution to their educational civil rights. So far the efforts of the CAF on the educational front in Ontario, supported by the

Ontario Alliance for Christian Schools (OACS) and coordinated by John Olthuis, its legal counsel, have not met with success. Plans are now afoot to launch a lawsuit against the Government of Ontario on the grounds that the working constitution of the Dominion of Canada, the British North America (BNA) Act of 1867, does not forbid support for an alternative system of public education.

For several years the CAF published *The Christian Vanguard* in Edmonton. It dealt with a broad variety of social issues. Edited until 1970 by James Visser of Edmonton, this periodical was the pioneering forerunner of VANGUARD, which today is not linked with any organization but is responsible for its own editorial direction. The occasion for making VANGUARD independent was the union between the CAF and the CJL. Since 1971 the leadership of the new organization has been studying steps to broaden its purpose and its constituency so that it can begin to act as an articulate Christian political movement in Canadian national and provincial politics.

## THE DEVELOPMENT OF POLICY

All the groups just mentioned assert that the Gospel is integrally related to politics. No doubt by now most of them have also discovered that it is quite another thing to show explicitly what that integral relation is to the concrete issues that must be debated in the actual political process. This is not an easy matter, as was evident in the analysis of the scope of politics in the first article of this series. What is needed is a Christian political *policy* which translates the heart of the Gospel into a conception of justice that, in turn, is related to the solution of problems in a specific time and place. What I mean by a political policy will be explained as we go along. But first I want to direct myself to the question of who is responsible for the development of a Christian political policy.

### Who is Responsible for Policy?

One might argue that a practical political action movement ought to limit itself to matters of organization, propaganda, and concrete efforts to influence political decision-makers, somewhat like a lobby or a pressure group. The articulation of an overall frame of reference and the exploration of detailed principles relevant to specific issues — this is what policy is all about — could then be left to other bodies, such as the institutional church (with its assemblies, synods, councils, etc.) or the Christian academic community. How should we understand both the distinction and the connection between the tasks of activation and articulation?

To begin with the institutional church cannot and should not be isolated from politics. For its task lies in the proclamation of the Word of Life, Christ crucified and risen. With divine authority, and thus great courage, it must dare proclaim that politics can heal if it is subject to the great Healer, the Savior, and conversely that politics is on the way to death if it does not share in the Life which the Healer brings to mankind. The church brings the Good News to politics that the Lamb of God is King of kings, that justice issues from His throne, that men can be authentic citizens of their nation in the final analysis only when their citizenship, their ultimate loyalty, is in heaven, where their Master rules. That kind of proclamation will bring life to the land, vigour to present bureaucracies, and light in the labyrinth. For through such proclamation the institutional church calls men to political repentance, political salvation, and political discipleship. Through such proclamation the citizen is beckoned to "Follow Me" in the exercise of his civil responsibilities.

S.U. Zuidema summed up the matter in the last paragraph of his essay "Church and Politics" in *Communication and Confrontation:* "The church is here in order that political life may be religion," that is, service to God. If the institutional churches in the US and Canada do not accept this as part of their task in preaching, missions, and pastoral care, citizens will not hear the Word of the Lord for this facet of their actual life, they will stumble along in darkness without Light, subject to all the propaganda and lies of the Prince of Darkness and his co-belligerents. If the institutional churches, with their prophets and preachers, do not understand that political life is religion, service to God or to idols, these churches are serving themselves and not their Master, the Head.

But when the institutional churches in the US and Canada again assume their all-important office of ministering to the Word of Life, then God's People will be challenged and revived to assume *their* office of serving the Master in their daily actions, their schooling, their citizenship, their economies. Grasped by the sovereign and healing Word brought by their minister and missionary, pleading forgiveness for their self-seeking sins at the foot of the Cross, they will become seekers of the Kingdom, salt of the earth, light upon a hilltop, leaven in society. In the maturity of faith the office of all believers can come to fuition. In the unity and fullness of faith, growing up in every way into Him Who is the Head, each part of the Body will begin to work properly (Eph. 4). That work includes subjecting our politics to the Word, to Christ.

In this light we can say that our task as *citizens* is not to be executed within the institutional church, but within the state. As mature members of the Kingdom of God we must become responsible citizens of the state. There we must learn to lead lives of sanctification, that is, lives of dedicated and humble service to Christ and, through Him, service to our fellow citizens. Our civil responsibility includes competence to judge legal and political matters and to act upon them. That competence and that activity require a Christian political vision, policy, and programme that express throughout the Gospel's concern for justice. The first task of a Christian political organization whose members have been gripped by the vision of the Lordship of Christ lies in the formulation of a political policy. In policy formulation the growing maturity of our faith can begin to express itself in political competence.

### Towards Non-Pragmatic Politics

There is another consideration that ought to be kept in mind here. Most political parties and organization in the US and Canada are "pragmatic." This is generally looked upon as a virtue, not a vice. They are largely oriented to the immediate application of political power to the realization of concrete aims and objectives. They are hardly interested in relating goals to principles, to basic and underlying starting points of reflection and action. Reflection, indeed, is often divorced from action. The former may deal with principles (or with "theories" as they are wrongly called); the latter deals with goals. No wonder that often one can not distinguish between political parties and pressure groups. Our parties, it is said with pride, are and should remain non-ideological.

Many Christians who are active in the political arena look upon this pragmatism with great enthusiasm, for it supposedly creates the possibility of making a concrete contribution without engaging in ideological hassles, without debate on principles which might lead to conflict.

Principles, it is asserted, divide; goals unite.

In response to this it must be said that pragmatic politics is by no means non-ideological. Its ideology is one of non-ideology; its principle is one of non-principle. It proceeds from a distinct view of man and his social environment. Man in pragmatism is not a responder to the Word of the Creator-Redeemer who in that response shapes creation into culture. No, man is viewed as a responder to (the stimulii received from) his physical and social environment. This environment offers certain potentials for man's existence; it also puts obstacles on man's path that threaten his life. Thus for his own well-being man must learn to cope with both potentials and obstacles. This "learning to cope" is man's progress in the process of evolution. This "learning to cope" sets the goals that must be achieved in his pragmatic existence. Tools, science, technique, organization, industry, and politics are the avenues by means of which man can learn to cope with his physical and social environment.

These features of political pragmatism help explain why so many are so highly interested in the "mere" manipulation of political power for the achievement of aims and objectives. The widespread commitment to pragmatism also explains the degree of confusion and aimlessness in the direction of the affairs of state. It gives at least some hints about the self-seeking character of the political system where public power, under the mask of public purpose, can so easily be used for the realization of private ends. Because there are so many private ends, pragmatic politics has failed to achieve political unity and cooperation.

From the very outset a Christian political movement will want to break radically with this conception of a supposedly non-ideological pragmatic politics. It must not leave the formation of principled policy to other bodies, but make it part of its own organization. This means that from the start and for the duration of their existence associations like NACPA and the CJL should assume responsibility for the acquisition of principled political ideas, and the translation of these ideas into policy and action programmes directed to immediate and concrete goals which they desire to realize. These and similar bodies should now establish a division or a centre where competent persons — we have too abominably little talent right now! — can systematically cement together the building blocks for an all-round Christian political option related to the most urgent questions of practical politics. The viable fusion of Christian principle and its realization in action must become a vital concern for a Christian political movement so that it can avoid the pitfalls of pragmatic activism unequally yoked to principial sloganeering.

## The Search for Building Blocks

Where should a Christian political movement start in the formulation of policy? Must it start from scratch? Not really! As there are some skeletal organizations that provide links with the past, so there are also meaningful elements in the history of Christian social reflection that can and must be used as stepping stones in the formation of policy. From the times of the early Church Fathers there has been a long tradition of social thought that anchors us in the biblical teachings on justice and stewardship. That tradition is partially revived for our generation in Roman Catholic and neo-orthodox Protestant circles. Witness the Second Vatican Council and the proceedings of the various social conferences of the World Council of Churches. Within the evangelical wing of the Anglo-Saxon countries there is also a growing awareness of the "social relevance" of the Gospel. Of the many publications that give evidence of this, I will mention just a few: C.F.H. Henry, *Aspects of Christian Social Ethics* (1964); R.G. Clouse, R.D. Linder, and R.V. Pierard, eds., *Protest and Politics: Chrisianity and Contemporary Affairs* (1968); Edward Coleson, *God, Government and the Good Life* (1970); Francis Schaeffer, *Pollution and the Death of Man* (1970); Vernon C. Grounds, *Revolution and the Christian Faith (1971)*; John H. Redekop, ed., *Labor Problems in Christian Perspective* (1972); and Brian Griffiths, ed., *Is Revolution Change?* (1972).

Despite these and many other explorations in the field, if we limit ourselves to evangelical thought we must in all honesty admit that our tradition does not provide a Christian theory of law and the state providing the building blocks of a policy for political action. Why is this so? Why is the main focus of evangelicalism, even after it transcended the narrow confines of fundamentalism, largely limited to "the salvation of individual souls" and "the defense of the faith?" There is a strange and certainly un-biblical confusion of issues that keeps evangelicals from developing a Christian notion of the state and a policy for political witness and action. In discussing the need for such witness and action in the areas of industry, education, and politics, the traditional evangelical will often answer: "Our method of social action is personal evangelism." This seems to be the conclusion, for instance, of Brian Griffiths, the editor of the recently published *Is Revolution Change?* (Inter-Varsity Press, 1972). After arguing that revolution is not the answer to social injustice, he asks, "What then is the Christian way?" His reply is that "the Christian starts not with society and its problems but with the individual. It is he himself who first needs to be changed."

(p. 108). But in my opinion this answer simply misses the point. No disciple of Christ will deny the neccessity of conversion, of a radical change of heart commitment. But a strategy of personal evangelism and missions — today as imperative as ever! — is not a Christian *political* strategy, nor a policy of *industrial* reform, nor an *educational* philosophy. The latter indeed presuppose the former. But how do we move from *conversion* by the Holy Spirit to a *life* where Christ is Lord to the *glory* of the Father? Or, how do we move from conversion to politics — a vital part of the life which the Man of Nazareth claims as His own?

The move from conversion to politics can only be made when there is no dualism in our conception of the relation between redemption and creation. Conversion is a phenomenon of redemption; and politics is a matter of creation (and its history). How are they related? I have dealt with this question extensively in, "Thy Word Our Life," an essay published in the 1972 summer issue of the *International Reformed Bulletin* (1677 Gentian Dr. S.E., Grand Rapids, Mich. 49508). Briefly put, redemption (conversion) makes it possible for the new Christian to understand the creation where his life is lived. Redemption makes it possible for the convert to walk in the Lord's *ways* of creation, and one way of creation is political. For redemption makes it possible for the convert to see that all creatures, including the state, are *structured* to be servants of the Creator. Thus the convert knows that God's Order or Plan or Word for conversion is the same as God's Order or Plan or Word for creation. This Word simply is, "Be My servant, and you will have life." This Word is addressed to man as a person, calling for repentance and service. This Word is also addressed to all other creatures, made after their kind, each with their peculiar structure, demanding obedience to the sovereign Master. When Christians, often with the best of intentions, drive a wedge into this single Order or Word of God for creation and redemption, they introduce a dualism between conversion and the life inescapably lived in creation. This dualism accounts for the absence of a Christian conception of law and the state among evangelicals today.

## Structural Analysis of the State

We have spoken of the need for a policy that directs the activities of a Christian political movement. At this point we can describe more precisely what that means. The state displays a *structure* that makes it suitable as one of the Creator's servants for the good of men (cf. Rom. 13). The state structure is an avenue of blessing.

What do we mean by "structure"? "Structure" derives from a Latin verb meaning "to pile up, put together, put in order, and thus to build or arrange." Two uses of the term "structure" are relevant here: (1) the arrangement of particles or parts in a substance or body, and (2) the interrelation of parts dominated by the general character of the whole.

When, in harmony with biblical revelation, we say that reality is creation, we confess that material things, plants, animals, human beings, and social institutions (all things "visible and invisible, whether thrones or dominions or principalities or authorities," Col. 1:16) are so built, arranged, and structured after their kind by the Creator as to make their unique and distinctive blessing possible to the glory of God. In this sense the state, for example, is not a human invention instituted by a dictatorial fiat or in a democratic social contract. It is a creature, a divine institution with a unique structure making possible its obedience to the

order of the Creator-Redeemer, and thus becoming a blessing to mankind. In the light of the written Word enlightening their hearts, Christian citizens have the task of discovering that peculiar arrangement of parts in the body politic and the unique interrrelationship of structured elements dominated by the general character of the whole that can make the state a minister of good for the entire citizenry.

This path of discovery on the part of Christians we have come to call *structural analysis* of the state, of its internal coherence and its external relationships. This type of structural analysis was already involved in the first installment of this series dealing with the scope of politics. Structural political analysis attempts to find coherent answers to questions such as these: (1) Should there be states at all in human society? If so, why? What are they supposed to accomplish? (2) How can a state achieve its purpose? What kind of power does it need? Who may wield this power? How does a person assume a position of power in the state? Are there limits to state power? (3) Who are the members of the state? Who are entitled to benefit from the state? What are rights? Do rights derive from the state itself or can the state only recognize rights inherent in human beings simply because they are persons? (4) What are the duties of citizens toward the state? Who determines these? What happens if there is a conflict in loyalties? Should a Christian obey God rather than the government? Or should he give Caesar what belongs to Caesar anyway? (5) How should a state be divided into parts? Are there a variety of ways of doing this? How should the powers of the whole and its parts be distinguished and still coordinated? (6) How should states get along together? Should there be a super-state? Can Christians support war between states? (7) What should a state *not* try to accomplish? Should it educate children? Should it support the poor? Should it determine when a person can get a divorce or use drugs? How should the state relate itself to all those areas of society which are not primarily political but moral, economic, environmental, social, medical, educational and ecclesiastical? How can we make distinctions here? Where is the overlap? How can we find avenues of cooperation rather than opposition?

## Structure, Principle, Theory, and Policy

To formulate and pursue a political policy, the following points should be clearly kept in mind.

First, one cannot answer these and similar political questions off the cuff. Rather, pooled answers to the questions above must form a *coherent* picture of the *foundations* of politics. In other words, they must be related to the one *structure* of the state, the institution responsible for the establishment of an order of public justice.

Second, the answers to these questions concern matters of *principle.* A principle is a point of departure for action. Principles are indispensable if one is not to get lost in action without direction. A principle is a human guideline, formulated in response to the unchanging divine norm of justice for concrete political action in a specific time and place. A set of political principles itself is not yet a political policy; it gives *direction* to policy.

Third, The Christian academic community can assist a Christian political movement in finding answers to political questions. Scholars thus contribute to the formation of policy. The relationship between the academy and political action is a debated one. President Eisenhower shunned the academics; Kennedy welcomed their contribution: George

Wallace is suspicious of professors; George McGovern is their friend. The question is important for a Christian political movement if only for the simple reason that there are hundreds of Christians teaching in the departments of political science and economics in both public universities and private Christian colleges. I would suggest that a Christian political movement and the Christian academic community ought to cooperate with the following distinctions in mind: The (Christian) academic community is responsible for the development of *theory.* With reference to our topic, political theory is concerned with the analysis of the general structure of states, the coherent principles of political action and organization, and the variable forms of government. The Christian political theorist and the Christian politician have two vital convictions in common: both proceed from the same biblical view of life and an all-controlling commitment to Christ. And both are interested in making a contribution to a meaningful politics. But the political theorist, as a member of an academic community, is not responsible for implementing his insights in political action. That is the politician's job. Nevertheless, the theoretical insights of the political scientist are of immense value to a political action movement as well as to the government, especially in a complex society. For the theorist can often relate and identify the principles, social forces, components, consequences, and possible options for action in a complex situation more easily than a political activist.

In view of this I would suggest close cooperation between Christian political action movements, like NACPA, CGM and the CJL, and those members of the academic world who are highly concerned about a Christian reorientation in society. Teams of activists and theorists should be formed by NACPA, CGM and the CJL (and perhaps other groups — like the People's Christian Coalition) to formulate the foundations, principles, and directives for Christian political action. These teams should include political scientists, economists, theologians, ecologists, etc.

Finally, principles plus theories still do not constitute a policy. A policy is the direction given in an actual issue by a set of principles. An actual issue, for example, may be the war in Viet Nam, Canada's participation in NATO, the size of the army, the use of nuclear weapons, the sources of governmental revenues, or the use of public funds to relieve unemployment, poverty and urban decline. A policy cannot be formulated in the abstract, that is, without having all the relevant facts of an issue on the table. Research into facts will be imperative for policy formulation. A good deal of information on public issues is easily available; much is not — as Daniel Ellsberg revealed to us in the Pentagon Papers.

## Conclusion

In sum, the development of policy is the first main item on the agenda for NACPA, CGM, the People's Christian Coalition, the CJL, and similar organizations. One reason why followers of Christ took the initiative to establish these bodies is the absence of a scripturally mature social policy that can direct us in the execution of our civil responsibilities. Now these Christian political agencies should take steps to fill this policy vacuum by founding and funding an inter-agency policy-research centre.

Will that then be enough? No. A policy, I said, is the direction of a set of principles for an actual issue. But that still isn't political action. The policy must be related to political decisions. That means that politicians must be influenced by the policy. At present I would suggest the following general avenues which can be pursued by a Christian political movement in order to influence actual decisions of legislative bodies, administrative organs, and the courts. (1) The building of a broad supportive constituency at the grassroots level; (2) influencing public opinion in the "hearing constituency" of the citizenry at large by means of the media, publications, conferences, demonstrations, etc.; and (3) developing an action front in those areas of political life and around those issues where a redirection is most feasible. We will have to pay attention to these aspects in the growth of a Christian political movement at a later time. Meanwhile, let us take those steps that are an indispensable prelude to Christian political action: the formation of a coherent policy.

# But does this mean a Christian PARTY?

Roger Dewey

There are several directions in which the Christian community can develop in order to declare openly in the political arena that Christ is Lord of all sectors of life. Some are heading in the direction of a Christian political party, following the apparently successful example of Abraham Kyper in Holland in 1874. Others speak of a political *movement, not,* however, to result in a Christian *party.* Still others conceive of a "national coalition" growing out of numerous neighborhood and metropolitan-wide coalitions organized to solve local problems of poverty, prejudice and injustice. National political action would be one part of its overall program. My own view leans strongly toward the third alternative. While these different visions are not mutually exclusive, I do believe that the concept of a Christian political party contains several extremely negative factors (not simply difficult, but negative). My purpose in this essay will be to spell out some of the factors leading me to this tentative conclusion. I will also make one suggestion which should enable those holding these different visions to act in concert, together deciding which direction the Lord would have us take for the long run.

Most of this issue of *Inside* has been devoted to exposing the dualistic assumptions so prevalent within Christianity today but so contrary to the Scripture. We have tried to allay fears that this would in any way water down the gospel, undermine evangelism, question the divine inspiration of the Scriptures or jeopardize our relationships with God. It was to show that the opposite is the case – that God's vision for this age can best be seen by those whose sight is not distorted by dualism – that we have so belabored the point of Christ's Kingdom over all of life.

We should point out that the rejection of dualism does not in itself lead to any one particular political viewpoint. In fact it is the philosophical starting point

INSIDE, July, 1972, 38-47.

for groups across the entire political spectrum; let me quote a recent editorial from the very conservative *Christian Economics:*

> The Bible's appeal is to the whole individual, including his intellect, emotions, will and conscience. . . Either explicitly or implicitly, directly or indirectly, it provides a firm and reliable basis for every decision which an individual must make — in his personal life, his family life, his business life, his social life, his community life, his economic and political life.

# Political Divergence Among Christians

Having accepted the principle of the authority of Scripture over all areas of life, the editors of *Christian Economics* then derive specific political positions on matters as diverse as welfare and South Africa, which are directly contrary to those *we* hold in *our* attempts to submit to the Lordship of Christ. Why is this so?

A partial response has already been given ("Christian Economics?" in *Inside,* November, 1971, p. 28), suggesting that they have raised both the free market economy and the "right" to hold private property to virtually the level of "articles of faith," creating an unholy alliance between service to God and service to Mammon. It is interesting that our views on this coincide with those of the very conservative Pastor Wurmbrand (anti-communist author of *Tortured for Christ*), who strongly and repeatedly challenges the concept of private property with statements such as, "True Christians give everything they have to the Lord, considering themselves *not as owners, but as stewards* of material riches,"[1] (emphasis is added). The centrality in Scripture of this rejection of true ownership should need no defense, yet it is ignored by *Christian Economics* since it conflicts with their philosophy. (Needless to say they do not stress very highly the obligation, "Give to every man that asks of you," Luke 6:30. A major reason, therefore, but hardly the only one, for the political divergence of opinion among Bible-believing Christians is the fact that all of us interpret Scripture from the perspective of our own culture. Since American culture is based on many non-Christian philosophies — materialism, humanism, dualism, pragmatism and others — our interpretation will usually reflect those concepts unless we are unusually perceptive in detecting their subtle influences. It is clearly essential, therefore, to disenculturate the gospel — to begin the hard work of distinguishing between those Christian truths which are universally applicable and those aspects of American (or European, or African) culture which have become a part of our value system and even of our worship, but which would only be a "stumbling block" to the presentation of Christ to someone of another culture (be it

[1] THE VOICE OF THE MARTYRS, Feb. 1972, p. 1.

Chinese, Latin American, or the youth culture). So much of evangelical writing looks at the *universal* aspects of the gospel and the plan of salvation that I feel free here to concentrate on the cultural stumbling blocks.

# Relationship Between Faith and Culture

What do the Scriptures indicate about God's perspective on the relationship between His message and human culture, one aspect of which is civil law?[2] To the Old Testament Jews, God spoke with great clarity, not only setting standards for personal morality and corporate worship but also establishing the details of civic law — holidays, economic structure, codes of conduct toward strangers and the poor, marriage regulations, foreign policy, etc. God was the head of their government, and so injustice was sin against *Him* — one of the most grievous ones to judge from reading the prophets. Jewish faith was deliberately enculturated by God. To become one of Jehovah's people, one had to become *culturally* Jewish — through circumcision as well as through adherence to all the civic laws. There was no evangelism outside of that one culture!

By the time of Christ, the Pharisees had taken the Word of God and had expanded it many times. Every place questions remained as to whether one should or should not take a certain action, the Pharisees defined the issues more closely. General principles were made more and more specific; specific statements were detailed in their application to more and more situations, until a body of laws so complete had been formed that the "correct" response had been worked out for virtually every conceivable occurance.

When Christ came along, He took a rather ambivalent attitude toward these laws — many he obeyed (attendance at the Synagogue, most of the dietary laws, the observances of the Passover) and many He did not (generally overruling any law which would interfere with His relationships with others). The Pharisees must have found this the most disturbing of His attributes, as well as the one which most conclusively proved that He was not from God. I can hear them so clearly: "He says he is from God, but he disregards the very obvious working out of the principles and laws God has given us in the Scripture." Yet Christ saw through their pious talk, saw that they had distorted God's word until man had become made for the laws instead of the laws being made for man. And worse, the fact that they had detailed "correct" responses for every situation, meant that one no longer required communication with God to know God's will — one had only to "follow the book." Faith in God had become faith in a mediator, the law. Christ, as the Word of God,

2 The following four paragraphs summarize the main argument of a paper by Dr. Richard Lovelace of Gordon-Conwell Seminary, presented at the Penial Ministers' Conference of 1971. It is soon to be published within a book titled, THE GOSPEL AND THE CULTURE CRISIS.

was replaced by the words of the law. God's people became people of the book.

The tie between faith in God and faith in the Jewish culture was broken for all time by God Himself in a dream to Peter (Acts 10). A sheet was lowered from heaven containing all the animals considered unclean by Jewish culture. Peter at first refused to eat them, but finally obeyed when God said, "That which I have called clean let no man call unclean." And so for the first time the gospel went forth to the "unclean" gentiles. Culture was stripped away so the essential faith could go out to *all* cultures. One no longer had to be circumcised to follow God.

# Not directions, but Direction

The major point I would make is that God was now calling "clean" that which He Himself had called "unclean" in Leviticus. Faith must be in Him, not in the rules. God does not change, but He might decide to change the rules, or purposely to make them unclear, as in a parable. When we are uncertain of what our response must be to a given problem, the goal is not to study and define so we can find a "safe" response, but it is to make our best moral decision consistent with the light He has given us. But, having made the same decision twice, or ten times, we dare not make a rule that, "This is *always* the proper response." Although we would deny it, as did the Pharisees, our faith may then, like that of the Pharisees, be in the rule and not in the Lord! As someone has said, "The Bible does not give us directions, but *direction.*" This, of course, has a direct bearing on Christian life and Christian politics.

The culture around us would have us believe there are no absolutes, no good or evil, no truth or falsehood, no will of God or rebellion against Him. This we must reject outright. Christ spoke of the broad way and the narrow and we must trust Him to lead us into the Truth in the political sector as well. Yet there are a multitude of areas which the Lord purposely leaves vague in order to force us into greater dependence upon Him. The Bible never describes all the ways in which we should not commit larceny — it says simply, "Thou shalt not steal." Christ never details everything we should do for our neighbor, He simply says to love Him as ourselves. God respects our minds sufficiently (after all they are His handiwork) to let us determine when, for instance, taking advantage of completely legal tax breaks becomes stealing because we're no longer paying our share. It is up to us, in openness, honesty, and dependence upon Him, to determine whether or not love demands that we provide additional food or better housing for our needy neighbor. The Bible will never give a simple answer to these questions, not because they are unimportant but because *we* are *too* important for God to continue spelling everything out for us as though we were children. He desires that we progress to the meat of the Word. Christian politics must also allow this individual freedom to make moral decisions.

Let me interject that I am *not* saying that God casts us adrift, leaving us with an impossibly high moral standard and asking us to do it ourselves. Part of the Christian message is that "Christ lives His own life inside of me,"(Gal. 2:20). Yet as we are "transformed by the renewing of our minds" by Christ, we will find it harder and harder to distinguish between the security which comes from Him and the security building within ourselves. We will find it easier and easier to trust the visions God gives us through our renewed minds. I *am* saying, however, that it borders on virtual superstition to believe that this supernatural insight comes as though a separate mind within us can think for us without our needing to think or to take any of the responsibility for the thoughts. The Galatians verse continues: "The life *I* live, *I* live by faith." Decisions need to be made by us: "Work out your salvation..."

# WHAT did THE schoolteacher teach?

In the Old Testament Theocracy, the Law was given as a "schoolteacher." Now what was the schoolteacher intended to teach? Simply that pork, idols and incest were bad? Or was there something more? Was not the law given so the Israelites would eventually learn to make independent moral decisions before God? Just as God does not force us to accept His gift of eternal life, being pleased rather to have us exercise our will, so He does not often spell out just exactly what position we should take on a multitude of issues. These issues range from the most peripheral cultural areas (clothing styles, drinking and dancing), to the typically "political" (social welfare, patriotism), to the very most personal matters (sex, abortion), to the most universal issues of life and death (participation in war). In each of these areas God has given us principles to guide our thinking, but He has not done our thinking for us. There is no blanket answer. He wants to encourage us to communicate directly with Him.

In each of those issues, the "answer" is a variation of that found in Romans 14, where the question was eating meat: "Let not him who eats despise him who abstains and let not him who abstains pass judgement on him who eats... He who eats, eats in honor of the Lord, since he gives thanks to God; while he who abstains, abstains in honor of the Lord and gives thanks to God." Apparently those who abstain from alcoholic beverages in order to honor the Lord, do in fact do Him honor. Those who drink, avoiding drunkenness, and give thanks to God for the fruit of the vine He has given, are also honoring Him. Neither of these is to pass judgement on the other. But if one were so convinced that his own standard were the only correct one that he attempted by law, (as in Prohibition or Sunday closing laws) to force that standard on the other, he would be wrong. He would be abrogating the other's freedom to make moral decisions, freedom which Christ died in order to give us. He would be guilty of re-enculturating the gospel, which God, through Christ (and in the dream to Peter) had broken free. He would be returning us to the realm of the law. This is not a "safe" position, but it is right. When we allow the possibility to morally decide to drink of the vine, we allow the possibility to abuse that right. But freedom always entails the knowledge that some will abuse it and be hurt by it.

As with wine, so more clearly with war. The U. S. government does not allow us to recognize *both* the basic principles God has given in this area. We must choose between them. Either we can stress "Thou shalt not kill" or we can emphasize "Render unto Caesar." But this means we are forced into choosing between ludicrous alternatives. To be a conscientious objector one must be a total absolute pacifist. Otherwise one must fight in any and every war the government ever tells him to, no matter what the moral complexities. By so limiting one's choice, the citizen has been denied the freedom of making a true moral decision. The right of *selective* conscientious objection, denied us by the government, is essential for the Christian. Each new war is a different moral decision. To establish THE Christian attitude towards war, one would have to delineate both principles and, in the end, leave it an open question for the individual to decide anew, each time, privately, as he stands before his Lord. This freedom is open to abuse *by Christian and non-Christian alike,* but the decision cannot morally be made for him.

The difficulty with Christian politics is that someone will try to do just that; on page 49 of this issue a Dutch Reformed pastor enlightens us on the Biblical principle regarding pants suits for women. Another Reformed pastor has criticized the ordination of women as elders and deacons as "symptomatic of a growing disregard for the Word of God. (He ignores the implications of Phil 4:3.) The temptation to take generalized statements and turn them into specific *laws* is just too strong. We are not that far from the Pharisees. *We seem to fear the freedom that Christ died to bring us* and we yearn for the safety and convenience of the old laws. We have flunked a grade in school and we are being put back a year. God, in his compassion for our weaknesses, allows us to exist in that realm of law if we wish to.

He will give us those laws as our "schoolteacher" once again until we can finally learn to make moral decisions.

# The Direction of Christian Politics

Many of the major decisions which affect the entire *direction* of a movement are made in the beginning when the foundation is being laid. Just such a fateful decision for the future of Christian politics appears imminent — NACPA is apparently close to coming out with a position paper forbidding abortion in all but the most extreme situations. (We are truly sorry to hear this.) The moral decision as to whether to abort or not to abort is a terribly serious one, but the Scripture is no more clear on that issue than on pant suits, liquor or warfare. It will be disastrous for the future of Christian politics if one of its first pronouncements in the name of Eternal Truth is, instead, a step toward the re-enculturization, the legalization, of the gospel. While ostensibly based on Scripture, is this position instead simply a reflection of the middle-class, white, conservative culture of those who are drafting it?

NACPA is one of those few tiny bands of Christians who have been working with great energy and speaking out fearlessly to show all Christians that Christ is King also of the political sector of life. We support each others' efforts. One of their articles forms the core of this issue (p. 10). Yet we must disagree strongly with this indication of their approach to Scripture. Abortion is an issue on which spiritually sensitive evangelicals can disagree. We *cannot* pass laws which would foreclose the very possibility of some Christians' moral choices before God. In those areas which are unclear in Scripture, the Christian for whom a particular choice is immoral cannot be forced to participate in it, but neither can he pass legislation forbidding others to do so (and he would be wrong to think *them* immoral).

The anti-abortion argument always rests on the questionable definition that a fertilized ova is a living human being, so its right to life outweighs the mother's right to abort unless her own life is endangered. The alternative definition is that it is a potential but not an actual human individual. Abortion is therefore not murder but the termination of a fetus. All of us make this distinction between potential and actual human life, whether we recognize it or not; we count age from date of birth, not conception; no one has funerals (or inquests) for natural miscarriages; we do not allow income tax deductions for fertilized ova. Even under the harsh "eye-for-an-eye" law of Exodus, only a fine was to be levied against a person for accidentally causing a miscarriage, as long as no harm came to the mother (21:22). But accidental harm to a *real human being* (the mother) was to be dealt with by that life-for-a-life code (21:23)! The only Scriptural limitation on this could possibly be derived from the story in which, "Elizabeth heard the salutation of Mary and the babe leaped in her womb," (Luke 1:36). But that particular fetus was about six months developed. There is no precise moment biologically when a fetus becomes viable — able to exist independently of the mother's womb — but this, historically, has been the definition of the beginning of life. The opponents usually respond, "As long as we cannot be sure, let's be safe." Thus admitting that the debate is open, they attempt to force their moral decision upon others, when Scripturally they would be wrong to even *think* the Christian immoral who has an abortion. Let not her who aborts not judge her who aborts honoring the Lord and and giving thanks to God, for God hath received her. But instead this anti-abortion law would replace a free moral decision before God with one imposed by the State. What a disasterous beginning for "Christian" politics!

This highlights my own difficulty with accepting the idea of a Christian political *party* as opposed to some other type of communal Christian political action. If a *party* is controlled by those who, before God, support regulated abortion, then self-excluded would be those who could not morally accept it. If, however, the positions were reversed, the party could not be supported by those others of us who believe that an abortion is sometimes the best moral solution to an agonizing problem. Any Christian political effort must allow for these differences.

What happens to those holding the minority position within a Christian political party? I'm sure there would be some! Do they find themselves support-ing a party which officially states *as a moral rule* that which they had tried unsuccessfully to defeat? That may be all right in "secular" politics, where positions are not promoted as being "God's moral voice," but in Christian politics majority rule is an invalid concept for determining morality. This is simply using the same reasoning within the Christian party as others use to condemn the two-party system because it does not allow for a distinctive Christian moral expression. I cannot change a moral opinion simply because I am out-voted. Therefore, if a Christian political party takes this cultural stance as being *the* Christian position, I can only support them with the same kinds of public reservations as they now express toward the present humanistic parties. This would rapidly become unwork-able and unnecessarily divisive.

It is for this reason that I pose an alternative. I would begin with Craig Ellison's concept (May-June *The Other Side*, p. 42) of a national coalition formed hierarchically of neighborhood groups, metropolitan-area coalitions (such as ECUMB), and regional (multi-state) organizations. "The national group would not be a 'working arm' in the sense of running specific programs but would be a planning and educational body." The coalitions would pull together the broadest possible spectrum of evangelical resources – political, educational, financial, technical, spiritual and personal.

Each political issue the coalition attempted to influence would then be formulated in relation to its experience at the neighborhood and city levels, rather than being simply theoretical. This could help prevent the coalition from becomming narrowed in scope or overweighted (as are the current fledgling efforts) with representatives from one race, socio-economic class, denomination, or ethnic or regional background. I feel certain, for instance, that if a reasonable percentage of those presently involved were black or poor that some basic assumptions would change and that we would be moving much more quickly to identify specific injustices which are amenable to rapid change. At any rate, the best wisdom of all those Christians who were struggling with any specific problem would be compiled by the national groups, and sent to all members, who would come to individual moral decisions and communicate their opinions to the proper public officials. The letter writing lobby of the National Rifle Association is one of the most effective in the country and a good model for us. In this way we could influence the votes of many politicians on specific issues without endorsing all their other positions. They woudl soon realize, and so would the country, that we were acting collectively in allegiance to the Lord. Those few politicians who were attempting to give public expression to the Lordship of God would be prevented (by the variety of this mail from Christians) from too easily assuming one rigid position and calling it "God's way." Perhaps more importantly this could be a means for educating the Christian public. I do not see evidence that the majority of Christians are indignant towards the injustices of our land, simply waiting for a chance to express this in a distinctively Christian way. I'm afraid the racial attitudes of the present national administration are a fairly accurate reflection of those held by most evangelicals. As *Time* magazine has said, "Political activity does not so much *produce* change in the society as to ratify change which has already occurred."

In the final analysis I believe the power of Christ in politics may be felt much more strongly if we recognize that we will never constitute more than an extremely limited percentage of the population and begin to act like the minority we are. We can never dominate through force of numbers even in the ballot box. But that seems to be God's way of doing it. Remember Gideon? If we were ever to dominate through numbers we would likely begin to take the credit for our actions ourselves. Besides, we do not simply need more laws — though I could easily name twenty major injustices upheld by the laws of our land, which need legal rectification. There is much legal work for us to do. Yet we Christians could do much to leaven this society even before we help to pass a single law. Just think what would happen if we lived, wrote, organized and voted as though injustice were as immoral as sexual immorality (which it certainly is)? What if the populace of our country, non-Christian as well as Christian, realized that "stealing" can be legal and still unjust, as in the abysmal quality of urban education? What if all Christians (even considering how few there are ) realized that, through the vote, they are personally responsible for the unjust situations resulting from our political leadership? And what if those who talk about the "local" body of Christ recognized that there is only *one* body — that it includes the black and the poor whom they never even see — and that those members of the body are hurting because of our indifference? If these were true, American evangelicals would rise up in unified horror at *our immoral collusion in the massive stealing* from the black members of the body by: (1) racially and economically segregating the suburbs, (2) providing inferior education in the ghetto, and (3) raising the false issue of bussing to eliminate the only possible means for alleviating the situation immediately. *For these problems to be changed, the Church must be changed, nor simply organized.* No president could continue to be apathetic or hostile if these cries for change came, not just from the NAACP but as an expression of the *ecclesia,* a prophetic "Thus saith the Lord." No president or congressman can allow himself to be recognized as immoral, as participating in exploitation. The cries of the *ecclesia* would influence many other "religious" people, enough to form the balance of power in the voting booth. We would have produced not just another law, which could be ignored, but a change. And the country would know that it was because *some* people knew that the Lord is King of all of life.

# WILL THERE BE A CHRISTIAN PROBLEM

## by Theodore Plantinga

The title of this series of articles ("The Jewish Problem as a Challenge for Christians") might seem to imply that the Jewish problem is not the Jews' problem but our problem. This is indeed the view of some writers who have dealt with this question. Louis Golding, in a little book entitled *The Jewish Problem* published just before the second World War, writes:

"The Jewish Problem is in essence a Gentile problem. . . . I mean that the Jewish Problem has been a Gentile Problem from the very first decades in which it raised its baneful head, and will remain so until the Gentiles themselves have solved it. There is no contribution the Jews themselves can make toward a solution which is not sooner or later pronounced an aggravation." As we have seen, Jean-Paul Sartre holds a similar view, arguing that the Jew as Jew is a

creation of the anti-Semite. If this is indeed the truth about the Jewish problem, a commitment on the part of non-Jews to halt anti-Semitic thinking, talk and behaviour should suffice to solve the Jewish problem.

Eminent Christians have been known to take similar attitudes. In a book entitled *A Christian Looks at the Jewish Question* (1938), the French Catholic philosopher Jacques Maritain quotes with approval a statement of Pope Pius XI, who had declared in September of 1938: "Anti-Semitism is unacceptable. Spiritually we are Semites." Maritain adds: "No stronger word has been spoken by a Christian against anti-Semitism. . . ." The Pope, of course, is correct in declaring that anti-Semitism is unacceptable to Christians, for there is a definite spiritual kinship between Christians and Jews,

VANGUARD, April/May, 1973, 11 ff.

193

between Christianity and Judaism. Furthermore, as human beings Jews are entitled to the same rights and protections that the law affords any other citizens, and hence the restrictive measures that have been taken against Jews in many countries are wrong. Many of the Christians of occupied Europe during the second World War realized this, and therefore they resisted Nazi anti-Semitic policies; the King of Denmark even went so far as to wear a yellow star of David in public when this traditional Jewish emblem was made mandatory for all Jews.

Those Christians who insist that there is room for Jews to live as Jews in western Europe and North America today do so on the basis of an old notion of religious tolerance. A sharp distinction is drawn between the public sphere and the private sphere, and religious faith and practice are relegated to the latter. Christians have long lived with such a reduction of the meaning of their own faith, and many of them see no reason why the Jews cannot do the same. This way of thinking, of course, has its roots in certain views about the relation between revelation and reason, faith and culture, that arose during the Middle Ages. On this question there are striking parallels between Christian, Jewish and Islamic thinkers, for many of these thinkers freely borrowed ideas from thinkers of opposing faiths. Thus we find the same kinds of views that are expressed in Christian circles about the relation between religious faith and public life also being voiced is a private matter, we are told, then Jews in their public lives can be faithful, participating members of the communities in which they live, just as Christians have done for the last two centuries.

Most Jewish writers, however, realize that there is more to the matter. They realize that the Old Testament and the Talmud are concerned not only with ritual observances but also with questions of social justice and the everyday affairs of the human community. Therefore they admit that the Jewish tradition can and does conflict with the political and social ideals and values of some nations (e.g., Nazi Germany). Milton Steinberg, a liberal American Jew and the author of *A Partisan Guide to the Jewish Problem* (1945), is well aware of the potential conflict. Describing himself as a "survivalist" rather than an assimilationist, Steinberg raises the question whether Judaism or being a Jew is compatible with "Americanism" (a term that he does not hesitate to use). His answer:

Let it be recalled that I acknowledge only one political allegiance — to America; just as I profess only one religion — the Jewish. Here there is certainly no cause for conflict. Beyond that, I have two heritages — the American and the Hebraic. English is my language and that of my children. I was educated in the public schools of my community. The history of America is my history. But Hebrew is my tongue too, and Jewish history my background also. Lincoln and Jefferson are my heroes together with Moses, Akiba and Maimonides. They all get along in my imagination most companionably. When I read Van Wyck Brooks on New England in its flowering and autumn it is in my own literary past that I am being instructed. I have studied Spiegel's *Hebrew Reborn* with the same sense of identification. I sing Negro spirituals, American ballads and Hasidic or Palestinian fold songs with equal ardor. On the Fourth of July I set off fireworks and attempt to transmit to my children an appreciation of the significance of the occasion. With equal earnestness I kindle Hanukkah lights and discuss with them the meaning of that festival. At no time am I conscious of strain between the two worlds. I move from one to the other with such naturalness that I am scarcely aware of the change in spiritual locale.

The process is immensely facilitated by the essential sympathy in spirit between the two traditions. Both are democratic. Both emphasize the worth of the individual and his right to freedom. In both there is passionate devotion to the ideal of social justice. And the vision of the more abundant life is a secularized parallel of the ancient Jewish dream of the Kingdom of God on earth.

This striking statement, like much of Jewish thinking, runs closely parallel to the thinking of some Christians. The prevalent Christian dichotomy between "public" school education (for training in the Canadian or American heritage) and "religious" instruction in the church and home (for training in the Christian heritage) is based on just such thinking.

The difficulty with Steinberg's answer to the Jewish problem, which amounts to a semi-assimilationism, is that it has not worked out in history. The balance between assimilation and separation has not been and can never be maintained for long. Some Jews who have attempted it have eventually become totally assimilated and virtually indistinguishable from their non-Jewish neighbours. And those who have managed to remain faithful to the Jewish religion have earned the hostility of their neighbours and have thereby wound up living the life of separation.

## Jewish public witness leads to hate

We have seen that writers like Golding and Sartre look for the roots of anti-Semitism in the non-Jew. But anti-Semitism can be better understood on the basis of the Jewish religious message. It appears that wherever a public witness to the Jewish faith has been raised, it has given rise to antagonism — and even hatred. As long as the western world was dominated by the Christian faith, the existence of the Jews as Jewish believers was a public testimony against that faith, and the inevitable result was hostility, distrust, suspicion, and antagonism. In the eighteenth century the leadership of western civilization was taken over by a new faith, Humanism, which has become ever more secularized and radicalized as time passed. The existence of the Jews as Jewish believers was also a public testimony against the truth of this faith, and again there was a hostile reaction. But with this new faith the rationale for anti-Semitism underwent a change, and with it the recommended solution to the Jewish problem. The anti-Semitism of the Christian era had reproached the Jews for crucifying Christ and rejecting the gospel, and it demanded the conversion of the Jews. But because the new Humanist faith was not entirely willing to admit that it was also a faith, the anti-Semitism of the Humanist era brought absurd, pseudo-scientific racial charges against the Jews. For the adherents of this essentially intolerant faith conversion was no longer an adequate solution; its more radical members demanded the elimination of the Jews from public life — by physical confinement, emigration, or extermination. Consequently, the anti-Semitism of the Humanist era has led to some of the most savage butchery that the world is ever likely to witness.

Some Jews, then, believe that their Jewish culture and beliefs are fully compatible with the religious worldview and beliefs of the dominantly Humanistic communities in which they live, but judging by the course of history during the last 100 years we must conclude otherwise. Public profession of Jewish belief is an offence to Humanism, just as

Elijah's taunting of the priests of Baal was an offence to the worshippers of Baal (see I Kings 18). Thus race is not the most basic issue in the Jewish problem; the real issue is the stubborn refusal of certain Jews to worship the gods of our day and to publicly approve the prevailing way of life. As long as Jews continue to resist the dominant Humanist faith, it is likely that they will be maligned. What this all adds up to is that there is no easy solution to the Jewish problem, for the cost of the solution (i.e., complete assimilation and acceptance of the Humanistic way of life) is more than believing Jews would be and should be willing to pay.

## At ease in Zion?

But the Jews are not the only religious community in North America whose principles and confession of faith stand opposed to the dominant Humanist faith. There are also millions of Christians in Canada and the United States. Do they earn the enmity and hatred of the Humanist community by refusing to worship the Humanist gods? Or is 'hatred' too strong a word to use in this connection? Many Christians would insist that it is, and that Christians must think only in terms of love. They would have us believe that if the Christian lives his life in love and obedience to God's will, he can expect only love and acceptance from his non-Christian neighbours. But this is hardly what Jesus said to his disciples when he spoke to them at length before his crucifixion: "If the world hates you, it hated me first, as you know well. If you belonged to the world, the world would love its own; but because you do not belong to the world, because I have chosen you out of the world, for that reason the world hates you" (John 15:18-19). Is this our situation as Christ's followers in North America in the twentieth century? And if not, is it because we are not living in obedience to

his commands?

'Hatred' is indeed a strong word, but we must not be afraid to use it in describing the attitudes of the many false faiths to the true faith. Liberal Protestants would have us believe that the "essence" of Christianity (its ethical content) is virtually identical with the ethical content of Humanism, and that the full blossoming of both can only lead to à *detente* and full reconciliation between them. But this way of thinking is far from the truth that Christ spoke, for he emphasized that he is the *only* way to the Father. If we take Christ at his word, we must face up to the fact that antagonism – and even hatred – will result whenever Christians stand up honestly in the face of Humanism. As long as Christians stay within their churches, the Humanist community will probably be tolerant. But once the Christian faith is carried into public life, tolerance breaks down and is replaced by fury, as some courageous members of the Christian Labour Association of Canada can testify.

## Will there be a Christian problem?

The title which I have chosen for this article is not "The Christian Problem" but "The Christian Problem?", for, unlike the Jews, the Christians in this part of the world simply do not constitute a recognized problem with a name of its own. Therefore we can only *ask* if there is – or perhaps should be – a Christian problem. At present the North American Humanist community simply does not recognize a Christian problem; Christians may be laughed at, but they are seldom taken seriously. No one would think of asking what is to be done about the Christians. But I am fully convinced that if Christians, as witness to the Way, the Truth and the Life, speak out about North American public life on the basis of a scriptural view of man and society and act according to their convictions, there will be a Christian problem. In this regard our Christian forefathers had more courage than we possess. The Christians in the time of the Roman emperor Nero refused to take part in the pagan religious rites of Rome. The Roman empire thus had a Christian problem, and many Christians lost their lives as witnesses to their faith. But here in North America we are content to believe that the demands which our faith lays upon us are perfectly compatible with "Americanism" and the democratic way of life. And as for the world hating us — that must be a reference to the communists in Russia, China and Vietnam!

As *Vanguard* has continually stressed, it is time that the Christians of North America give full expression to their faith — not only in their churches but also in the public life of this continent, both by speaking out on public issues and by taking concrete action. If we as Christians commit ourselves to such a program, then the Jewish reaction to the Jewish problem has some lessons and a challenge for us.

First, it is striking that many of the Jewish leaders, as well as their supporters, were led to do something about their situation because of anti-Semitism and anti-Jewish actions. Moses Hess and Theodor Herzl did not become Zionists by attending synagogues or reading books. Hess's thinking was changed by the Damascus blood libel of 1840, and Herzl became a Zionist only when he experienced the depth of anti-Semitic feeling as a witness to the Dreyfus affair. Eastern Europe, the traditional stronghold of Zionism, is also the area where the Jews have suffered the most during the last two centuries. And the murder of millions of Jews during the second World War finally succeeded in making virtually every surviving Jew a supporter of the idea of a Jewish state in Palestine. Yet, by the time that this broad support was finally achieved, the battle for Israel had in principle been decided.

## Action plus results lead to growth

If there is a real parallel between Zionism and what some radical Christians in North America are trying to achieve, the following lesson can be drawn. Christians will, in general, be convinced of the necessity of Christian social, cultural and political action only after they have seen such action and its results. Christian schools get broader support once they have shown what they can achieve. Even such confrontations as those between the Christian Labour Association of Canada and the huge, secular labour unions are useful, for they reveal an ugly side to our society which is apparently unknown to many unsuspecting Christians. Hence the struggle for equality and religious freedom under the law should continue in areas like labour, education and politics. Many Christians fear conflict, but we must learn to distinguish carefully between the conflict that is carried out in courts, legislatures and the press and the violence used by many revolutionary groups to attain their goals.

## Don't postpone responsible action

Second, the story of the success of Zionism suggests that it would be a mistake to postpone action until all — or even most — Christians are agreed on what must be done. If the Zionists had waited for full support, there would be no state of Israel today. They eventually got broad support and should not expect to be able to talk the majority of their fellow believers into agreement.

By calling for action before the support of the majority is gained, I am not opening the door to irresponsible decisions. The Zionists achieved their

197

ultimate success only because their support grew as the years went by. And one of the main reasons for the increase in their support was that Zionists had shown that their proposals were responsible and feasible, relative to the circumstances in which the Jews found themselves. At the beginning many skeptics laughed at the idea of a Hebrew-speaking Jewish nation and state in the barren land of Palestine. It took decades of work to prove that the skeptics were wrong, that it could be done. Similarly, Christian action in the fields of labour, education, politics, and communication media will gain the success envisioned at the outset only if its proponents are able to convince their skeptically inclined fellow believers that a Christian university, a Christian political party, a Christian labour union, and a Christian public press are indeed feasible. If they are not able to prove this within a reasonable period of time, the movement will fail and become a mere footnote to Christian history. But if they wait for broad support before trying to prove their point, they will not even rate a footnote.

Third, it would be instructive to consider the role of the leaders of the worship institutions in the Zionist struggle and in the struggle of North American Christians committed to Christian action. It is noteworthy that we find very few rabbis in the ranks of the Zionists. The rabbis were more inclined to advocate the kind of semi-assimilationist position expressed by Milton Steinberg in the quotation above or the traditional view that the return to Zion will be accomplished only through divine intervention and the coming of the Messiah. Thus, the Association of Rabbis in Germany condemned Herzl's First Zionist Congress. Even rabbis in Palestine took a dim view of the energetic efforts of early Zionist colonists there to lay the foundations for a Jewish state.

There was a reason for this opposition on the part of the rabbis. When the Jews of the modern era accepted the reduced role which religious observance was to play in life according to the Humanist vision of society, the Jew's life as Jew came to be concentrated almost completely around the activities of the synagogue (a sharp contrast with Jewish life in the Old Testament). This naturally enhanced the power and prestige of the rabbis in the Jewish community. Many rabbis saw the growth of Zionism as a threat to the *modus operandi* that had slowly been worked out with the Gentile world, as well as a threat to their own leadership. Futhermore, some of them had accepted the Humanistic way of thinking about religion (i.e., the equation of religion with worship activities), and thus they could not see the Zionist enterprise had anything to do with the Jew as believer. Many of them therefore opposed Zionism for entirely honest reasons: they feared that it would distract the Jews from religious observance and eventually destroy the Jewish faith community.

Many of the Zionist leaders seemed to realize that the rabbis could hardly be expected to be whole-hearted supporters of Zionism, and hence they did not make too much of the issue. They generally ignored the attacks of the rabbis and issued their appeals directly to the Jewish people. Consequently, tensions between the Zionist leaders and the Jewish clergy were never strained to the breaking point, and as time went by more and more of the rabbis went over to the Zionist position.

The parallel with the Christian situation is direct and obvious. Christians in the modern world are forced to live with the same equation of religion and worship activities, and they too tend to concentrate their lives as believers around institutions of worship. It should therefore come as no surprise that the leaders of these institutions of worship tend to view Christian action in non-ecclesiastical areas as a potential or actual threat to the health of the church. It is true that movements for Christian action have nonetheless been able to count clergymen and church leaders among their most faithful supporters, but it is also true that the emergence of various non-ecclesiastical Christian organizations in North America has had a disrupting effect on the lives of many churches whose members have been involved. That the clergy associated with such churches become suspicious and somewhat hostile is only to be expected. By virtue of their office, they bear a tremendous responsibility to the institutional church. Therefore they are rightfully fearful of anything that might in any way undermine the position of the church in the Christian community or in society in general.

## Little to be gained from stirring up clergy

Some clergy, of course, have accepted the Humanistic vision of religion as a private, optional matter involving only worship, and hence they will not become supporters of Christian action unless there is a major change in their thinking. But most Christian clergy in orthodox churches do confess that obedience to Christ involves the entirety of human life and thus cannot be locked up in any "private" sector of our lives. These Christians should be supporters of Christian action, and in time most of them probably will be — as long as it is demonstrated that what is proposed is both feasible and responsible, given the present situation of Christians in North America. Meanwhile, their seemingly excessive concern for the welfare of the church should not become an occasion for quarreling among Christians. There is little to be gained from confrontations that pit Christians involved in Christian action over against members of the clergy.

A final question that must be raised is whether we should follow the example of the Jewish Zionists to the point of becoming "Christian Zionists." This idea has arisen in a number of minds, and is already being discussed in guarded terms. What the ultimate answer to this question might be will depend heavily on events in North America over the next decade or two. If North American democracy lives up to its proud boasts and grants its citizens the full range of civil and religious freedoms and rights, there will be no need for Christians to consider "Zionism." But if Christians are to be denied a place to stand, they may eventually decide — as many Christians before them have decided — to move on, either to a more hospitable country or, perhaps, to a homeland of their own. It would be highly ironic if the descendants of the Pilgrims (i.e. the "wasp" establishment) were to force the Christians living in their midst to go elsewhere in search of religious liberty, but such irony is the fabric of history.

## Prayer without action?

The Zionist movement has lessons for us, then, and it also poses a challenge. Through hard work, determination and a great deal of suffering, the Zionists of the twentieth century have succeeded far beyond the dreams of many of their founders. Triumph has been stained by tragedy, but the great Zionist aim of a Jewish state in Palestine has been realized. Are the Christians of North America willing to work as hard as the Zionists to make North America a good place to raise a child in the fear of the Lord? Or will they restrict themselves to prayer, in the hope that there will be another generation of Christians to do what must be done? Will prayer without action be any more effective than faith without works? ∎